THE PRESIDENT AND THE SUPREME COURT: GOING PUBLIC ON JUDICIAL DECISIONS FROM WASHINGTON TO TRUMP

When presidents take positions on pending Supreme Court cases or criticize the Court's decisions, they are susceptible to being attacked for acting as bullies and violating the norm of judicial independence. Why then do presidents target Supreme Court decisions in their public appeals? In this book, Paul M. Collins, Jr. and Matthew Eshbaugh-Soha argue that presidents discuss the Court's decisions to demonstrate their responsiveness to important matters of public policy and to steer the implementation of the Court's decisions. Using data from Washington to Trump, they show that, far from being bullies, presidents discuss cases to promote their reelection, policy goals, and historical legacies, while attempting to affect the impact of Court decisions on the bureaucracy, Congress, the media, and the public.

Paul M. Collins, Jr. is Professor of Political Science and Legal Studies and the Director of Legal Studies at the University of Massachusetts Amherst. He has published extensively on the U.S. Supreme Court in a variety of journals and is also the author of two award-winning books: *Supreme Court Confirmation Hearings and Constitutional Change* (2013), coauthored with Lori A. Ringhand, and *Friends of the Supreme Court: Interest Groups and Judicial Decision Making* (2008).

Matthew Eshbaugh-Soha is Department Chair and Professor of Political Science at the University of North Texas. His research focuses on American political institutions, specifically the presidency and mass media, and public policy. He is the author of nearly three dozen scholarly articles and two books: *The President's Speeches: Beyond "Going Public"* (2006) and *Breaking through the Noise: Presidential Leadership, Public Opinion, and the News Media*, coauthored with Jeffrey S. Peake (2011).

The President and the Supreme Court: Going Public on Judicial Decisions from Washington to Trump

PAUL M. COLLINS, JR.
University of Massachusetts Amherst

MATTHEW ESHBAUGH-SOHA
University of North Texas

CAMBRIDGE
UNIVERSITY PRESS

CAMBRIDGE
UNIVERSITY PRESS

University Printing House, Cambridge CB2 8BS, United Kingdom

One Liberty Plaza, 20th Floor, New York, NY 10006, USA

477 Williamstown Road, Port Melbourne, VIC 3207, Australia

314–321, 3rd Floor, Plot 3, Splendor Forum, Jasola District Centre, New Delhi – 110025, India

79 Anson Road, #06–04/06, Singapore 079906

Cambridge University Press is part of the University of Cambridge.

It furthers the University's mission by disseminating knowledge in the pursuit of education, learning, and research at the highest international levels of excellence.

www.cambridge.org
Information on this title: www.cambridge.org/9781108498487
DOI: 10.1017/9781108682428

First published 2019

A catalogue record for this publication is available from the British Library.

Library of Congress Cataloging-in-Publication Data
NAMES: Eshbaugh-Soha, Matthew, 1972–, author. | Collins, Paul M., Jr., author.
TITLE: The President and the Supreme Court : going public on judicial decisions from Washington to Trump / Matthew Eshbaugh-Soha, Paul M. Collins.
DESCRIPTION: New York : Cambridge University Press, 2019. | Includes index.
IDENTIFIERS: LCCN 2019027926 (print) | LCCN 2019027927 (ebook) | ISBN 9781108498487 (hardback) | ISBN 9781108723893 (epub)
SUBJECTS: LCSH: Executive power – United States. | Political questions and judicial power – United States. | Presidents – United States. | United States. Supreme Court – History. | Judicial review – United States. | Separation of powers – United States.
CLASSIFICATION: LCC KF5053 .E84 2019 (print) | LCC KF5053 (ebook) | DDC 342.73/062–dc23
LC record available at https://lccn.loc.gov/2019027926
LC ebook record available at https://lccn.loc.gov/2019027927

ISBN 978-1-108-49848-7 Hardback
ISBN 978-1-108-72389-3 Paperback

For Mom and Dad
– PMC
For Ethan and Rowan
– MES

Contents

Figures

Tables

Preface

The original idea for this book came in a conversation we had the day after President Obama gave his State of the Union Address in 2010. During that speech, Obama sharply criticized the Supreme Court's decision in *Citizens United* v. *FEC* (2010), with six of the justices sitting just a few feet in front of him. It appeared that Justice Alito in particular was not prepared for this, as he mouthed "not true" and shook his head after Obama condemned the decision. Two years later, President Obama took what many believed to be the unprecedented step of taking a firm, public position on a pending Supreme Court case involving the Patient Protection and Affordable Care Act. Both of these actions created a firestorm of debate throughout the country, with many harshly criticizing the president for violating the norm of judicial independence and trying to bully the justices.

As scholars of the presidency and the Supreme Court, these events piqued our interest. Was President Obama really a bully? Were these actions truly unprecedented? What are the costs and benefits to presidents who engage in this rhetorical strategy? Does this type of position taking undermine the norm of judicial independence? How often do presidents comment on Supreme Court cases, and what are their motivations for doing so? Inspired by these questions and others, we set out to gather the empirical evidence necessary to shed light on this unique and previously unexplored form of presidential-judicial relations.

In an effort to provide a comprehensive treatment of presidential speeches on the Court's decisions, we were guided by three main principles. First, we recognized that there are substantial normative concerns implicated in presidents discussing the Court's cases in their public remarks. Chiefly, we were aware, that when presidents engage in this form of speechmaking, they might offend the norm of judicial independence, which holds that judges should be free to render decisions without interference from the elected branches of government. Although some empirical social science work avoids thorny normative questions such as this, we felt it appropriate to address the judicial independence problem directly.

Second, we acknowledged early on that the issue of presidential position taking on the Court's decisions has the potential for broad appeal. Though this is a scholarly work, we sought to make the book as accessible as possible. To do this, we present almost all of the empirical data in an easy-to-understand graphical format, instead of relaying information in complicated tables of coefficients, standard errors, and the like. For those readers uninterested in the technical aspects of our data collection and coding protocols, we are confident that the data and methodology sections that appear throughout this book can be skipped without losing a grasp of the main conclusions. For those readers concerned with the more technical aspects of our analyses, we have included the traditional coefficient tables in the appendices of the relevant chapters and provide footnotes to various decisions related to statistical modeling.

Finally, we recognized that for us to answer the questions tackled in this book, we needed to draw insights from a wide range of literatures, both theoretical and empirical. At its core, this called for a thorough understanding of the public presidency (Eshbaugh-Soha's specialty) and the Supreme Court (Collins's specialty). But it also required speaking to research on Congress, the media, public opinion, constitutional interpretation, judicial independence, the separation of powers, and executive-judicial relations more generally. Although we are aware that scholars working within a single one of these areas might not be completely thrilled with how we treat their area of specialization, our purpose was to fairly incorporate a wide array of scholarship related to presidential discussions of Supreme Court decisions. Ultimately, whether we were successful at this endeavor will be left to the reader.

As we have been working on this book in one form or another for almost a decade, it has many precursors. Earlier versions of various chapters were presented at meetings of the American Political Science Association (2013, 2014, 2015, 2017) and the Law and Society Association (2016, 2018), as well as the UMass Interdisciplinary Legal Studies Colloquium (2016) and the University of Georgia Separation of Powers Conference (2016). A previous version of Chapter 3 appeared in *Presidential Studies Quarterly* (Eshbaugh-Soha and Collins 2015). We are very grateful to the chairs, discussants, and audience members who provided us with feedback on this work at these venues.

In addition, we thank our many colleagues and friends for their valuable help, including Zack Albert, Jennifer Balint, Bethany Blackstone, Scott Blinder, Jon Bond, Todd Collins, Pam Corley, Dennis Coyle, Denis De Castro Halis, Jolly Emery, Lee Epstein, Alan Gaitenby, Justin Gross, Rebecca Hamlin, Lori Hausegger, Lisa Holmes, Tim Johnson, Ray La Raja, Daniel Lempert, John Maltese, Alyx Mark, Wendy Martinek, Lauren McCarthy, Ali Masood, Dan Miller, Paul Musgrave, Tatishe Nteta, Lori Ringhand, Jesse Rhodes, Doug Rice, Meredith Rolfe, Jamie Rowen, Jeff Segal, Libby Sharrow, Matthew Steilen, Sharece Thrower, Alicia Uribe-McGuire, Dominick Usher, Rich Vining, Art Ward, Howard Wasserman, Leah Wing, Chad Westerland, and Miranda Yaver. We are particularly grateful to Eileen Braman, Kaylee Johnson, and Brian Schaffner for their exceptional advice on the design and execution of our survey experiment. Many thanks go to Thomas Marshall for sharing his data on public opinion and the Supreme Court with us. We are also incredibly indebted to our team of research assistants who helped compile the data used in this book. At the University of Massachusetts Amherst, we thank Emilia Beuger, Brian Carchedi, Joe Dolciotto, Thomas Kennedy, Brianna Owen, Taylor Smoske, Chelsie Trombly, and Michal Wojewodzic. At the University of North Texas, we thank Ron McGauvran, Evan Lowe, Antonio Molinar, Wei-Feng Tzeng, and Ben Vail. We are also grateful to John Berger, the team at Cambridge University Press, and the anonymous reviewers, whose insightful comments helped make this a stronger book.

We also acknowledge our childhood heroes who flamed out (due to one drug or another) and failed to fulfill their potential as Major League Baseball hall-of-famers. Both of us were so traumatized by their failures that we gave up our dreams of playing professional baseball and pursued doctoral degrees instead. In many ways, therefore, we owe a debt of gratitude to Jose Canseco, Dwight Gooden, Mark McGwire, and Daryl Strawberry for this book.

Paul expresses his sincere gratitude to his family and friends who have put up with him talking about this project for almost a decade. He is particularly grateful to the Campions, Caseys, Collinses, Haggertys, and Solowiejs, whose companionship and generosity are beyond reproach. Paul also thanks his two kind, funny, and inquisitive daughters, Rose and Maggie, and his exceptional wife, Lisa, for their support on this project. Paul dedicates this book to his parents, Lea and Paul, without whose love and guidance none of this would be possible.

Matt thanks all who have asked about this research, provided encouragement and advice, and wondered aloud how difficult it is to complete any research while department chair. Part of his gratitude, therefore, goes to his colleagues at the University of North Texas who always gave him just enough time to complete this project. Matt is deeply grateful for the support of his family, their inspiration, and patience. Shelly is and always will be the reason why Matt has the time to read, write, and teach political science. Although Ethan and Rowan may never find the topic of presidential leadership meme-worthy, it is to them that Matt dedicates this book.

1

Going Public and the Supreme Court

On April 2, 2012, President Obama commented publicly on the pending US Supreme Court decision involving whether the "individual mandate" requirement of the Patient Protection and Affordable Care Act was constitutional. The president remarked that:

> Ultimately, I'm confident that the Supreme Court will not take what would be an unprecedented, extraordinary step of overturning a law that was passed by a strong majority of a democratically elected Congress. And I'd just remind conservative commentators that for years what we've heard is, the biggest problem on the bench was judicial activism or a lack of judicial restraint, that an unelected group of people would somehow overturn a duly constituted and passed law. Well, this is a good example. And I'm pretty confident that this Court will recognize that and not take that step.[1]

The following day, Obama clarified his comments in stating, "the Supreme Court is the final say on our Constitution and our laws, and all of us have to respect it, but it's precisely because of that extraordinary power that the Court has traditionally exercised significant restraint and deference to our duly elected legislature, our Congress."[2] Obama made a similar argument in June of 2015, when he said that it should be an "easy decision" for the Supreme Court to uphold the Affordable Care Act in the face of another statutory challenge.[3]

These remarks generated much discussion in the news media and political circles about whether it is appropriate for presidents to comment on pending Supreme Court decisions. Critics of the president argued that he was trying to bully the justices (Fabian 2015; Ferris 2015; Wallsten and Barnes 2012). Representative Lamar Smith (R-Texas), Chairman of the House Judiciary Committee, authored an op-ed condemning the president for his "disturbing" comments about the case, which he said revealed "a fundamental lack of respect for the judicial branch" (Smith 2012). Senate minority leader Mitch McConnell (R-KY) said the president tried to "intimidate" the Court and "crossed a dangerous line" in his statements, warning the president to "back off" (Associated Press 2012). South Carolina Governor Nikki Haley accused the president of "bullying the Supreme Court" (Swaine 2012), and Senator Chuck Grassley (R-IA) called the president "stupid" for his remarks (Daily Mail Reporter 2012). The *Chicago Daily Herald* (2012) took the president to task for not respecting the nation's system of checks and balances, while others referred to the president's statements as "extraordinary" (Presser 2012), "dangerous" (Agence France Presse 2012), and "virtually unprecedented" (Wolf 2012). Things got so bad for the president that a Fifth Circuit Court of Appeals panel of judges required the Department of Justice to prepare a three-page, single-spaced letter addressing whether the president believes that courts have the power of judicial review (Mears 2012).[4]

Despite the outrage targeted at President Obama, he is far from the only president who has commented on pending Court cases. George H. W. Bush indicated he wanted to see *Webster* v. *Reproductive Health Services* (1989) mark the first step toward the end of legal abortion in the United States.[5] Bill Clinton argued in favor of upholding the background checks found in the Brady Handgun Violence Prevention Act at issue in *Printz v. United States* (1997).[6] George W. Bush took a position against affirmative action in *Gratz v. Bollinger* (2003) and *Grutter v. Bollinger* (2003).[7] Indeed, every president since Eisenhower has taken a public position on at least one pending Supreme Court case during their time in office.

Thus, it is evident that modern presidents have targeted the Court's decisions using their public rhetoric, a strategy known as "going public." And this makes sense: the Supreme Court is typically viewed as the final arbiter of the Constitution and many presidential policy goals are subject to judicial interpretation, hindering or facilitating presidential success. If presidents can leverage their power to affect the Court's adjudication of policies that they support or oppose, this would be a significant feature of presidential leadership.

In addition to taking public positions on pending Supreme Court cases, presidents also comment on cases the Court has already decided. In fact, this is the much more common strategy, dating back to President Andrew Jackson. For example, President Ronald Reagan expressed his "profound disappointment" with the Court's decision in *Akron v. Akron Center for Reproductive Health* (1983), and called on Congress to "to restore legal protections for the unborn whether by statute or constitutional amendment."[8] President George W. Bush praised the Court's opinion in the school choice case of *Zelman v. Simmons-Harris* (2002), stating that the decision "gave a great victory to parents and students throughout the Nation" in a manner comparable to *Brown v. Board of Education* (1954).[9] As these examples demonstrate, presidents use their public rhetoric to both criticize and praise the Court's decisions.

Regardless of whether presidents should or should not target Supreme Court cases in their public remarks, we know relatively little about when and why presidents make public statements about pending or decided Supreme Court cases. Thus, we lack answers to pressing questions involving this rhetorical strategy: Do presidents speak about pending Court cases to influence Supreme Court justices, as Representative Smith's comments suggest? What are the presidents' motivations for commenting on cases after they have been handed down? How often do presidents comment on cases and how do these statements affect Congress, the news media, and the public? What are the consequences of these types of comments for our understanding of American democracy and judicial independence?

The purpose of this book is to thoroughly investigate why presidents talk about Supreme Court decisions in their public rhetoric. To this end, we address when presidents speak about cases, the tone they take when they speak, and the impact presidential rhetoric has on the Court's decisions, Congress, the news media, and the public. We examine spoken and written remarks by presidents, and explore the extent to which presidents discuss both contemporary and historical cases. In commenting on Supreme Court cases, we show that presidents are primarily motivated to demonstrate democratic responsiveness by talking about issues that are important to the American public (Dahl 1957). This is evinced by the preponderance of case mentions that occur after the Court has issued a ruling, and by our revelation that even when presidents comment on pending cases, they are not generally trying to affect case outcomes. Moreover, we show that, when presidents discuss recently decided cases, they often do so to shape the implementation of Court decisions by the bureaucracy and Congress. In doing this, we argue, presidents are exercising their legitimate constitutional function to "take Care that the Laws be faithfully executed" (U.S. Constitution, Article II, Section 3). Thus, far from being bullies, when presidents speak about Supreme Court decisions, they are performing a perfectly acceptable role in American democracy.

In the next section, we explain our motivation for writing this book, focusing on why we believe it is significant to understand presidential rhetoric regarding Supreme Court cases. Next, we discuss why presidents make public appeals generally and who they target in those appeals. We then present a sketch of our theoretical framework for understanding why presidents discuss Supreme Court decisions in their public rhetoric, including a treatment of the norm of judicial independence. This is followed by an introduction to the data used throughout this book and a brief analysis of the frequency with which presidents discuss pending and decided cases. We close with an overview of the chapters that follow.

THE IMPORTANCE OF UNDERSTANDING GOING PUBLIC ON SUPREME COURT DECISIONS

We are motivated to write this book for a number of reasons. First, exploring presidential rhetoric concerning Supreme Court cases helps us to illustrate a significant, but previously understudied aspect of the interrelationship between the executive and judiciary. Public remarks made on Supreme Court cases are important to the president's governing strategy vis-à-vis the Court, particularly because the Court can strike down executive and legislative policies supported by the president. Because of this fact, presidents are not, and need not be, neutral in relation to cases pending before the Court, even in the face of allegations of violating the norm of judicial independence. By examining presidential rhetoric on cases, this study moves beyond previous examinations of presidential-Court interrelations that focus primarily on the Office of Solicitor General (Black and Owens 2012; Nicholson and Collins 2008; Pacelle 2003) or presidential nominations to the federal courts (Cameron and Park 2011; Holmes 2007, 2008; Johnson and Roberts 2004; Maltese 1995a; Yalof 1999). Although this prior research offers much insight into executive-judicial relations, our understanding of this relationship will be enriched by exploring presidential position taking on Court decisions via a president's spoken and written remarks. This allows us to link one of the president's primary governing strategies – going public – to the Court's primary means of policy making – the decisions it renders.

This book also speaks to the larger issue of how presidents view the norm of judicial independence and their role in the coordinate construction of the Constitution. On the one hand, when presidents take a position on pending judicial decisions, they are susceptible to charges of violating the norm of judicial independence, which concerns the capability of judges to issue rulings free from interference by either Congress or the presidency (Reddish 1995, 699). On the other hand, the coordinate construction view holds that when presidents discuss Supreme Court decisions, they are not violating the norm of judicial independence. Instead, they are engaging in their own, perfectly appropriate, efforts to reach a common understanding of what the Constitution stands for at a given moment in time (Meese 1987; Paulsen 1994; Whittington 2001). By investigating a yet unexamined aspect of the relationship between the president and the Court – going public on Supreme Court decisions – we introduce new evidence to the debate between these opposing viewpoints.

This book also expands on our knowledge of the president's role in implementing Supreme Court decisions. Because it lacks the power to execute its rulings, the Court must rely on other actors, including the executive and legislative branches, to enforce its opinions. Presidents can assist the Court in obtaining public support for its decisions by speaking favorably about them. Presidents can also use public statements to lead the implementation of policy and the enforcement of the Court's decisions by the executive branch (e.g., Bullock and Lamb 1984). Conversely, presidents seeking to hinder the implementation of judicial decisions can criticize the Court's opinions to encourage public resistance or congressional efforts to limit or overrule those decisions (Canon and Johnson 1999; Epstein and Knight 1998). Thus, by investigating this topic, we bring new evidence to bear on the president's role in the implementation of judicial decisions. This speaks directly to the ability of the president to engage in constitutional construction by attempting to shape the way the public, media, bureaucracy, and Congress understand the Constitution, as well as set the agendas of those institutions (Cohen 1995; Edwards and Wood 1999; Edwards and Barrett 2000; Whitford and Yates 2009). Indeed, although presidents are often seen as the primary movers of the national policy debate (Baumgartner and Jones 1993; Kingdon 1995), it remains to be seen how presidential remarks on Supreme Court cases shape the national conversation on the issues considered in those cases or whether these remarks are effective tools for presidential agenda-setting.

This book also contributes to our understanding of the effects of presidential speeches on the media. Although there has been a great deal of research on presidents' ability to lead the media (e.g., Cohen 2008), this is the first book to examine the ability of presidents to shape newspaper coverage of speeches involving Supreme Court decisions. Thus, it sheds new light on the effectiveness of presidential strategies for influencing media coverage. That is significant because the news media represents one of the primary intermediaries by which presidents' messages are filtered to the public (e.g., Eshbaugh-Soha and Peake 2011), a particularly important role given the limited attention the public pays to the Supreme Court (Dost 2015; Hoekstra 2003).

This works also clarifies whether presidents can shape public attitudes on the Court's decisions, and whether they lead or follow public opinion on the Court's cases. To do this, we present a first-of-its-kind survey experiment that investigates whether presidential position taking on the Court's cases shapes the way the public views those decisions, and the Court itself (e.g., Armaly 2018;

Clark and Kastellec 2015). We pair our experimental survey with observational data on whether presidents try to lead or follow public opinion in their public remarks on the Court's cases, thus providing a rich look into the relationship between the president and the public as it involves public rhetoric on the Court's decisions.

Finally, this book expands our knowledge of the public presidency to include the Supreme Court. Going public is the foundation of presidential leadership, and public speeches are the primary means by which presidents attempt to influence public opinion (Edwards 2003), news coverage (Eshbaugh-Soha and Peake 2011), and their success in Congress (Canes-Wrone 2001; Kernell 1997). Despite the large literature devoted to this topic, we do not yet know how often presidents speak about Supreme Court cases, why they do so, or whether these comments have any substantive impact on judicial decisions, the media, Congress, or the public. Thus, this book adds to the larger going public literature by extending our understanding of the president's public commentary to an investigation of Supreme Court cases.

PRESIDENTIAL PUBLIC APPEALS

One of the president's most commonly employed strategies of leadership is "going public." It is by going public that presidents take advantage of their central role in American democracy. Presidents go public in an effort to further their policy goals, reelection prospects, and historical relevance. Since 1953, presidents have spoken nearly 310 times per year, peaking at 449 speeches per year during the Clinton Administration (Ragsdale 2014). Below, we detail some of the reasons that presidents go public in general. Because this book is the first to focus specifically on why presidents go public on the Court's decisions, we flesh out our detailed theoretical explanations for this type of going public in the chapters that follow.

Why Do Presidents Go Public?

Presidents have numerous motivations for public speaking, and the primary incentives for doing so arose relatively recently in the long history of the American republic. Since Nixon's creation of the Office of Communications, which helped to facilitate public relations – and certainly since Ronald Reagan stressed public outreach to achieve his goals – presidents have emphasized public relations to generate support, meet public expectations, and otherwise campaign continuously to promote their presidencies, policies, and reelection campaigns outside Washington, DC. As much research has illustrated (Hager and Sullivan 1994; Powell 1999), the increase in presidential speeches over time marks a central characteristic behind the leadership strategies of modern presidents.

There are several reasons why presidents have increased their speechmaking since the early 1970s. Kernell (1997) initially observed an institutional change in Congress that precipitated a shift in the president's target audience, from members of Congress to the American people. Simply, as Congress decentralized into myriad points of access and divided government became more common, bargaining with a few party leaders and committee chairs proved to be insufficient for presidents to achieve their legislative policy goals. Thus, we observe a shift from what Kernell calls institutionalized pluralism to individualized pluralism. Coupling this to changes in the party nomination process, which encourages outsider presidential candidates who need support from the party rank and file, not party leadership, is a decentralized Congress that encourages presidents to go public to build the public support necessary to break legislative gridlock. Moreover, the creation and evolution of the Office of Communications, which correlates with the rise in public speeches (Eshbaugh-Soha 2011), provided more recent presidents with the institutional tools and resources necessary to continue to deliver more speeches than their predecessors.

Other changes external to the institutions of Washington, DC, further facilitated the rise of the public presidency. Improved communications technology made it more feasible for presidents to reach large, national audiences. Reagan, in particular, took advantage of national addresses to pressure Congress in a prototypical going public strategy: to motivate the public to demand that their legislative representatives support the president. Although the effectiveness of public outreach is limited (Edwards 2003), technological advances that eased public access to television significantly increased the number of presidential speeches over time (Hager and Sullivan 1994).

Who Do Presidents Target with Speeches?

With more speeches have come more opportunities for presidents to reach a variety of target audiences. One of the president's primary targets, of course, is the American public. Presidents target the public in their speeches in an effort to raise the salience of issues (Canes-Wrong 2001), build support for their policy agendas (Rottinghaus 2010), and increase their approval ratings (Cohen and Powell 2005). In so doing, presidents can promote their reelections, enhance their ability to make public policy, and advance their presidencies in the eyes of history (Light 1999; Moe 1985).

Presidents also use speeches to influence the media, and they do so in a variety of ways. Typically, presidential speeches designed to increase the amount of news coverage of the president are successful (Cohen 2010), whether by setting the media's agenda on domestic policy issues (Edwards and Wood 1999), or by generating more local news coverage in a strategy some call "going local" (Eshbaugh-Soha and Peake 2006). Further, added media coverage can benefit presidents as it often enhances the salience of policies to the public, making presidential priorities public priorities (Cohen 1997). The evidence of presidential leadership of the news media therefore points to speeches as an essential source of power for presidents that allows them to generate public interest in a policy, which in turn may give presidents the weight of democratic legitimacy in pursuit of their policy goals (Eshbaugh-Soha and Peake 2011).

Presidents additionally use speeches to influence the legislative process (Kernell 1997). In an effort to pressure Congress to support their policy priorities, presidents target bills before Congress with their public rhetoric, which increases their legislative success rate (Barrett 2004). Given the role of public opinion in the going public strategy, presidents are most likely to go public – and be most successful influencing Congress – on policies that already enjoy popular support (Canes-Wrone 2001). In other words, presidential speeches do not necessarily change legislative preferences. Rather, speaking frequently about an issue increases the salience of that policy to the public. If the public already supports the president's position, the decision for a legislator to support that position is an obvious one. Relatedly, public appeals can affect the legislative agenda (Edwards and Barrett 2000), a precursor to enhanced legislative success. Although increasing partisanship may actually encourage presidents to revisit traditional bargaining strategies in pursuit of legislation under unified government (McGauvran and Eshbaugh-Soha 2017), presidents have continued to speak frequently for a variety of other reasons that we have listed.

Speeches can influence the bureaucracy, too. By affecting an agency's policy priorities, speeches increase the consistency between bureaucratic policy decisions and the president's policy preferences (Whitford and Yates 2009). That is, the more the president prioritizes an issue on his policy agenda, the more likely relevant bureaucratic agencies will follow the president's leadership on that issue. Presidents may also affect the implementation of public policy more directly. For example, among policies that are salient and relatively uncomplicated to bureaucrats and the American public, the president's positive rhetoric enhances bureaucratic activity (Eshbaugh-Soha 2006).

Presidential Speeches Involving the Judiciary

It is evident that presidents have multiple motivations and audiences for going public. Though we have a fairly comprehensive understanding of why presidents go public to influence the public, media, Congress, and the bureaucracy, we have very limited knowledge of why presidents target the Supreme Court in their public appeals. One body of work on this topic focuses on presidents going public in support of their judicial nominees. Maltese (1995b) initiated this line of research by showing that Ronald Reagan was the first president to go public to influence Supreme Court confirmation votes, a strategy that later presidents followed. Specifically, he studied how Ronald Reagan issued a number of public appeals in response to the contentious judiciary committee hearings that eventually brought down Judge Robert Bork's nomination to the Supreme Court. Reagan spoke about the Bork nomination in 34 public remarks,[10] which included mentions in several radio addresses and was the sole subject of a national address on October 14, 1987.[11]

The Bork case helps to illustrate later work on the effectiveness of going public on Supreme Court nominations more generally. Johnson and Roberts (2004) demonstrate that presidents more often go public on their Supreme Court nominees when those nominees are less likely to be confirmed by the Senate. Holmes (2007, 2008) extended this line of inquiry to US court of appeals judges and found that, although the frequency of public utterances is minimal for these nominees, it has increased over time, and is driven in large part by the nomination's vulnerability in the Senate. Finally, Cameron and Park (2011) found that going public on behalf of Supreme Court nominees occurs most frequently when the nominee's confirmation is in danger, such as during contentious confirmation hearings (e.g., the nominations of Robert Bork and Clarence Thomas).

The question of whether presidential speeches increase the likelihood that the Senate will approve a judicial nomination is also important. On the one hand, Krutz, Fleisher, and Bond (1998) show that the length of the president's announcement of a nominee is correlated with a higher likelihood of that nominee's success in the Senate. Johnson and Roberts (2004) refine this approach by analyzing all remarks prior to a nominee's Senate vote. They demonstrate that more presidential remarks on a nominee leads the Senate to cast fewer no votes than would be expected without going public. On the other hand, both Holmes (2007) and Cameron and Park (2011) find that going public is negatively related to the success of judicial nominations. This follows from their expectations concerning why presidents go public on judicial nominees.

Although presidents hope to influence Senate confirmation votes with their speeches, presidents have spoken most often about judicial nominees when such speeches are deemed necessary to deflect criticism away from a vulnerable nominee with the goal of ensuring confirmation.

There is little research that examines the tendency for presidents to target the Court more generally and outside of the nomination process through their rhetoric. Among this small body of literature, Blackstone and Goelzhauser (2014) find that presidents deliver more negative sentences about the Court in the year after the Court makes decisions that are contrary to the president's own policy preferences. They discover that presidents speak more about the Supreme Court when a vacancy arises and during reelection years, but devote less attention to it during wartime. Presidents who are lawyers also speak more often about the Court than other presidents. Blackstone and Goelzhauser (2014) look more broadly at mentions of the Supreme Court, which include comments about Supreme Court nominations or, in the case of Franklin D. Roosevelt, several mentions of his plan to increase the number of justices on the high bench (i.e., his "Court-packing plan"). They do not focus specifically on presidential mentions of Supreme Court cases that are the primary vehicles by which the Court makes policy. Nevertheless, their attention to tone is important and helps extend our understanding of presidential rhetoric generally and as it relates to the judiciary more specifically.

In addition, two studies explore whether presidential attention to certain issue areas in public speeches influences decision-making in the Supreme Court. First, Wahlbeck (1997) shows that presidential discussions of crime fighting in State of the Union Address is correlated with the evolution of search and seizure law in the Court. Second, Rogol, Montgomery, and Kingsland (2018) illustrate that the volume of attention presidents devote to civil rights and liberties in their State of the Union addresses influences the ideological direction of the Court's decisions in those policy areas. Although neither of these studies deals directly with presidential statements on the Court's decisions, they nonetheless provide evidence that presidents target the issues areas handled by the Court in their public speeches and that the justices may be responsive to presidential rhetoric.

WHY PRESIDENTS SPEAK ABOUT SUPREME COURT CASES

Our theoretical framework to answer how often and when presidents speak about Supreme Court cases is built upon several key assumptions of presidential behavior. At base, we contend that presidents are strategic actors who have limited time and resources. They will therefore act purposively to achieve their goals, which we generalize to include reelection, good public policy, and historical achievement (Canes-Wrone 2001; Light 1999; Moe 1985), and use their legitimate power and authority to realize those goals. Although presidents may be forced to respond to situations that arise outside of their control, these goals guide our explanation of presidential leadership of constitutional interpretation via the discussion of Court decisions.

One of the president's primary tools to accomplish these goals, of course, is his public speeches. Given the potential relevance of Supreme Court cases to the president's policy agenda, reelection prospects, and historical significance, presidents have many reasons to speak about them. Most notably, presidents know that the Court has the authority to restrict or expand the chances of their goal achievement. The Supreme Court can bolster or counteract presidential policy making, including domestic policy initiatives (e.g., *National Federation of Independent Business* v. *Sebelius*) and unilateral actions undertaken as Commander in Chief (e.g., *Hamdan* v. *Rumsfeld* 2006). The Court can issue rulings that give the president a campaign issue to generate electoral support (e.g., *Roe* v. *Wade* 1973). And the Court may support or oppose matters that speak to the president's historical significance (e.g., *United States* v. *Nixon* 1974).

Even though we think that these goals apply to presidential rhetoric that occurs before and after cases are decided and for both historical and modern presidents, there are key variations in these motivations. First, there are differences concerning the president's goal of achieving good public policy. Presidents who speak on pending cases are trying to influence the adoption of policy. So long as these speeches occur before the Court has made a decision, then presidents are arguably trying to pressure the Court to see their perspective, in an attempt to influence the Court much as the president may speak to pressure Congress to adopt their policy priorities (Rogol, Montgomery, and Kingsland 2018). Presidents who speak about decided cases are also interested in influencing policy. But in these speeches, presidents are often trying to affect the *implementation* of policy. For example, when presidents speak about recently decided cases, they can call on Congress to respond with additional legislation or the bureaucracy to carry out the policy in a manner consistent with the presidents' points of view. In both situations, presidents are attempting to influence how Court decisions will be carried out, which is, by definition, the implementation of public policy.

In addition, presidents can use their public speeches about the Court's cases in an attempt to shape how the public understands the Constitution. If presidents are successful at bringing the public on board with their constitutional understandings, this too can affect the implementation of policy by encouraging the public to support the president's preferred understanding of the constitutionality of particular policies. For example, if the president can successfully convince the public that bans on so-called assault weapons are consistent with the Second Amendment and the Court's decision in *District of Columbia* v. *Heller* (2008), this can shape the means by which such restrictions are supported, enacted, and implemented throughout the country.

Second, there are differences concerning the president's goal of achieving reelection. Presidents who speak on pending cases may have little reason to believe that they can affect the outcome of a case (as we demonstrate in Chapter 2). Even so, they may find it advantageous to take positions on cases relevant to their electoral bases when the Supreme Court is about to address a topic of national concern. It is even more likely that presidents who speak on decided cases have their electoral bases in mind when considering which cases to address and how to address them. Of course, the specific cases that presidents reference is a function of when the Court decided those cases. Presidents can reference historical cases (those cases that the Court decided before the president's term in office) to motivate key constituencies. Cases such as *Roe* v. *Wade* and *Buckley* v. *Valeo* (1976) are common references for those who either oppose or support abortion rights, or who consider campaign finance reform to be a significant issue. In addition, there are often high-profile cases, such as the two Affordable Care Act cases, that are decided during a president's tenure and can be used to excite the electorate.

Third, historical achievement is central to a president's legacy, a goal that presidents tend to focus on in their second term in office. Thus, presidents may speak about pending cases that are highly significant to their policy legacies. One prominent example is the second of the two Affordable Care Act cases (*King* v. *Burwell*), in which the president took a clear position in favor of his own signature domestic policy achievement. Although such a strategy is rare, and is one that could also tie in with his goal of achieving (or, in this case, maintaining) good public policy, the relationship to his historical legacy is clear. Presidents may also generate historical benefits by referencing high-profile decided cases that have historical significance. Although we would not necessarily contend that these references are designed to directly improve the president's own historical ranking or improve his legacy in that way, the president can act, well, presidential by referencing cases such as *Brown* v. *Board of Education* (1954) in a manner that reflects broadly on important developments in American history.

Of course, each of these goals and their relationship to Supreme Court cases are tempered by overall institutional norms in different eras of the presidency. Whereas modern presidents have increasingly seen the Court as a vehicle for achieving their goals, historical presidents may not have viewed the Court in this way. The norms guiding executive-judicial interactions differed for historical presidents, after all, which contributed to presidents having a limited relationship with the Court (Scigliano 1971). Presidents also spoke publicly less often in the nineteenth century (Laracey 2002). As a result, they are likely to have spoken infrequently about Supreme Court cases (something we show in Chapter 8). Thus, we are careful to build our theoretical framework in the context of the modern presidency because historical presidents are unlikely to have referenced cases frequently enough to argue that they viewed Court cases through the same lens as modern presidents.

Taken together, we think that the president's three primary goals of good public policy, reelection, and historical achievement guide the frequency, timing, and type of rhetoric on Court cases. The specific aspects of achieving those goals vary by several key factors that we will identify and use to structure this book. Whether the president speaks about a case before or after it its decided influences whether a president's goal of policy achievement, for example, is centered on affecting a policy's adoption or implementation. The same is true of reelection and historical achievement goals, just as the president's references to historical or recent cases may deviate from some standardized general approach to speaking about Court cases. Thus, our theoretical approach to why presidents go public on Supreme Court cases is specified later in each chapter with regard to the focus of each chapter.

THE NORM OF JUDICIAL INDEPENDENCE

Throughout this book, we frame going public on Court cases within the larger debate about whether presidents *should* comment publicly on the decisions of the Court. We compare the competing views of the coordinate construction of the Constitution perspective of presidential relations with the Supreme Court to the more popular judicial supremacy view. Whereas the former gives presidents license to comment on Court cases as they see fit, the norm of judicial independence may inhibit the willingness of presidents to deliver speeches about Court cases. This book thus speaks to the larger issue of how presidents view the norm of judicial independence, whether they adhere to it, and whether it is a reasonable constraint on presidential leadership.

On the one hand, when presidents take a position on pending judicial decisions, they are susceptible to charges of violating the norm of judicial independence, which concerns the capability of judges to issue rulings free from interference by either Congress or the presidency (Reddish 1995, 699). Though this norm is a central feature of an independent judiciary (e.g.,

Bermant and Wheeler 1995), we show that presidents are willing to make comments that may appear to violate this norm on occasion. Thus, we seek to understand why presidents risk the possibility of infringing on this norm when doing so may leave them open to criticism for meddling with the independence of the judicial branch. In so doing, we shed important light on how presidents understand the concept of judicial independence. Far from only an academic matter, this concern has substantial practical relevance given recent comments made by President Donald Trump, and previous presidents, regarding federal court decisions that did not go their way (Brennan Center for Justice 2018; Lithwick 2017).

On the other hand, there is an alternative view of the appropriateness of presidential discussions of both pending and decided cases. The coordinate construction, or departmentalism, view is that each branch of government has the duty to engage in constitutional interpretation (Calabresi and Yoo 2008; Corwin 1957; Murphy 1986; Whittington 1999). This view holds that each branch of government plays an important role in interpreting what the Constitution means to the American people at a given moment in time. In other words, the president, Congress, and the Supreme Court possess independent and coordinate authority to interpret the Constitution. This can prevent a form of tyranny of the majority in that no single branch is charged primarily with constitutional interpretation (Farber and Sherry 2009, 15; Johnsen 2004; Kramer 2004; Post and Siegel 2004; Whittington 2009).

Thus, according to this view, when presidents discuss Supreme Court decisions, they are not violating the norm of judicial independence. Instead, they are engaging in their own, perfectly appropriate, efforts to reach a common understanding of constitutional meaning (Meese 1987; Paulsen 1994; Whittington 2001). As the *Baltimore Sun* (2012) stated in describing President Obama's April 2, 2012, speech, "it was the nation's chief executive exercising his own constitutionally protected right to express an opinion that he believes in passionately." This perspective is in stark contrast to the more common view of judicial supremacy, which holds that the judicial branch has the final say on the interpretation of the Constitution (Gant 1997). By probing a yet unexamined aspect of the relationship between the president and the Court – presidential speeches regarding Supreme Court decisions from Washington to Trump – we introduce new evidence to the debate between these opposing viewpoints.

One such piece of evidence involves how the public thinks about the appropriateness of presidential position taking on the Court's pending and rendered decisions. To explore this, we asked survey respondents about the appropriateness of these rhetorical strategies.[12] On a 1–7 scale from "strongly disapprove" to "strongly approve," respondents were asked: 1) "Sometimes, presidents of the United States praise or criticize the Supreme Court's decisions in their public speeches *after* the Court has decided cases. Do you approve or disapprove of this presidential behavior?;" and 2) "Sometimes, presidents of the United States urge the Supreme Court to decide cases in a certain way in their public speeches *before* the Court has decided cases. Do you approve or disapprove of this presidential behavior?"

Figure 1.1 provides a look at Americans' answers to these questions. Each bar in the graph represents the percentage of respondents who fit into each of the seven categories (with higher values reflecting more approval). Respondent's attitudes toward presidential positon taking on the Court's pending decisions appear in the top graph, and their attitudes toward presidential position taking on the Court's decided cases appear in the bottom graph. As these graphs make clear, the public is much more supportive of presidential remarks on decided, rather than pending, decisions. On a 1–7 scale, average public support for position taking on decided cases is 4.3, compared with 3.5 for pending cases, a statistically significant difference ($p < 0.001$, one-tailed). Perhaps more tellingly are the distribution of respondents. For example, more than 35 percent of respondents either "strongly disapproved" or "disapproved" with presidents taking positions on the Court's pending decisions, compared with only 13 percent for decided cases. Moreover, a majority of respondents disapproved of presidents urging the Court to rule in a particular manner on its pending cases (51.5 percent), while only 26.1 percent of respondents disapproved with presidents taking positions on the Court's decided cases. Thus, it is evident that presidents are much more at risk for public condemnation when they take positions on the Court's pending decisions, as opposed to the Court's decided cases, something we explore throughout this book.

Some work on the coordinate construction of the Constitution has focused primarily on conflicts between the executive and the courts, often in the form of debates about whether the Court's decisions constrain the president (e.g., Calabresi and Prakash 1994; Calabresi and Yoo 2008; Easterbrook 1990; Paulsen 1994; Steilen 2013, 2014). Here, we take a broader view of the coordinate construction of the Constitution by conceptualizing both the Court and the president playing a role in helping to define constitutional understanding. Thus, our approach to the coordinate construction used throughout this book is closer in line with the views expressed by scholars such as Chemerinsky (1997), Kramer (2004), and Tushnet (1999), who posit that presidents, other political leaders, and the public play an important role in constitutional interpretation (e.g., Gant 1997, 383–389).

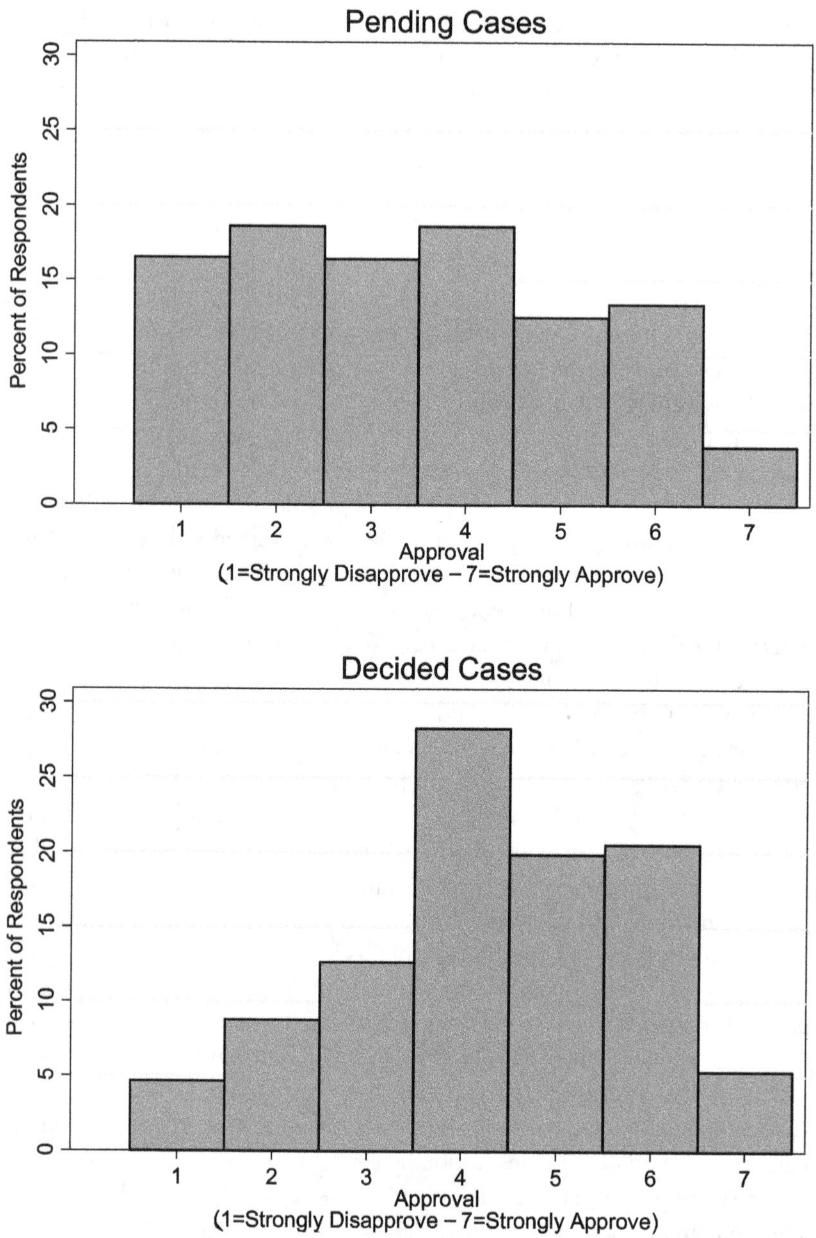

FIGURE 1.1. Public approval of presidential position taking on the Supreme Court's pending and decided cases

As it pertains to the focus of our study, the extent to which presidents work against, or with, the Court depends on the particulars of the Court's decision and the views of the president. As we demonstrate, presidents who disagree with the Court's decisions can use their public rhetoric to criticize those decisions in an effort to undermine them in the eyes of the public. Not infrequently, presidents go the extra mile and call on Congress to alter the Court's decisions with which they disagree, either by legislation or by initiating the constitutional amendment process. Conversely, presidents who agree with the Court's decisions can use their public statements to express support for those decisions, thus helping to legitimize the decision in the eyes of the public. Further, presidents can call on the bureaucracy or Congress to swiftly implement decisions with which they agree. Irrespective of whether the president disagrees or agrees with particular decisions, when presidents take public positions on the Court's decisions, they are playing an important and public role in helping to shape how Americans understand the Constitution. This, we argue, is engaging in the coordinate construction of the Constitution alongside the Court.

A NEW DATABASE OF PRESIDENTIAL COMMENTS ON SUPREME COURT CASES

To bring empirical evidence to bear on why presidents discuss Supreme Court decisions in their public rhetoric, we have compiled a first-of-its-kind database on all presidential mentions of Supreme Court cases from the presidencies of George Washington through Barack Obama (1789–2017). Given major differences in how the Court and the presidency operated across United States history, we divide our analysis into two time periods. First, the bulk of our analysis center on data that span from January 20, 1953, to January 19, 2017. This represents the eras of the modern presidency (e.g., Neustadt 1990) and Supreme Court (e.g., Pacelle, Curry, and Marshall 2011), and covers all 11 presidencies since Eisenhower and including Obama. We use the online *Public Papers of the Presidents* database available at the American Presidency Project (2017) to collect data for presidents in the modern era. Save for a handful of off-the-record speeches at fundraisers, which are not published, the *Public Papers of the Presidents* contain all public presidential remarks, spoken and written (Doherty 2012).

Second, we examine presidential discussions of Supreme Court decisions in what we call the historical era of the presidency and Supreme Court. This era begins with George Washington and ends with the conclusion of the Truman Administration. Because the *Public Papers of the Presidents* were not published until the Hoover Administration in 1929, we only use these volumes (also available online at the American Presidency Project) to collect data on Hoover, Roosevelt, and Truman. The remainder of the papers are also available at the American Presidency Project, but were originally published as *A Compilation of the Messages and Papers of the Presidents* by the Bureau of National Literature in New York, edited by James D. Richardson. Like the *Public Papers*, these historical papers represent the president's public record – not private remarks or other communications archived at presidential libraries. Our decision to focus on presidents' public speeches, as opposed to private correspondences, is motivated by our desire to investigate how presidents use the going public strategy in relation to the Supreme Court. While we recognize that presidents may discuss Supreme Court decisions in their private correspondences (Scigliano 1971), this is a different form of engagement with the Court than using public rhetoric to discuss judicial decisions.

To identify presidential mentions of Supreme Court cases, we searched for the term "Supreme Court" in both databases. These searches produced a list of speeches that contain this term, and we read through each speech to ensure that the president was in fact referencing a Supreme Court case. Based on information provided in these speeches, most notably the topic of the case and the timing of the president's remarks, we connected the president's speeches to one or more Supreme Court decisions. In developing this data collection strategy, we realized that presidents frequently discuss Supreme Court cases without directly mentioning them by name. For example, President Obama discussed *National Federation of Independent Business* v. *Sebelius* in four speeches where he never mentioned the name of the case. Similarly, searching for the term "Supreme Court" using our search strategy reveals 11 speeches involving *Texas* v. *Johnson* (1989), the case involving the constitutionality of anti-flag burning laws, while searching for *Texas* v. *Johnson* reveals a single speech (which was accompanied by the term "Supreme Court").

Nonetheless, we sought to ensure the validity of our search strategy. To do this, we extracted a random sample of 78 case names (approximately 30 percent of all cases mentioned in speeches) from the modern-era dataset we collected (1953–2017). This gives us precision of ±10 percent at 95 percent confidence. We then searched for each case name in the *Public Papers of the Presidents* using two techniques. First, we searched for the case name in a single search box without using quotes (e.g., *Texas* v. *Johnson*). Second, we searched for the case name in two search boxes using the Boolean connector "AND" (e.g., Texas AND Johnson). Based on this analysis, two significant discoveries were made corroborating the validity of our search strategy. First, presidents rarely mention case names in their public speeches on Supreme

Court decisions. Searching for the case name using either strategy identifies only 19 of 78 cases (although the exact cases identified depend on the search strategy). Second, all of the speeches mentioning the case name also contained the term "Supreme Court." Thus, we are highly confident in the validity of our search strategy.

To ensure that our data identifying the cases presidents discuss are reliable, we extracted a random sample of 87 speeches (approximately 9 percent of speeches) from the modern-era dataset (1953–2017). This gives us precision of ±10 percent at 95 percent confidence. We then re-read each speech to identify the name of the Supreme Court case mentioned by the president. Of the 87 speeches, there were two discrepancies between the original coding of the data and the reliability analysis. Thus, we have 97.7 percent agreement, indicating our data on the cases mentioned by presidents are highly reliable.

Having identified presidential speeches that mention Supreme Court decisions, we next coded several important features of the president's remarks that are explored throughout this book. For example, we coded the timing of presidential remarks, which allows us to investigate whether presidents more frequently discuss pending or decided cases. We coded the tone of presidential statements, which provides us with the opportunity to examine why presidents praise or criticize decisions. And we coded whether the president called on Congress to legislatively or constitutionally alter the Court's decision, which sheds light on how the president can bring Congress into the picture regarding the Court's decisions. In addition, to explore whether presidential speeches can influence public attitudes toward the Court and its decisions, we present the results of an original survey experiment. Thus, the data used throughout this book provide a host of novel information regarding presidential discussions of Supreme Court decisions.

WHEN DO PRESIDENTS SPEAK ABOUT SUPREME COURT DECISIONS?

Although presidents speak often and do so frequently to affect others in and outside of government, we know little about presidential efforts to speak about Supreme Court cases. Despite accusations that presidents use their rhetoric to "bully" the Court as they might Congress, there is no systematic evidence that presidents do this. We simply do not know whether the examples cited in the introduction to this chapter are common or whether they are exceptions to more general patterns of executive-judicial relations. Nevertheless, we do know that presidents speak about Supreme Court cases, and we posit that presidents are motivated to speak about the Court's pending or decided cases for one of two principle reasons.

First, presidents might use their speeches to influence cases *before* the Court renders its decisions, much as they attempt to influence legislation pending in Congress (Barrett 2004; Canes-Wrone 2001; Kernell 1997). In this mode, presidents seek to push the Court to rule in a manner that reflects their policy preferences and goals. They might highlight public support for their position knowing that justices are receptive to public opinion on pending cases (McGuire and Stimson 2004). In addition, presidents might signal to the Court the extent to which they are willing to enforce a decision, or remind the justices of their duty to faithfully interpret the Constitution, to help shape the Court's decisions (Epstein and Knight 1998). If seeking to influence the Court's decisions is the primary force driving presidential references to judicial decisions, we expect the vast majority of presidential references to Supreme Court decisions will come *before* the Court offers its opinion in a given case.

Second, presidents might comment on Supreme Court cases *after* they have been handed down in an effort to promote their reelection, policy goals, and historical legacies. Given the excitement that landmark Supreme Court cases, such as those involving abortion, gun rights, and health care, can generate in the context of a presidential election campaign, referencing Supreme Court cases may benefit presidents as they pursue reelection. By taking positions on such high-profile cases, the president can communicate to the public his position on the policies underlying those decisions, thereby addressing salient matters of public concern. This might have the effect of shaping public understanding of the constitutional issues implicated in the cases. Presidents might also write about Court decisions as a way to ensure that the executive branch implements the policies underlying those decisions in a manner consistent with his preferences, or address recent cases to influence the Court's decisions in future cases touching on a similar subject matter.

Using our database in the era of the modern presidency, we coded whether the president's remarks occurred before or after the Supreme Court's decision by comparing the date of the speech with the Court's decision date (Spaeth et al. 2018), allowing us to determine how frequently presidents speak about pending or decided cases. Figure 1.2 presents the number of Supreme Court cases mentioned by presidents from 1953 until 2017. The white portions of the bars are the number of cases referenced before they were decided, while the black portions of the bars indicate the number of cases discussed after the opinions were handed down. Overall, presidents have mentioned 937 Supreme Court cases in their public remarks, comprising 256 unique cases.

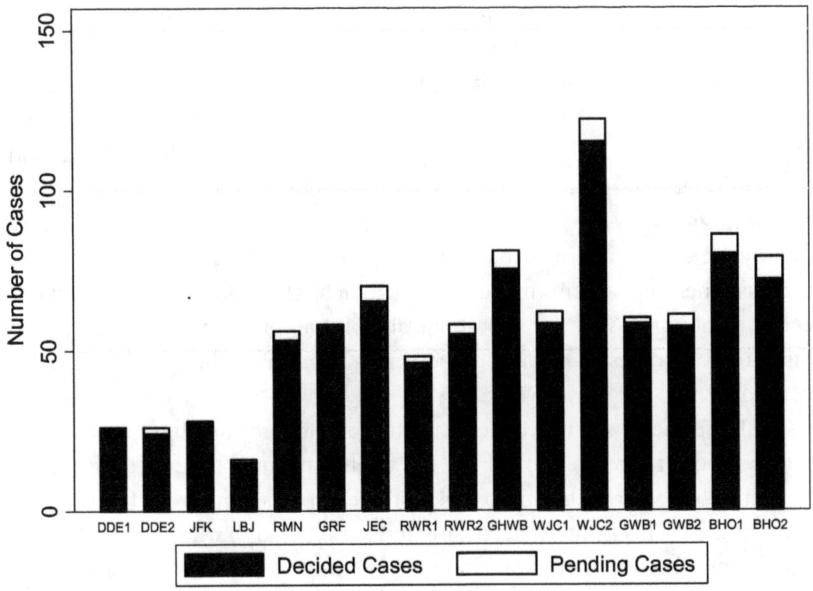

FIGURE 1.2. Presidential remarks on the Supreme Court's pending and decided cases, 1953–2017

As Figure 1.2 illustrates, nearly all of the president's comments concerning Supreme Court cases occur after the Court has ruled. On only 54 occasions – or 5.8 percent of the time – has the president mentioned a Supreme Court case prior to a decision. There is considerable variation by presidential term, with President Clinton speaking the most about decided cases during his second term in office. Although presidents paid relatively limited attention to Court cases during the 1950s and 1960s, presidents since Nixon have referenced publicly Supreme Court cases more frequently.

Although it has become somewhat more common since the Carter Administration for presidents to address cases prior to a ruling, no president has made more than 13 appeals. Among these cases, most centered on a handful of pending cases that a president referenced several times. Presidents Reagan (*Bowsher* v. *Synar* 1986), George H. W. Bush (*Webster* v. *Reproductive Health Services*), and Barack Obama (*King* v. *Burwell*) each mentioned one case three times. Presidents George W. Bush (*Hamdan* v. *Rumsfeld*) and Barack Obama (*National Federation of Independent Business* v. *Sebelius*) both mentioned one case four times before the Court handed down its ruling. In one way or another, these cases were central to a president's policy agenda or historical legacy, and presidents used their public platform to state their positions accordingly.

Our data thus show that presidents do not speak about Supreme Court cases in a manner consistent with how scholars envision that presidents go public on legislation before Congress – to put public pressure on legislators to support the president's positions (Kernell 1997). Presidents are generally not actively attempting to bully the Court as critics contend, or to marshal public support to sway the Court's decision-making. Rather, they tend to speak about cases for reasons other than attempting to influence the Court. Although they do speak about pending cases, the vast majority of the president's comments on Supreme Court cases – almost 95 percent – occur after the Court renders its decisions.

That presidents do not typically comment to pressure the Court is not unexpected for three reasons. First, presidents' primary motivation for using speeches to pressure others is to make public appeals to improve their legislative fortunes. This is likely, according to Kernell (1997), when the traditional bargaining environment with Congress has broken down (Kernell 1997). If presidents cannot secure support from legislators or exact concessions on policies by negotiating with key legislators, then they are more likely to go public to pressure Congress to assent to their policy preferences. Because presidents do not bargain with the Supreme Court regarding its decisions (and are, in fact, forbidden from doing so), the environmental context regarding executive-judicial relations differs from that governing executive-legislative interactions. Therefore, presidents are unlikely to see speeches as an effective means to pressure the Court and are unlikely to use their speeches to do so.

Second, although going public to influence the Court's decisions is perfectly within the bounds of the law, the norm of decisional independence appears to frown on such activity. Indeed, this norm is so strong that Bermant and Wheeler (1995, 836) refer to decisional independence as the "*sine qua non* of the judicial function." The strength of this norm no doubt motivated in part the harsh criticism President Obama received from the media and politicians regarding the appropriateness of his comments about the pending *Sebelius* case (e.g., Editorial Board 2012; Hartman 2012). Thus, our findings suggest that presidents generally refrain from discussing pending cases in their public rhetoric to avoid violating the norm of decisional independence, lending support for research that shows how norms shape the behavior of political actors (e.g., March and Olson 2004; Peters 2012).

Finally, the president has an institutionalized mechanism that obviates the need to go public to influence the Court: the Office of Solicitor General. As the principal attorney for the executive branch in the Court, the Solicitor General acts in part as an agent of the president, expressing presidential preferences to the Court (e.g., Nicholson and Collins 2008; Pacelle 2003). Thus, rather than going public to influence the Court, the president can simply direct the Solicitor General to appeal or defend cases that further the president's policy agenda or file amicus curiae ("friend of the court") briefs in cases in which the federal government is not a party (Collins 2008a). This is a particularly effective strategy for influencing the Court's decision-making because of the Court's deference to the Solicitor General (Black and Owens 2012).

Based on the universe of presidential remarks on Supreme Court cases as summarized in Figure 1.2 from 1953 to 2017, we conclude that presidents rarely speak to pressure the Court to decide in their favor. This initial look at our data also allays some concerns that President Obama violated the norm of judicial independence with his remarks on the Court's pending decision regarding the Affordable Care Act. If Obama had overstepped bounds (e.g., Blackman 2016), he appears to be unique in this regard, being the only president to speak about a signature domestic policy achievement that was scrutinized by the Supreme Court. This does not mean that our presentation of these initial data explains why presidents talk about pending cases and why they speak in overwhelming numbers about cases already decided by the Court. The remainder of the book does this, and does so around a broad theoretical framework centered on the president's purposive behavior to achieve several goals.

PLAN OF THE BOOK

Although our data show that presidents rarely take positions on pending Supreme Court decisions, given the controversy surrounding this rhetorical strategy and its implications for judicial independence, we devote Chapter 2 to examining presidents' motivations for going public on pending cases. To do this, we investigate the types of speeches in which presidents mention cases, whether presidents take strong positions on case outcomes, the length of statements on pending decisions, the timing of statements, and the outcome of the cases presidents discuss in their public commentary. Based on these analyses, we conclude that presidents' primary motivation to speak about pending cases is not to influence their outcomes, but rather to take public positions that demonstrate their commitment to the policies implicated in the litigation, including shaping how the public understands the constitutional issues involved in the cases.

Chapter 3 explores presidential rhetoric on cases that have already been decided by the Supreme Court. Although this type of commentary receives less attention in the popular media, it is far more common. Thus, exploring why presidents speak about decided cases is significant since it sheds new light on the most common strategy presidents use for discussing Court cases, which can influence how their presidencies are viewed and affect the implementation of the Court's decisions and how the public understands the Constitution. We differentiate written and spoken comments and show that while the former are used almost exclusively to direct the implementation of the Court's decisions, the latter are designed to allow presidents to take positions on Court cases that are important to their electoral bases given the primacy of presidential speeches to presidents' permanent campaign for public support (Doherty 2012). Often, presidents will comment on recently decided cases to speak of issues that are timely and salient to the national policy conversation in an effort to guide those conversations. Indeed, we find that the presidents are especially likely to discuss Supreme Court cases during reelection years and when those cases garner media attention.

Chapter 4 examines the tone of presidential discussions of Supreme Court cases, focusing on why presidents discuss decided cases in positive, negative, and neutral ways. We argue that presidents alter the tone of their remarks about the Court's decisions in an effort to build public support for their presidencies, shape how the public views the constitutional issues at play, and influence the implementation of the Court's decisions in the bureaucracy and in Congress. For example, a president happy with the Court's decision can praise the decision and assure the country that he will take all steps necessary to ensure it is implemented. Conversely, a president displeased with a decision can criticize that decision and encourage Congress to take steps to alter or reverse the decision, thus signaling that the fight over the case has not ended. Consistent with our theoretical expectations, we find that presidents criticize cases they disagree with ideologically, those that declare laws unconstitutional, and those decided by minimum winning coalitions. Conversely, presidents tend to praise salient Supreme Court decisions that support their preferred ideological positions.

Throughout the book, we are interested in both why presidents talk about Supreme Court decisions in their public rhetoric and the impact of that rhetoric. In Chapter 2, we examine the latter with respect to whether presidential position taking on pending cases influences the outcome of those cases. In Chapter 5, we expand our analysis to include the effect of presidential speeches on Congress. To do this, we explore instances in which presidents call for congressional action, such as passing a piece of legislation or proposing a constitutional amendment. Our results show that these types of calls to Congress occur in about 20 percent of presidential speeches regarding decided cases. We then follow up on these pleas to Congress by investigating whether Congress acted on the presidents' requests by introducing legislation or constitutional amendments to alter the Court's decisions. Thus, this chapter contributes to our understanding of how the executive, legislative, and judicial branches do and do not coordinate to interpret the constitution (e.g., Epstein and Knight 1998; Johnson 2003; Murphy 1986; Paulsen 1994).

Chapters 3 and 4 have one primary finding in common: media attention strongly affects presidential attention to Supreme Court cases. This follows from our contention that presidents go public on Supreme Court cases to demonstrate their democratic responsiveness to issues of public importance. In Chapter 6, we investigate the relationship between presidential remarks on specific cases and news coverage of those remarks pertaining to speeches on both pending and decided cases. We argue that presidents make concerted efforts to affect media coverage of their perspectives to achieve their goals and shape how the public thinks about the constitutional issues involved in the Court's cases. To do this, we scrutinize the relationship between the president's remarks on Court cases (both pending and decided) and the volume and tone of that newspaper coverage. Although presidential attention increases the amount of news coverage of their discussions of Court cases, the president's tone has little effect on the tone of news coverage. Even so, our findings with respect to presidents' abilities to increase the volume of news coverage demonstrates support for a key argument of the book: that presidents are motivated to speak publicly about Supreme Court cases to demonstrate democratic responsiveness on important national issues.

Chapter 7 sheds light on whether presidents can influence public attitudes toward the Court and its decisions when they discuss the Court's cases in their public rhetoric. To do this, we present an original survey experiment that allows us to manipulate the statements made by presidents on the Court's decisions to evaluate what effect, if any, those statements have on the public. We find that presidents can influence public attitudes on the Court's low-salience decisions, but that they have a hard time motivating opinion change on the Court's high-salience cases. In addition, we examine whether presidents tend to take positions on the Court's cases in an effort to lead or follow public opinion. We find that the vast majority of positions presidents take on the Court's cases – more than 80 percent – are congruent with the public's preference on those issues. This provides evidence that presidents take positions on the Court's decisions in an effort to demonstrate that they are democratically responsive actors.

Our penultimate chapter provides a historical view of presidential remarks concerning Court cases. This enables us to put modern presidents in historical perspective and to illuminate how constitutional and political concerns motivated early presidents to discuss Court decisions. The data collection examines all presidential remarks related to Supreme Court cases from 1789 through 1953. We show in Chapter 8 that, excluding Franklin Delano Roosevelt (FDR), Presidents Hoover, Theodore Roosevelt, and Truman devoted more attention to Supreme Court cases than all of their predecessors combined. Like modern presidents, they rarely took positions on pending decisions, opting instead to comment on the Court's already decided cases. In this chapter, we pay particular attention to FDR's remarks concerning Supreme Court cases. Given the frequency of speeches concerning his Court-packing plan (Blackstone and Goelzhauser 2014), one might expect that FDR would have spoken a great deal to influence judicial decisions or their implementation. Our data reveal that, while FDR spoke more about Supreme Court decisions than any other president from 1789 to 1953, he never took a public position on a pending Supreme Court case. Instead, like modern presidents and those before him, he opted to comment on the Court's recently decided cases, frequently to criticize the Court's decisions that struck down New Deal legislation, in an effort to advance his policy goals and mobilize public support behind the New Deal.

We conclude the book in Chapter 9. We begin by presenting data on the first 21.5 months of the Trump Administration and situate that information in light of our findings with regard to previous presidents as a way of bringing our empirical conclusions to life. We find that President Trump's remarks on the Court's cases are similar to previous presidents in many ways, but his rhetoric toward courts as institutions and lower court judges is more vitriolic than his predecessors. We then review our key findings with regard to normative theoretical debates about judicial independence and the coordinate construction of the Constitution, and discuss their contributions to the study of the rhetorical presidency. We ultimately conclude that taking positions on Supreme Court decisions is a perfectly appropriate presidential governance strategy. We close by offering suggestions for future research on the important subject of executive-judicial relations in the US and across the globe.

2

Going Public on Pending Decisions

On January 15, 2003, President George W. Bush held a press conference on *Gratz* v. *Bollinger* and *Grutter* v. *Bollinger*, the affirmative action cases pending before the Supreme Court.[1] These cases involved challenges to two University of Michigan affirmative action policies on the grounds that they violated the Fourteenth Amendment to the Constitution and the Civil Rights Act of 1964. In his seven-minute speech devoted solely to the cases, the president spoke out in favor of the importance of racial diversity in higher education, but argued that the university's affirmative action policies were "fundamentally flawed" because they "amount to a quota system that unfairly rewards or penalizes prospective students, based solely on their race" (Goldstein and Milbank 2003). Bush further announced that his administration would file an amicus curiae ("friend of the court") brief arguing that the policies are unconstitutional.

Outside of his conservative base, the president's speech did not go over well (Greenhouse 2003). Civil rights groups attacked the president for trying to end diversity in our nation's institutions of higher education (Goldstein and Milbank 2003). The president was also criticized for putting the interests of conservative Republicans over those of racial and ethnic minorities, who the party was trying to court (Wilson 2003). Senate Minority Leader Tom Daschle (D-SD) questioned the president's claim that he was committed to diversity, but against programs with track records for increasing diversity (Clymer 2003). The *New York Daily News* (2003) went further, arguing that Bush's rhetoric was "cheap, shallow, disingenuous."

In addition, the president was condemned for the timing of his speech on two fronts. First, the speech fell on Martin Luther King Jr. Day. This point was not lost on Representative John Lewis (D-GA), a celebrated civil rights activist who was a victim of America's Bloody Sunday. He penned a scathing editorial condemning the president for seeking racial division in the country and using racial innuendo (J. Lewis 2003; Moore 2003). Second, the speech came only a few weeks after Senator Minority Leader Trent Lott (R-MS) resigned from his leadership position after expressing support for the 1948 racial segregationist presidential bid of Strom Thurmond, further alienating racial minorities in the Republican Party (N. Lewis 2003). The *St. Louis Post-Dispatch* (2003) went as far as to write that the president "threw away an opportunity to send the message that the Republican Party is the party of Lincoln, not Lott."

Even some of his supporters were disappointed or surprised by Bush's intervention in the cases, particularly as moderate Republican senators had asked the administration not to get involved, fearing electoral backlash from black and Hispanic voters (Wilson 2003). Secretary of State Colin Powell voiced his disapproval with the president's position, arguing that "race should be a factor among many other factors in determining the makeup of a student body of a university" (Loughlin 2003). The litigant in one of the cases, Jennifer Gratz, expressed her astonishment that the president weighed in on the cases, particularly as the administration had no obligation to participate in the disputes (Laurence 2003; Mercer 2003).[2]

As this example makes clear, President Bush's decision to speak on the pending Supreme Court affirmative action cases generated a substantial amount of backlash and surprise from a variety of quarters. Interestingly, however, Bush was not widely criticized for violating the norm of judicial independence. For example, the *New York Times* extensively covered the speech (e.g., Clymer 2003; Greenhouse 2003; N. Lewis 2003; Nagourney 2003; New York Times 2003; Stevenson 2003), but made no reference to judicial independence at all. To the contrary, the *Times* editorial board referred to Bush's personal involvement in the cases as "entirely appropriate" (New York Times 2003).

This stands in stark contrast to the response President Obama received in reaction to his comments about the Affordable Care Act cases described in the opening of this book (e.g., Bravin 2015). Because of his position taking, Obama faced a great deal of public outcry and pushback, particularly involving claims that he violated the norm of judicial independence and engaged in the bullying of Supreme Court justices. Although we speculate that this is yet another example of how the presidency has changed as American politics have become more partisan, it is a notable distinction. Besides, it demonstrates that the type of uproar and consternation concerning questions of judicial independence and executive overreach that Obama faced may not be reflective of other presidents.[3] That is, while all presidents face the potential for some sort of backlash for their public remarks on pending Supreme Court decisions, that backlash can vary and it may not outweigh the benefits of this type of position taking.

The purpose of this chapter is to shed light on why presidents discuss pending Supreme Court cases in their public commentary, and what effect, if any, this commentary has on case outcomes. To vet why presidents speak about pending cases, we explore two primary motivations for going public on pending Supreme Court decisions. First, the popular expectation generated from Obama's remarks prior to the Affordable Care Act cases is that presidents target decisions to influence the outcome of those cases (Rogol, Montgomery, and Kingsland 2018; Wallsten and Barnes 2012). Though this is a common strategy in terms of using presidential speeches to shape the actions of Congress and the bureaucracy (Canes-Wrong 2001; Edwards and Barrett 2000; Whitford and Yates 2009), this is a risky tactic with regard to the Supreme Court since it makes the president susceptible to attacks for violating the norm of judicial independence, alienating segments of the population, and other criticisms. Moreover, it is not entirely evident why a president would turn to public speeches to influence the justices when the Office of Solicitor General is available to litigate cases or file amicus curiae briefs before the Court on behalf of the administration (Black and Owens 2012).

Given this, we explore a secondary reason to explain why presidents go public on pending Supreme Court decisions: to demonstrate their commitment to issues important to the American people. By discussing pending cases in their public remarks, presidents are able to show that they are willing to defend those positions in the face of legal challenges. This might be a particularly useful strategy for motivating public support for presidential priorities or to inspire partisan enthusiasm for the president. At the least, by commenting on important cases, presidents demonstrate that they are committed to the democratic norms of responding to issues of public concern and acting as the leaders of their political parties.

To evaluate these motivations, we have cataloged the number of times presidents discuss undecided Supreme Court cases during the Eisenhower to Obama administrations (1953–2017). Because presidents rarely go public on pending cases, inferential statistical models are inappropriate for our analysis. Accordingly, we present descriptive data that provide leverage over why presidents discuss pending cases. Our data allow us to examine the timing of statements, the types of speeches in which presidents mention cases, whether presidents take strong positions on case outcomes, the length of statements on pending decisions, and the outcome of the cases presidents discuss in their public commentary. Based on these analyses, we conclude that presidents' primary motivation to speak about pending cases is not to influence their outcomes, but rather to take public positions that demonstrate their commitment to the policies implicated in the litigation.

PRESIDENTS' MOTIVATIONS TO TARGET COURT DECISIONS

Presidents are purposive actors who have significant time and resource constraints. Thus, any action by the president should be geared to achieve some end, as part of a larger strategy, and with the intent of minimizing costs. As with all other aspects of presidential leadership, therefore, we think that presidents are motivated to target pending Supreme Court decisions in their public remarks so long as doing so helps the president to obtain good policy, reelection, and/or historical achievement (e.g., Moe 1985). Furthermore, presidents are only likely to engage in a discretionary activity, such as speaking publicly about a Supreme Court case, when they perceive some benefit to these efforts, and that this benefit outweighs the potential costs. As it relates to discussing pending cases, the primary costs are the time and energy spent preparing and delivering remarks about the cases, the negative impression that may come from violating the norm of judicial independence, and any loss in public support for the positions they take. The potential benefits to the president include influencing the outcome of the case and thereby influencing policy, building electoral support, and achieving some historical benefit, such as being associated with the establishment of a landmark Supreme Court decision.

The Costs of Going Public

While the burden of researching cases largely falls on White House staff, and is thus a minimal cost to the president individually, if presidents are viewed in a negative light for discussing pending cases, this might affect their public support and historical legacy. In particular, the norm of judicial independence coupled with the constitutional separation of powers insinuates that presidents should not actively lobby the Court via public appeals (Reddish 1995). Indeed, President Obama's remarks on the *Sebelius* case were seen by critics as "unprecedented" and in violation of the norm of decisional independence (Wallsten and Barnes 2012). For example, Laurence Tribe suggested that "Even if such comments won't affect the justices a bit, they can contribute to an atmosphere of public cynicism that I know this president laments" (Wallsten and Barnes 2012). Consequently, there is a risk to presidents' reputations as guardians of democratic and constitutional norms when they speak about cases pending before the Court.

Similarly, presidents might be criticized for the positions they take on pending cases in their public speeches. As noted on p. 27, Bush faced a host of criticism for his strong public position on the University of Michigan affirmative action cases, including claims that his position was disingenuous, abandoned racial minorities, and turned off political moderates. Further, Democrats were particularly vocal in their opposition to Bush, illustrating how members of the opposite party of the president can seize on such speeches in an effort to hurt the president in the eyes of the public.

The Role of the Office of Solicitor General

In addition to these costs associated with taking public positions on pending cases, the Office of Solicitor General (OSG) provides another reason why presidents may only sparingly use this rhetorical tactic. As the principal attorneys for the executive branch in the Supreme Court, the OSG limits the need to make public appeals since it litigates cases on behalf of the president (Nicholson and Collins 2008; Pacelle 2003). What's more, because the Solicitor General serves at the pleasure of the president, the president can communicate directly with the OSG to ensure the office takes positions in important cases consistent with the president's policy preferences (Caplan 1987; Days 2001; Salokar 1992). If the federal government is a direct party to the case, the OSG represents the interest of the president as a litigant; if the federal government is not a direct party, the OSG can file amicus curiae briefs to make the justices aware of the president's position in the case (Collins 2008a). Thus, the OSG provides a direct and formal mechanism by which presidents can make their positions known to the justices.

Importantly, there is evidence that the justices grant the OSG a substantial amount of deference, ruling in favor of the positions advocated by the OSG in approximately 70 percent of cases (Black and Owens 2012). Further, because the OSG is institutionalized, presidents face little risk of being accused of violating the norm of judicial independence by relying on the OSG to communicate their preferences to the justices. Accordingly, this office may obviate the need for presidents to take public positions on pending cases, or at least minimize the frequency with which they do so.

The Benefits of Going Public

Just as there are costs to going public, and a clear institutional reason – the Office of Solicitor General – why presidents have little need to speak about pending cases, there are several reasons why presidents may be motivated to discuss pending cases. In determining whether to take public positions on pending cases, we posit that presidents will be motivated by two primary factors. First, presidents may take positions on pending cases in their public remarks to influence the outcome of cases through public leadership. This is consistent with the classic going public strategy (Kernell 1997), in which presidents use public pressure to influence the Court to support the president's position, much as they do with respect to influencing legislative outcomes. It is also in line with the popular view that presidents who speak about pending cases are trying to pressure the Court to adopt the president's position. And there is some evidence that presidential power does extend to influence over judicial decisions. Yates and Whitford (1998) and Yates (2002) show, for example, that more popular presidents are more likely to see their preferences adopted by the Court (see also Ducat and Dudley 1989 with respect to federal district courts; but see Nicholson and Collins 2008 on Supreme Court amicus briefs). As well, Rogol, Montgomery, and Kingsland (2018) demonstrate that, when the Court is ideologically unaligned with the president, the justices are more likely to rule in favor of the president's policy preferences in civil rights and liberties cases when the president devotes a relatively large amount of attention to those issue areas in his State of the Union Address.

Obviously, this potential for influence proceeds differently from what Kernell (1997) suggested would motivate a legislative response to presidential remarks. Recall that Kernell expected presidential speeches to create a groundswell of public support on behalf of the president's position. In turn, the public would contact their legislators or otherwise put pressure on them to support the president or face electoral retaliation. This, for Kernell, is the mechanism that allows for going public to be successful in the legislative arena.

For the Court, presidential influence over public opinion would work in a different way. We would not expect the public to respond to presidential speeches by contacting the justices. But, there is fairly compelling evidence that the Court is receptive to public attitudes and tends to follow general trends in public opinion (e.g., Epstein and Martin 2010; Friedman 2009; Giles, Blackstone, and Vining Jr. 2008; McGuire and Stimson 2004). Building off these literatures, we believe that presidential speeches about pending decisions may increase the salience of those issues to the public and motivate them to support the president's position, while further encouraging the justices to consider public opinion as they deliberate over those issues. This approach to going public is more akin to Canes-Wrone's (2001) model of influence through speeches, which also hinges on issue salience. Presidents, undoubtedly, are going to raise this when they use scarce resources to highlight a pending Court decision and so this approach would be plausible in theory, and consistent with previous research on presidential leadership through speechmaking. Under this theory of going public, of course, the ultimate target of the president's speeches is the justices and the potential benefit is a favorable decision.

The second reason why presidents may speak about pending cases is to demonstrate their commitment to issues important to the American people and the democratic process. The public expects presidents to address issues of top concern to the nation (Waterman, Silva, and Jenkins-Smith 2014). As a result, presidents may feel compelled to talk about cases prior to a decision. Such speeches might include explaining to the public the position taken in a legal brief filed on behalf of the federal government, or educating the public as to why the executive branch believes a case should be decided in a particular way. Doing so is consistent with the foundations of the permanent campaign (Doherty 2012), a president's relentless pursuit of public support through travel and public speechmaking.

Both of these reasons for presidential action are consistent with the coordinate construction, or departmentalism, view of constitutional interpretation. Unlike the judicial supremacy perspective, which posits that the judicial branch is the primary arbiter of constitutional meaning, this view holds that all three branches – the executive, legislative, and judicial – play a role in constitutional interpretation (e.g., Scigliano 1971; Whittington 2007). Thus, when the president takes a public position on a pending Supreme Court case, he is not violating the norm of judicial independence. Instead, he is fulfilling his duty as a legitimate interpreter of the Constitution who is engaging in an open dialogue with the judicial branch regarding how best to apply the Constitution to a given dispute. Besides, when the president takes a public position on a pending case, the president can address issues of significance to the public. Because the president, unlike the justices, is elected, this can potentially provide the opportunity for democratic input into constitutional interpretation (e.g., Kramer 2004; Steilen 2013). Though presidents vary with respect to whether they follow departmentalism or judicial supremacy views of constitutional interpretation (Whittington 2001), it is evident that all presidents can claim at least some authority over constitutional interpretation if they see fit. One way that they can do this, largely absent from scholarship on the coordinate construction of the Constitution, is by going public on pending decisions.

In addition, presidents might discuss pending cases to appeal to their partisan bases and motivate these voters. After all, presidents are most likely to represent partisan preferences in their public rhetoric (Wood 2009), something that should be reflected in their position taking on pending cases. Thus, presidents can show their partisan supporters that they are aware of the issues important to them and are willing to take public stances on those issues, which may increase or maintain their co-partisans' support for the president. Under this theory, the ultimate target of these speeches is the public, not the justices, and the potential benefit is mobilizing public support behind the president's positions for reasons other than to influence case outcomes. Indeed, many of the newspaper articles involving President Bush's position on the University of Michigan affirmative action cases made this very point – that presidents can take clear ideological positions that appeal to their bases in a manner that is likely to generate media coverage (e.g., N. Lewis 2003; Stevenson 2003; Wilson 2003).

Discussing pending cases is not a cost-free activity, of course, and thus requires presidents to understand the costs and benefits of doing so. What's more, the ability of the OSG to represent presidents' interests limits the need to turn to public appeals on pending decisions, which supports the empirical data revealed in Chapter 1 that going public on pending cases is quite rare. Moreover, there is always the potential criticism that a president may be opportunistic and look to pander to the public by taking positions on high profile issues. This criticism may be unfounded, however, given that presidents are unlikely to speak about an issue simply to pander to public opinion (Canes-Wrone 2006; Jacobs and Shapiro 2000). Therefore, although we think that the decision to speak about cases is strategic – in that presidents will consider the potential costs and benefits of doing so – we also believe that presidential statements on pending Court cases reflect presidents' sincere preferences (Peterson 1990).

UNDERSTANDING PRESIDENTS' MOTIVATIONS FOR GOING PUBLIC

We have already established in Chapter 1 that presidents rarely go public on pending Supreme Court decisions. They do so, nevertheless, and there are two competing views that appear to best summarize presidents' likely motivations. First, presidents may go public in an effort to influence case outcomes. Second, presidents may go public in an effort to demonstrate that they are responsive to issues that are important to the American public. We explore how we might parse these two motivations. Note that we do not contend these motivations are always mutually exclusive. Rather, we believe that we can paint a picture of overall presidential behavior based on a variety of factors that are more likely to correspond to one approach or the other. With this information in hand, we believe we can then provide some generalizable insights about presidential motivations for position taking on pending Supreme Court decisions.

Timing of Remarks

If presidents' primary motivation for discussing pending cases in their public speeches is to influence the justices' decisions, their speeches should share several common characteristics. First, the timing of speeches on pending decisions may signal the president's intent in speaking about them. If presidents are primarily motivated to influence case outcomes with their speeches, those speeches should cluster within days of the date of oral argument. Such is the case because the justices meet in conference later in the week following oral argument to cast their initial votes and begin the opinion writing process (Baum 2013, 109). Further, the justices begin forming their opinions about the outcome of cases in the weeks prior to oral argument based on the legal briefs, lower court opinions, and bench memoranda that accompany the case (Corley, Collins, and Calvin 2011; Ward and Weiden 2006). Thus, the date of oral argument represents one of the last opportunities to shape the justices' decisions before they begin casting votes and writing opinions. Indeed, it is perhaps the point in which the justices' attention is most focused on a given case. Moreover, the media devote substantial attention to covering oral arguments (Clark, Lax, and Rice 2015). By taking positions on cases around the date of oral arguments, presidents are provided with the opportunity to shape the nature of that coverage, potentially putting their positions on the justices' radar. Conversely, speeches made months prior to oral argument might not permeate the justices' psyches since they are unlikely to have given the case close scrutiny at such an early date. Similarly, speeches made months after oral argument are probably not an effective means of influencing the justices since they would be inclined to have already joined drafts of the opinions by then. Accordingly, if presidents discuss pending cases in an effort to influence the justices, we expect that their speeches will cluster within days of the date of oral argument.

Types of Remarks

Second, we expect presidents to comment on cases in prepared remarks if they are attempting to influence case outcomes. There are three main means by which presidents can communicate: in spoken, prepared remarks, such as formal addresses; in written, prepared remarks, such as in memoranda or statements; and in unprepared, spoken responses, such as question and answer sessions with reporters. If presidents are trying to influence the justices, we expect them to develop this strategy, including their approach and choices of words, internally, and to communicate their position publicly in prepared remarks. Such is the case because prepared remarks may be more likely to set the media's agenda, therefore raising the salience of the case (Bradshaw, Coe, and Neumann 2014).[4] And since the media often drives the public's agenda (Iyengar and Kinder 1987), setting the media's agenda may motivate public interest in the case, which could affect the justices' decisions (McGuire and Stimson 2004).

Conversely, presidents are more likely comment on cases in response to reporters' questions when they are not trying to influence the outcome of cases. Although presidents often anticipate the topics reporters are likely to ask about (Eshbaugh-Soha 2013; Kumar 2007), a question-and-answer format allows the media to dictate the topic of discussion and guide the president's comments through their questions. Presidents may be compelled to answer reporters' questions about Court cases – even when they have no intent to affect the Court's decision – so as to demonstrate a democratic commitment to newsworthy issues that are also important to the public, with the added benefit, we think, of building public or partisan support for their position.

In addition, responses offer presidents less control over the exact language used in their comments than prepared remarks, which also suggests a weaker form of commitment to the positions taken on the cases. For example, President Obama misspoke when he described the administration's position in *United States* v. *Windsor* (2013) as follows: "In the meantime, we filed a–we filed briefs *[sic]* before the Supreme Court that say we think that any discrimination against gays, lesbians, transgenders is subject to heightened scrutiny, and we don't think that DOMA is unconstitutional."[5] Though the White House subsequently corrected this error regarding the constitutionality of the Defense of Marriage Act, it is unlikely that the president would have stumbled in this manner in a prepared remark. Accordingly, if presidents discuss pending cases for the purpose of influencing the justices, we expect to observe most comments come in the form of written or spoken prepared remarks.

Position Strength

Third, if presidents are primarily interested in influencing case outcomes, we expect that they will take strong positions on the outcomes in their public speeches. By taking unequivocal positions, in which there is no ambiguity as to the president's preferred outcome for the case, presidents send the public and the justices a clear signal that they have a strong preference over how the case should be decided. Further, the media may be more attracted to covering such speeches since they represent instances in which presidents take an unwavering public position on a case. This media coverage might increase the justices' awareness of the president's position. And, because the president plays a role in the implementation of the Court's decisions (Epstein and Knight 1998; Hall 2014), a strong public remark about a case may signal to the justices that the president will faithfully oversee the implementation of the Court's decision if the justices rule in favor of the president's view. On the contrary, if presidents are primarily concerned with addressing issues of public concern, they may avoid taking strong positions on cases for fear that doing so may offend some members of the public. Given this, if presidents discuss pending cases for the purpose of influencing the justices, we expect presidents will take strong positions on the outcome of cases.

Presidential Priorities

Fourth, if presidents chiefly use their speeches to influence the justices, we believe they will focus on cases involving presidential policy priorities. Presidents are most likely to go public on their top policy priorities because a defeat on these issues could damage their reputations and undermine their claims for historical relevance (Neustadt 1990). For example, should the Court strike down a president's signature policy achievement, not only is there an immediate loss in terms of eliminating the policy, but there is also the potential for historical damage in the sense that the president might be viewed as being ineffective (Light 1999). To counter such criticism, presidents may attempt to pressure justices to support presidential preferences on cases involving their top policy priorities. Conversely, if presidents are motivated to discuss cases primarily as a way of taking positions on matters of public concern, they will not limit their remarks to cases involving policy priorities. Instead, they can comment on a wider array of cases, many of which may be salient to the public and media, but that are not top presidential priorities. Accordingly, if presidents are primarily motivated to influence the justices, we believe they will tend to comment on cases involving presidential policy priorities.

Length of Remarks

Finally, if presidents' intent is to influence case outcomes, we posit that their remarks on pending cases will be relatively long. Presidents who devote comparatively extensive remarks to pending cases illustrate that they have thought in depth about the case and understand its implications. As it is, lengthier speeches provide presidents with the opportunity to explain why their preferred position has merit and is a better option for the justices than their opponent's position. Since Supreme Court justices are used to writing lengthy opinions (Black and Spriggs 2008), they may better appreciate the time and energy that go into lengthy remarks on pending cases more so than brief comments with little legal depth. Further, presidential influence through speeches centers on the attention presidents devote to an issue, such that presidents are more likely to increase their legislative success by going public more frequently (Barrett 2004) and increase public concern by devoting more sentences to a policy (Cohen 1997). Given this, presidents are likely to be familiar with the benefits of giving certain issues a great deal of attention and pursue this strategy in their efforts to influence the Court. Conversely, if presidents are primarily interested in addressing matters of public concern, the length of their comments is not as relevant as having taken a position, particularly given the media's tendency to cover soundbites, not lengthy explanations. Thus, if presidents discuss pending cases for the purpose of influencing the justices, we expect such speeches to be relatively long.

INVESTIGATING PRESIDENTIAL DISCUSSIONS OF PENDING CASES

To examine presidential motivations for going public on the Court's pending cases, we use the data described in Chapter 1. Figure 2.1 presents the number of presidential comments on pending Supreme Court cases. The black portion of the bars indicates the number of speeches in which presidents mention pending cases and take a position on those cases. The white portion of the bars indicates those speeches in which presidents mention pending cases, but do not take a position on the cases. For example, in response to a reporter's question about *Webster v. Reproductive Health Services* (1989), President George H. W. Bush made his position on the case evident:

> It is an emotional issue, and I am firmly positioned in favor of overturn of *Roe v. Wade*. And that's my position, and I'm not going to change that position. But I don't want to see the divisiveness that that whole issue causes split this country. And yet the decision is going to be – I don't know what they're going to decide, but my position on it is very clear.[6]

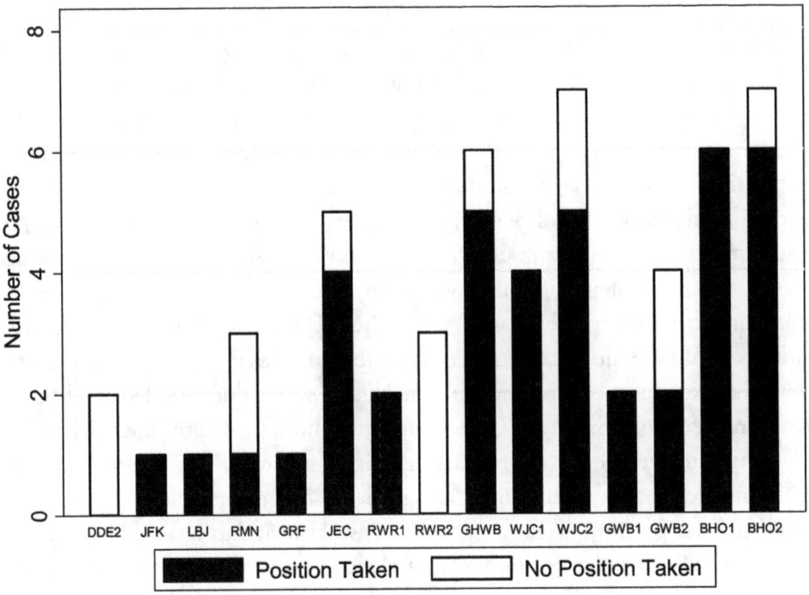

FIGURE 2.1. The number of presidential speeches on pending cases, 1953–2017

Conversely, President Obama discussed *United States* v. *Texas* (2016) in response to a reporter's questions about the case, but did not take a position on the case's outcome:

> So we put forward a plan. Part of it we were able to implement: the DREAM Act kids who we were able to make sure were treated like the young Americans that they are. We then had an additional program through administrative action that the Supreme Court put a stay on – or the lower courts put a stay on, and is about to go to the Supreme Court. In part, the process takes a long time generally. With the Supreme Court one Justice short, it will be interesting to see whether or not they can come to a ruling or whether they're – they arrive at a tie, a 4–4 tie. We don't know yet. That's pending.
>
> In the meantime, we're still implementing a number of reforms and changes to make the system – the legal immigration system smoother, not as expensive, fairer to people, to treat families with more respect. We have changed our priorities in terms of enforcement so that we're not deporting and separating families as much and more focused on going after criminals and people who pose a security threat to the community. But our hands are a little bit tied on some of the bigger things until the Supreme Court rules.[7]

Figure 2.1 reveals several important findings. First, presidential discussions of pending cases are rare. From 1953 to 2017, presidents discussed 36 unique pending cases in 54 speeches. (Appendix Table 2.1 provides a list of these cases.) Moreover, when they discuss cases, they do not always take positions on those cases. Of the 54 speeches that mention a pending case, presidents took a position on the case mentioned in 40 speeches (74.1 percent). Second, presidential discussions of pending cases have increased over time. Although each president in our sample commented on at least one pending Supreme Court case, recent presidents have commented on more pending cases in comparison with presidents who served before Carter. Prior to Carter, presidents from Eisenhower to Ford commented on cases in a single speech each, with the exception of Eisenhower and Nixon, who addressed two and three cases, respectively. Since the Carter administration, presidents have discussed cases in an average of approximately eight speeches per president, with Clinton and Obama mentioning cases in 11 and 13 speeches each. This finding also holds for position taking on pending cases. Presidents Kennedy, Johnson, Nixon, and Ford took a position on a single case each. Since Carter, presidents have taken positions on pending cases in an average of six speeches per president. Further, presidents have become increasingly accustomed to addressing the same case in multiple speeches. For example, President George W. Bush discussed *Hamdan* v. *Rumsfeld* in four speeches, and President Obama addressed *King* v. *Burwell* (2015) in three speeches and *National Federation of Independent Business* v. *Sebelius* in four speeches. This overall increase in going public with respect to the Court's pending decisions is consistent with the tendency of more recent presidents to speak about judicial nominations (Cameron and Park 2011) and the Supreme Court in general terms (Blackstone and Goelzhauser 2014). Besides, this figure should put to rest the claim that President Obama's position taking regarding the Affordable Care Act cases was unprecedented.

We continue our investigation by examining the characteristics of the speeches under analysis. Because we are most interested in those speeches in which presidents engaged in position taking on cases, we limit our remaining analyses to those instances in which presidents took a position on a pending case. As noted above, since presidents comment on pending cases very rarely, this small sample size necessarily limits the extent of our analysis. Therefore, the remainder of our discussion is also descriptive in nature.

We begin by examining the timing of presidential speeches on pending cases. To calculate this information, we compared the date of the speech to the oral argument date, as indicated in Spaeth et al. (2018). Figure 2.2 reports the number of days from the date of oral argument that the speech was given.

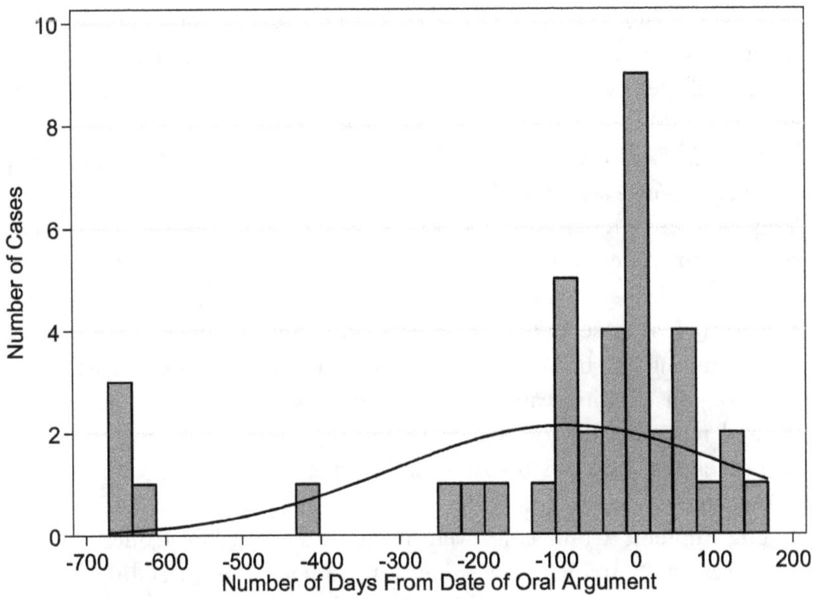

FIGURE 2.2. The timing of presidential speeches on pending Supreme Court decisions relative to the date of oral argument, 1953–2017

Note: Negative values indicate the number of days before oral argument that the speech was given, and positive values indicate the number of days after oral argument that the speech was given. The solid line indicates the scaled normal density curve.

Negative values indicate the number of days *before* oral argument that the speech was given, and positive values indicate the number of days *after* oral argument that the speech was given. The solid line indicates the scaled normal density curve.

On average, presidents take positions on cases 89 days before oral argument (standard deviation = 219), although there is some evidence that speeches cluster around oral argument.[8] For example, 11 of the 39[9] speeches (28.2 percent) were given within a month before or after oral argument. However, if presidents' motivation for discussing pending cases was to influence the justices, we would expect a much higher percentage of speeches to cluster around the date of oral arguments since that date marks the period in which the justices' attention is most focused on the cases. Indeed, even a generous calculation of ± one month around oral arguments indicates that only about one in four speeches coincide with this time period. This provides perhaps the most compelling evidence that presidents' primary motivation for position taking on pending cases is not to influence the justices, but rather to address matters of public concern and appeal to their political bases, as it indicates that presidential speeches are rarely timed to coincide with the period of time in which the justices are most engaged with their cases.

Figure 2.3 presents the types of remarks in which presidents discussed Supreme Court cases. Written, prepared remarks include messages to Congress, signing remarks, and, most commonly, policy statements. Spoken, prepared remarks consist of statements made during speeches, such as those with religious leaders and interest groups. Responses include unprepared oral remarks, such as those made during news conferences, interviews with reporters, and during question-and-answer sessions. Overall, presidents have taken a position on pending cases in 10 written, prepared remarks; 11 spoken, prepared remarks; and 19 spoken, unprepared responses. Thus, presidents discuss pending cases in prepared and unprepared remarks with roughly equal frequency. Indeed, 19 of the presidents' 40 (47.5 percent) mentions of pending Supreme Court cases were made in some form of question-and-answer session.[10] Among these, nine were responses to questions in more structured press conferences. Although presidents have some control over the subject of questions asked (Eshbaugh-Soha 2013; Kumar 2007) and are likely to be aware that a reporter will ask about a high-profile Supreme Court case, the president's decision to comment on pending cases in response to reporters' questions suggests that presidents often go public on Supreme Court cases to demonstrate a democratic commitment to address issues of public concern, not to purposively influence the Court's decision. If that was the case, we would expect to see substantially more discussions of pending cases in prepared remarks, as compared with 19 unprepared remarks. Instead, presidents address pending cases in almost an equal amount of prepared and unprepared remarks.

Figure 2.4 illustrates the frequency with which presidents take strong positions on pending decisions. Strong positions are coded as those in which presidents expressed an unequivocal and clear position as to their preferred outcome of the case. Strong positions often involve presidents detailing their stance on a piece of legislation being reviewed or specifically noting that the Court should rule in a particular way. Those positions not coded as strong include instances in which presidents suggest a law is constitutional, restate the position taken by the Solicitor General in a case without advocating for it, or make a statement from which the president's position can be inferred. For example, President Clinton's position on *Printz* v. *United States* (1997) is coded as strong:

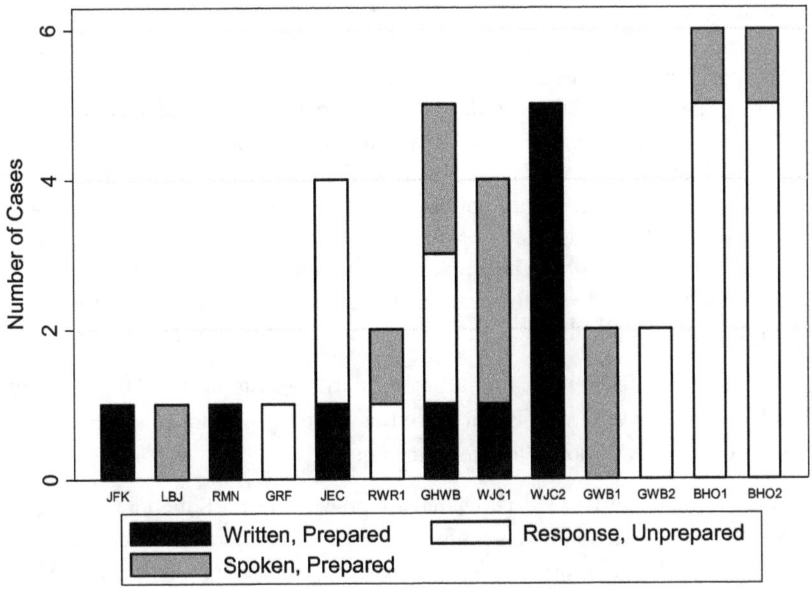

FIGURE 2.3. The number of presidential speeches by type of remark, 1953–2017

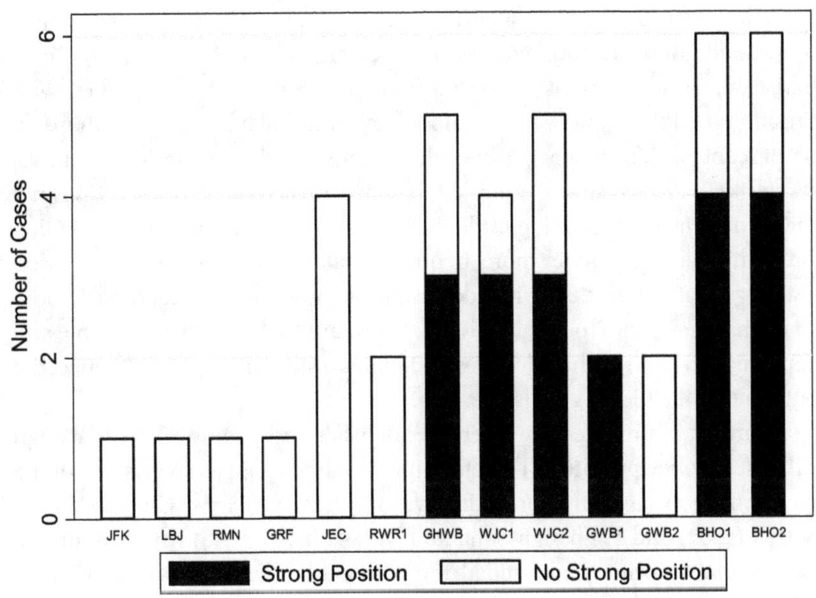

FIGURE 2.4. The number of strong positions taken on Supreme Court cases by presidents, 1953–2017

> Now the Supreme Court has agreed to review a case over the constitutionality of requiring local law enforcement officials to help make sure that a person buying a handgun is legally entitled to do so. Well, I just want to make clear I am going to do everything in my power to keep the Brady bill the law of the land. It's keeping people alive. It's a good thing. Convicted felons and fugitives and people who are a threat to the community or to their own spouses and children should not be out there, if we can keep them legally from having the handguns by a simple waiting period so that we can check whether they should have it or not. Every law enforcement organization in this country has endorsed the Brady Bill. And we dare not walk away from it. It is keeping people alive.[11]

Conversely, President Carter's position in *Regents of the University of California* v. *Bakke* (1978) is not coded as a strong position, as revealed in this portion of his response to a reporter's question:

> Well, as you know, we filed a brief that was prepared by the Solicitor General, Mr. McCree, which I think is compatible with what you would have wanted. This is the White House position, because I personally approved the brief. I am not a lawyer. And the Attorney General filed it on behalf of me and the entire administration.[12]

Overall, presidents took strong positions on pending cases in 19 of the 40 speeches in which they took a position on a case (47.5 percent). Interestingly, no president took a strong position until George H. W. Bush in 1989. Since that date, presidents took strong positions in 63 percent of speeches, with Presidents Clinton and Obama most frequently taking strong positions in 67 percent of their respective speeches. Considered as a whole, Figure 2.4 reveals that, though strong position taking has increased over time, this is not the dominant strategy for presidents when they take positions on pending cases. Instead, presidents more frequently take weaker positions on cases, a strategy that is consistent with addressing issues of public concern to demonstrate that they are in touch with issues important to the American people and appealing to their political bases, rather than attempting to influence the outcome of the Court's decisions.

Figure 2.5 illuminates how often presidents discuss pending cases that align with their policy priorities. To determine whether a case addresses one of the president's top legislative priorities, we matched our cases with Eshbaugh-Soha's (2005) and Eshbaugh-Soha and Miles's (2008–2009) lists of domestic presidential priorities, and added the Affordable Care Act for the Obama administration. We also matched one foreign policy priority not on these lists of domestic proposals – the War in Iraq – with one Supreme Court case

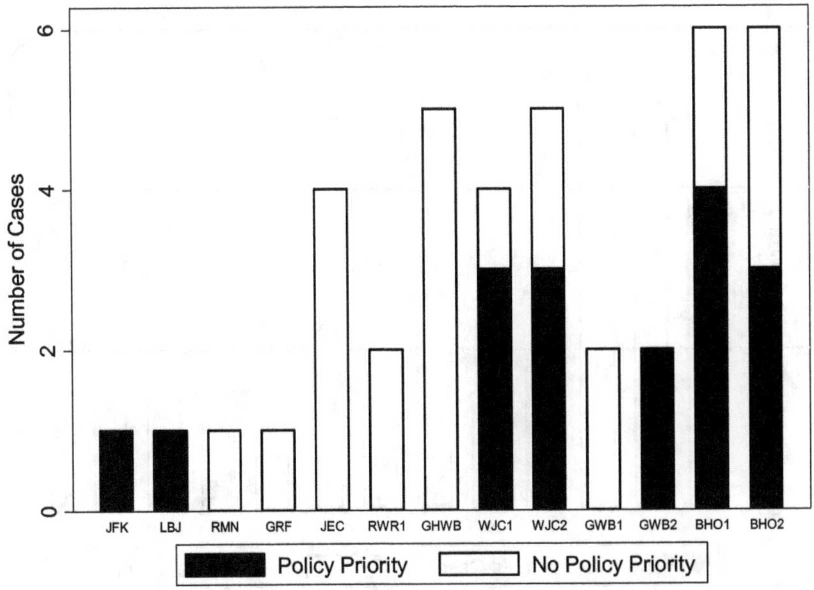

FIGURE 2.5. The number of speeches on Supreme Court cases involving presidential policy priorities by presidents, 1953–2017

during the George W. Bush administration – *Hamdan* v. *Rumsfeld* (2006) – to create a final list of cases that involved presidential priorities.

Figure 2.5 indicates that presidents addressed cases that aligned with their policy priorities in 17 of 40 speeches in which they took a position on a pending case (42.5 percent). Notably, only 5 of the 11 presidents in our sample discussed any cases involving their policy priorities. Of those that did, Presidents Clinton and Obama discussed the most priority-related cases, in 66.7 percent and 58.3 percent of their respective speeches. Overall, these results support the view that presidents do not discuss cases to influence the Court. If this were the president's primary strategy, we would expect to see far more attention devoted to cases that implicate their policy priorities. Instead, we find further evidence that presidents discuss pending cases to show the citizenry that they are responsive to matters of public concern, including those not involving policy priorities.

Figure 2.6 provides information regarding the length of presidential comments on pending decisions. The black portion of the bars indicates the average number of words in each remark that involved the discussion of the pending case, and the white portion of the bars indicates the average number of words in the entire remark.[13] The number of words devoted to the Court's

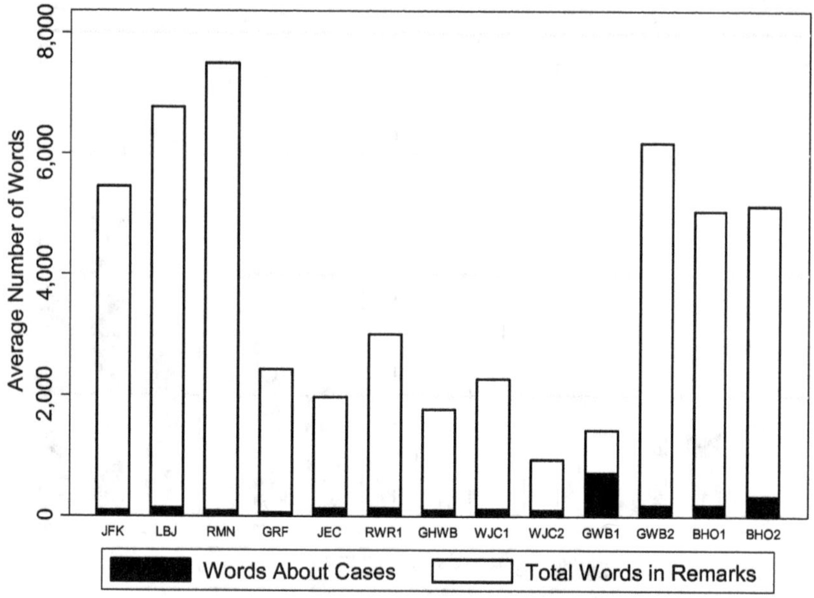

FIGURE 2.6. The average number of words in presidential speeches involving pending Supreme Court decisions, 1953–2017

decisions ranges from a low of a single word to a high of 712 words. On the low end, President George H. W. Bush took a position on *Webster* when he responded "Yes" to a reporter's question that asked whether he would like to see the case "be the first step in a move to ban abortion in this country?"[14] On the high end, President George W. Bush outlined his position on the University of Michigan affirmative action cases in 11 paragraphs, constituting more than 700 words.[15] The mean number of words devoted to pending decisions is 188 (standard deviation = 173). To put this in perspective, the average number of words in the whole of the remarks under analysis that mention cases is 3,225 (standard deviation = 2,793). This means that less than 6 percent of presidential remarks that involve position taking on pending cases are actually devoted to the case itself. If presidents' primary motivation for discussing cases was to influence the decisions of the Court, we would expect this percentage to be substantially higher, indicating that they devote much of their remarks to the cases themselves. Instead, we find less than 1 in 15 words touch on cases, which is more consistent with demonstrating their commitment to issues that are important to the American people and appealing to their political bases than trying to influence the justices.

THE IMPACT OF PRESIDENTIAL DISCUSSIONS OF PENDING CASES

Although we are chiefly interested in understanding why presidents discuss pending cases in their public rhetoric, we are also able to provide some evidence with respect to the impact of these speeches on case outcomes in Figure 2.7.[16] The white bars indicate the success rate of the Solicitor General in cases in which presidents took a public position, and the black bars indicate the Solicitor General's overall success rate, as reported in Black and Owens (2012, 26). Note that the Solicitor General either filed an amicus curiae brief or represented the government as a litigant in all of the cases in which presidents took a public position. In the cases in which the US filed an amicus curiae brief, the president's position emerged victorious in 71 percent of cases, compared with 75 percent of cases overall. In those cases in which the US was a litigant, the president's position was endorsed by the Court in 56 percent of cases, compared with 65 percent of cases overall. Thus, there is no evidence of a positive effect of presidential rhetoric on the justices.[17]

In fact, one might interpret these figures to imply that presidents take positions on cases they perceive as being at risk of losing. One way to look into this further is to examine instances in which presidents took positions in cases after the Solicitor General participated in oral arguments. Research

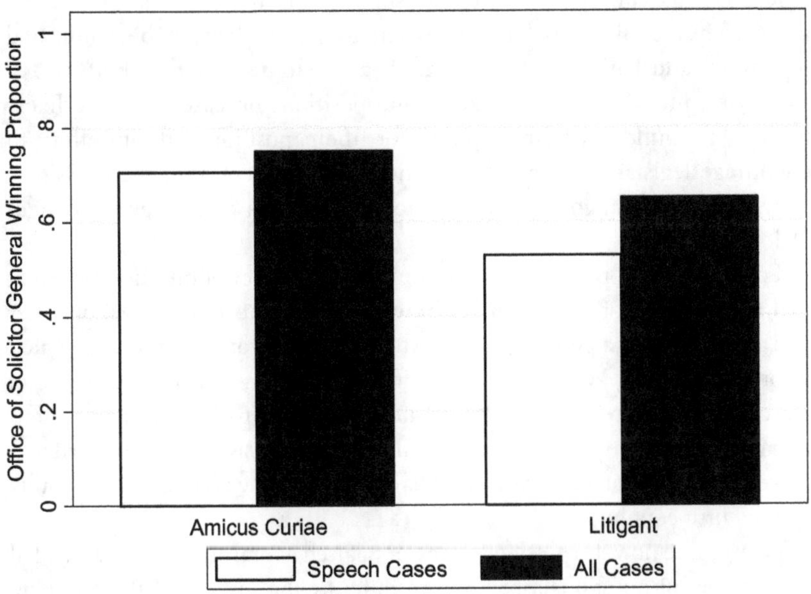

FIGURE 2.7. Solicitor General success in the Supreme Court, 1953–2017

demonstrates that case outcomes can be partially predicted by the number of questions asked at oral arguments, with the party receiving the highest volume of questioning more likely to lose (e.g., Epstein, Landes, and Posner 2010; Greenhouse 2004; Johnson et al. 2009; Roberts 2005). The logic is that, when the justices ask a particularly high volume of questions of an attorney, this signals their doubt as to the validity of that attorney's position. Conversely, when the justices ask few questions of an attorney, this is suggestive of agreement with that attorney's position. Applying these findings to the focus of this chapter, if presidents take positions on cases they believe they are likely to lose after oral arguments, we would expect the attorneys in the Solicitor General's office to be asked a higher volume of questions than their opponents at oral arguments in such cases.

From the president's perspective, taking a public position on cases they are likely to lose may be a strategic effort to relay to the justices that they have a strong opinion on the case and are willing to use the bully pulpit to communicate that position. Since it is so rare for presidents to take positions on pending decisions, the justices might view this as a credible signal that the president cares a great deal about the outcome of the case and may give the president's position additional consideration. Further, such a strategy by presidents is consistent with the manner in which they go public on judicial nominations. Research indicates that presidents tend to make public speeches in support of their judicial nominees when they are likely to fail, not when they are likely to be confirmed (Cameron and Park 2011; Holmes 2007, 2008; Johnson and Roberts 2004). Moreover, presidents might take public positions on cases they are likely to lose to build partisan support for their positions in an effort to encourage legislative or executive actions to reverse or alter the decisions. Thus, presidents might be expected to go public on cases they are danger of losing.

To evaluate this possibility, we examine the number of questions asked at oral arguments for those instances in which presidents took a position, after oral arguments, on a pending case in which the Solicitor General participated in oral arguments. We include cases in which attorneys from the Office of Solicitor General represented the United States as a party and as an amicus curiae at oral arguments. There is a total of only nine cases that fit our criteria, so we recognize that we have a very small sample size, which limits our ability to draw firm conclusions.

To examine how the president's position faired at oral arguments, we coded the number of questions asked, per minute, by the justices of the attorneys arguing in support of the president's position and the number of questions asked, per minute, by the justices of the attorneys arguing in opposition to the president's position. We use the per minute average to account for the fact that there are variations in the length of time granted to each litigant when the Solicitor General participates in oral arguments as an amicus. We also include the number of questions asked of the counsel supported by the Solicitor General as an amicus, since the number of questions that lawyer receives is also reflective of the justice's likely positions on the case.[18] We obtained the oral argument transcripts from Oyez (2018).

Figure 2.8 reports the number of questions asked by the justices of the attorneys advocating for the president's position and those asked of the attorneys advocating for the opposing position. In the nine cases under analysis, the justices asked the attorneys supporting the president's position an average of 1.9 questions per minute, compared with an average of 1.7 questions per minute for the opposing attorneys. A difference-of-means test reveals this distinction is not statistically significant. Moreover, looking at the individual oral arguments reveals that the attorneys representing the president's position were asked more questions than their opposition in only 4 out of 9 cases. Thus, there does not appear to be systematic evidence that presidents are more likely to take public positions on

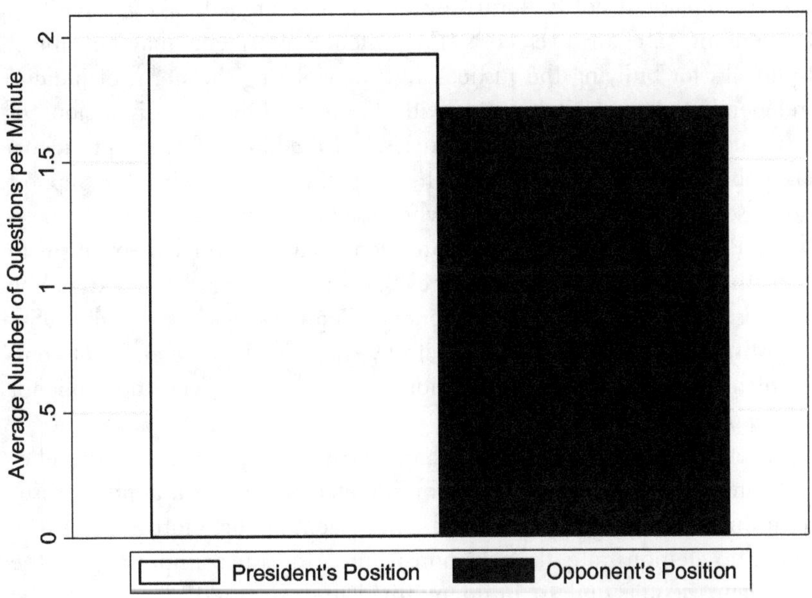

FIGURE 2.8. The average number of questions at oral argument supporting and opposing the president's position, 1953–2017

pending cases if the justices appear to oppose the presidents' positions at oral arguments. We believe this provides additional evidence that presidential remarks on pending cases are not primarily intended to influence the justices.

CONCLUSIONS

Speaking publicly is central to the president's governing strategy. Although we know that presidents speak to influence legislation, news coverage, and public opinion, the extent of our understanding of whether presidents speak to influence the Supreme Court has heretofore been limited. Having catalogued and analyzed the universe of cases in which presidents have spoken about pending Supreme Court decisions, we offer two primary conclusions concerning presidential efforts to target cases through public appeals.

First, such appeals are very rare. From 1953 to 2017, presidents discussed Supreme Court cases in only 54 speeches and took a position on the cases in only 40 speeches covering 28 cases. Thus, though presidents are occasionally willing to take public positions on pending cases, this is not a common rhetorical strategy. That discussions of pending cases are infrequent should not be surprising. As we have argued, taking a position on pending cases involves costs. For instance, presidents may be subject to attacks for bullying the justices and for violating the norm of judicial independence, as was the case with President Obama's discussions of challenges to the Affordable Care Act. In addition, when presidents take positions on pending cases, they run the risk of losing the support of those members of the public who disagree with the presidents' positions. Perhaps most importantly, presidents have a formal mechanism to relay their preferences to the justices that limits the need to make public appeals: the Office of Solicitor General. Significantly, because the OSG is institutionalized, there are few (if any) negative consequences of communicating the presidents' positions to the Court via the Solicitor General.

Second, our analyses of the characteristics of presidential speeches indicate that presidents do not primarily take positions on pending cases to influence the justices. Instead, they seem to be motivated by the desire to demonstrate their responsiveness to issues important to the American people and to build political and electoral support. To be clear, we are not concluding that presidents *never* take positions on pending cases in the hope that they will influence the Court's decision.

For instance, George W. Bush's speech on the University of Michigan affirmative action cases has many of the hallmarks of trying to the influence the justices: it was a prepared remark; it was lengthy, and the president took a strong position on outcome of the cases. Rather, on balance, our evidence reveals this is not the dominant strategy for discussing pending cases. For example, presidents take positions on cases with roughly equal frequency in prepared and unprepared remarks and do not overwhelmingly take strong positions on cases or primarily address cases touching on their policy priorities. Further, when they take positions on pending cases, presidents do not devote especially lengthy portions of their public remarks to the cases. Perhaps most tellingly, the timing of presidential positions on pending cases is not consistent with a dominant strategy of influencing the justices as only about one in four speeches fall within one month of oral argument. Thus, the weight of our evidence suggests that presidents do not go public on pending cases primarily to influence their outcomes. This suggests that presidents may view their role in the coordinate construction of the Constitution not as primarily involving efforts to shape the Court's pending decisions, but rather as efforts to influence the interpretation of already decided cases, as we demonstrate in the chapters that follow.

All of this makes sense and plays into a balanced approach to presidential relations with the Court. On the one hand, presidents run the risk of being criticized for violating the norm of judicial independence if they attempt to pressure the Court by taking public positions on pending cases. This is one reason why the president is not likely to attempt this strategy. But the president may still affect Court decisions through the Office of the Solicitor General, which provides the opportunity to engage in the coordinate construction of the Constitution in a different manner. What's more, presidents are fortunate that they do not have to speak about Court cases, as they might have to speak about pending legislation to influence its outcome. Thus, presidents are in an enviable position that enables them to protect the norm of judicial independence while still influencing the outcome of Supreme Court cases through the Office of Solicitor General. If this mechanism was not available to presidents, then they might have to reconsider using their public rhetoric to affect Court decisions. Of course, there is no reason to think that the Office of Solicitor General is likely to go away any time soon, so the patterns demonstrated in this chapter are likely to hold for future presidents.

APPENDIX TABLE.2.1. *Pending Supreme Court cases discussed by presidents, 1953–2017*

Case (Year)	President	Speeches	Position
Cooper v. *Aaron* (1958)	Eisenhower	1	0
US v. *Cannelton Sewer Pipe Co.* (1960)	Eisenhower	1	0
Peterson v. *City of Greenville* (1963)	Kennedy	1	100
Heart of Atlanta Motel v. *US* (1964)	Johnson	1	100
US v. *Nevada* (1973)	Nixon	1	100
US v. *Nixon* (1974)	,Nixon	2	0
Runyon v. *McCrary* ((1976)	Ford	1	100
Regents of California v. *Bakke* (1978)	Carter	2	50
New York Times v. *Jascalevich* (1978)	Carter	1	0
INS v. *Chadha* (1983)	Carter	2	100
Boston Firefighters v. *NAACP* (1983)	Reagan	1	100
Estate of Thornton v. *Caldor* (1985)	Reagan	1	100
Bowsher v. *Synar* (1986)	Reagan	3	0
Webster v. *Reproductive Health Services* (1989)	H. W. Bush	3	66.7
Michigan Dept. of State Police v. *Sitz* (1990)	H. W. Bush	1	100
Planned Parenthood v. *Casey* (1992)	H. W. Bush	2	100
Miller v. *Johnson* (1995)	Clinton	1	100
US v. *Lopez* (1995)	Clinton	1	100
Printz v. *US* (1997)	Clinton	2	100
Clinton v. *Jones* (1997)	Clinton	1	0
Raines v. *Byrd* (1997)	Clinton	2	50
Clinton v. *New York* (1998)	Clinton	1	100
Department of Commerce v. *US House* (1999)	Clinton	1	100
FDA v. *Brown & Williamson Tobacco* (2000)	Clinton	1	100
Bush v. *Gore* (2000)	Clinton	1	0
Gratz v. *Bollinger* (2003)	W. Bush	1	100
Grutter v. *Bollinger* (2003)	W. Bush	1	100
Hamdan v. *Rumsfeld* (2006)	W. Bush	4	50
al-Marri v. *Spagone* (2009)	Obama	1	100
NFIB v. *Sebelius* (2012)	Obama	4	100
US v. *Windsor* (2013)	Obama	1	100
Hollingsworth v. *Perry* (2013)	Obama	1	100
McCutcheon v. *FEC* (2014)	Obama	1	100
King v. *Burwell* (2015)	Obama	3	100
Obergefell v. *Hodges* (2015)	Obama	1	100
US v. *Texas* (2016)	Obama	1	100
Overall		54	74.1

Speeches represents the number of speeches in which presidents discussed each case. **Position** indicates the percentage of speeches in which presidents took a position on the case.

3

Going Public on Decided Cases

It is far more common for presidents to speak about cases already decided by the Supreme Court than it is for presidents to pressure the Court to side with their preferences by taking positions on pending decisions. Yet, among presidential remarks on decided cases, there exists fairly wide variation in the style of presidential comments. Consider, for example, statements made by Presidents Reagan and Clinton. President Reagan expressed his strong disdain for *Roe* v. *Wade* (1973) in 14 separate speeches. Reagan's speech at a March for Life rally in 1987 is emblematic of the type of rhetoric the president used in referring to *Roe*. In this speech, held on the fifteenth anniversary of *Roe*, Reagan denounced the Court's decision in no uncertain terms, calling it a "tragedy" that "has claimed the lives of more than 20 million infants."[1] Reagan's comments clearly targeted the Court and were highly critical of its landmark decision. Yet, his intent does not appear related to pressuring the Court on any immediate decision as the president made no reference to any pending abortion cases on the Court's docket. Rather, it appears that the president's motivation was to reach out to a committed constituency about a highly salient political issue, motivate support for his historical legacy, and communicate his policy position on the issue of abortion.

In contrast to President Reagan's harsh criticism of *Roe*, President Clinton took a more measured approach in his response to the landmark affirmative action case, *Adarand* v. *Pena* (1995). The president referenced the ruling a total of eight times, four of which came shortly after the Court's ruling in June of 1995. Clinton not only stated his commitment to following the Court's decision, but he also directed his Attorney General and bureaucratic agencies to ensure that the federal government complied with the ruling and implemented it "expeditiously." In addition, Clinton took the opportunity to provide his own opinion on affirmative action in light of the Court's decision:

> Affirmative action has been good for America. Affirmative action has not always been perfect, and affirmative action should not go on forever. It should be changed now to take care of those things that are wrong, and it should be retired when its job is done. I am resolved that that day will come. But the evidence suggests, indeed, screams that that day has not come.[2]

Given these statements, President Clinton's reasons for referencing *Adarand* appear to have been to take a position on a highly salient public issue and direct the federal bureaucracy in the implementation of the Court's ruling.

These two examples illustrate the different ways that presidents have responded to Supreme Court decisions. But why are presidents motivated to speak about these cases more generally? Appealing to key electoral constituencies, responding to salient issues, and guiding the implementation of Court decisions appear to be a few reasons why presidents do this. And although presidents can be quite critical of the Court in their public remarks, responding to the Court's decided cases in this manner does not appear to present the same challenge to the norm of judicial independence as pressuring the Court before it renders a decision might. Such is the case because, in these instances, presidents cannot be criticized for putting inappropriate pressure on the justices regarding the Court's pending decisions. Instead, they are contributing to the public debate about already-decided cases. From the coordinate construction of the Constitution perspective, such statements are perfectly legitimate and demonstrate how the president can play a role in constitutional interpretation as a coequal branch of government (e.g., Meese 1987; Paulsen 1994; Whittington 2001). Further, such comments allow presidents to demonstrate responsiveness to the American people on important issues facing the nation, and we argue that their incentives for doing so are driven by presidents' three primary goals: achieving reelection, good public policy, and historical recognition.

To investigate why presidents respond to Supreme Court decisions in their public rhetoric, we examine the amount of attention presidents devote per month to referencing decided cases, similar to research conducted on the number of presidential speeches generally (e.g., Eshbaugh-Soha 2010; Hager and Sullivan 1994; Powell 1999; Ragsdale 1984). We differentiate written and spoken comments and show that, although the former are used almost exclusively to direct the implementation of the Court's decisions, the latter are designed to allow presidents to take positions on Court cases that are important to their electoral bases given the primacy of presidential speeches to presidents' permanent campaign for public support (Doherty 2012). Often, presidents will comment on recently decided cases to speak to issues that are timely and salient to the national policy conversation. Indeed, we find that presidents are especially likely to discuss Supreme Court cases during reelection years and when those cases garner media attention. We further divide our cases into historic and recent decisions in an effort to demonstrate how presidential motivations may vary depending on the age of the case they are referencing. In addition to examining the factors that shape presidents' decisions to discuss the Court's cases, this chapter also provides an overview of the decisions presidents most commonly discuss. Our purpose in doing so is to provide the reader with a better understanding of the cases presidents deem salient enough to mention in their public rhetoric.

PRESIDENTIAL RESPONSIVENESS THROUGH PUBLIC COMMENTS

Presidents speak frequently, averaging over 300 speeches each year since 1953 and nearly 375 speeches per year since the Reagan Administration (Ragsdale 2014). Including written statements, as we do in our analyses, increases the yearly average by several hundred more public comments. Aided by the institution of the White House communications operation (Eshbaugh-Soha 2011), presidents have ample resources to use their spoken and written statements to govern. Indeed, an army of speechwriters and communications experts, as well as increased institutional capacity, has allowed presidents to use these speeches and written comments to maintain a public presence in an increasingly noisy political world.

In addition to having the means to engage in public outreach, presidents have had a strategy for making public appeals. Initially, scholars coined this strategy "going public," whereby presidents speak to lead the public in an attempt to pressure Congress to respond and support their legislative agendas (Kernell 1997). Subsequent research showed that because presidents are typically unsuccessful moving public preferences (Edwards 2003), the relationship between presidential speeches and increased legislative success was not necessarily coercive. Instead, it was done as a way for presidents to signal support for their agendas (Eshbaugh-Soha 2006) and, in so doing, increase the salience of issues on the legislative agenda (Eshbaugh-Soha and Peake 2011). By going public on issues already popular with the American people, presidents are able to use their power of agenda-setting to increase their success in Congress (Canes-Wrone 2001).

Scholarship now contends that the presidents' efforts at speaking publicly go well beyond presidential leadership of the agenda and efforts to enhance their success in Congress. Indeed, there are many times when the president's priorities fail to pass Congress, which is often a function of conditions over which presidents have very limited control, such as the partisan makeup of the House and Senate (Bond and Fleisher 1990). Thus, presidents also speak to generate news coverage (Cohen 2008), lead partisan public opinion (Cavari 2017), and, in some instances, shape public preferences (Rottinghaus 2010). This may be to build additional public support or, more than likely, to maintain the support the president already has (Edwards 2003).

Regardless of whom the president targets when speaking, the bulk of existing research on presidential public leadership assumes that the president's primary goal is to lead others (Neustadt 1990). Mounting evidence reveals the difficulty presidents have persuading through speeches, yet they continue to deliver an average of over one speech per day. Increasingly, scholars have found that when they speak, presidents also respond in their public speeches to others, including the media, Congress, and the public, all of which have important implications for the president's role as a democratic leader. In many ways, presidents respond to the public's preferences for popular policy solutions in Canes-Wrone's (2001) model of strategic action, even though they also attempt to increase the salience of those issues through public leadership (Eshbaugh-Soha and Peake 2011). Either way, what we know about presidential responsiveness through public comments primarily centers on the president's reaction to issues in the news. This literature has mostly overlooked whether, to what extent, and why presidents might respond to decisions of the Supreme Court, which is the focus of this chapter.

Presidential Responsiveness

The essence of presidential responsiveness may be explained by presidents' inability to stay out in front of many policy and political issues even though they speak frequently. Without a doubt, presidents successfully set the policy agenda by prioritizing issues not currently on the national agenda. For example, Edwards and Wood (1999) find that presidents lead the agendas of the news media and Congress when the issue was a policy that they initiated and not previously salient. One prominent example in their study is health care policy, which was not a salient topic prior to Bill Clinton's health care reform proposal, but became an important issue after the proposal was introduced. In turn, the president led media and congressional attention, although the relationship to congressional attention is relatively weak (Edwards and Wood 1999, 340).

More often than not, however, presidents respond to issues that arise independently of their efforts at public leadership or that are chronically on the political agenda. That is, when an issue is already salient – and may have become so regardless of presidential speeches – presidents tend to respond rather than lead those issues. For example, Edwards and Wood (1999) illustrate how the president's agenda on chronically salient foreign policy issues, such as the Arab-Israeli conflict, is responsive to the news agenda. Eshbaugh-Soha and Peake (2011) argue that issue salience is a key factor in whether presidents lead or respond in their public remarks, whereby issues that increase in salience independently of presidential leadership may encourage presidential responsiveness. This is often the case when it comes to issues such as the economy and especially when public concern for such an issue is high (Eshbaugh-Soha and Peake 2005). Interestingly, presidents rarely respond to the legislative agenda (Edwards and Wood 1999). Finally, the principle that presidents respond to salient issues extends to presidential responsiveness to the public. On highly salient issues, such as the economy, both Eshbaugh-Soha and Peake (2011) and Wood (2007, 51) demonstrate that presidents respond to public concern about economic issues. Echoing initial research into public mood (Erikson, MacKuen, and Stimson 2002), Wood (2009) also finds that presidents become more liberal when public opinion shifts in the liberal direction. Thus, it is evident that presidents react to a wide array of actors and situations in formulating their public appeals.

Responding to the Court

The same motivations that guide presidential responsiveness to other institutions, the public, and the news media may also drive their responsiveness to the Supreme Court. That is, when a salient issue attracts the attention of the Supreme Court, presidents are likely to respond to the Court's attention to the issue. To date, little research explores the presidents' responses to the actions of the judiciary (but see Blackstone and Goelzhauser 2014; Flemming, Wood, and Bohte 1999). It makes sense, on the one hand, that scholarship has not explored the public relationship between the president and Court at length. The Court is typically the least public of all governmental institutions. For example, the justices conduct much of their business behind closed doors, they do not allow cameras in the courtroom, and they engage the public much less frequently than their elected counterparts (Black, Owens, and Armaly 2016). Thus, as compared with the public, news media, and Congress, presidents often have little to respond to when it involves the Supreme Court.

On the other hand, however, this lack of research is surprising. The Supreme Court is often the final arbiter of the Constitution and is a coequal branch of government with enormous potential to shape major policy concerns and drive social change (Segal and Spaeth 2002). Particular to the president, the Court issues rulings that may affect presidents' policy priorities or their preferred outcomes associated with a case. Some high-profile recent examples of the Court deciding the fate of presidential policy priorities include health care reform under President Obama and President Trump's travel ban.

Despite our descriptive evidence presented in Chapter 1 that reveals presidents not infrequently comment on Supreme Court decisions, there is very little research that explores the relationship between the Court and the presidency in the public arena. One thread of research that does study the presidency and the Court examines agenda-setting, often focusing on the interrelationships between presidential, judicial, and congressional attention to various issues. For example, Flemming, Wood, and Bohte (1999) find that presidents are highly responsive to civil rights, one of the most salient issues of the 1960s and 1970s. They are also responsive to Supreme Court attention to civil liberties issues, but not to environmental issues. What is more, presidents do not lead the Court's attention on any of these issues. In a related article, but in which the authors exclude the presidency, Flemming, Bohte, and Wood (1997) look at how news coverage responds to significant Supreme Court decisions. Not surprisingly, several key Supreme Court cases, such as *Engle* v. *Vitale* (1962) and *Cooper* v. *Aaron* (1958), had positive and substantively significant effects on subsequent news coverage of related issues. This work suggests that news coverage of Supreme Court cases may be a driving factor behind those cases that presidents reference in their public remarks, something that we examine in this chapter and in Chapter 6.

Another thread of research looks more precisely at the president's rhetoric that references the Supreme Court. Blackstone and Goelzhauser (2014) examine all mentions of the Supreme Court by the president. They find that a number of factors encourage presidents to reference the Supreme Court in their public rhetoric. In brief, presidents who are lawyers are more likely to speak about the Supreme Court and presidents more frequently discuss the Court during presidential election years and when there is a vacancy on the Court. Whether presidents attempt to sway the Court or respond to its actions is uncertain from this approach, which also includes references to Supreme Court appointments. Thus, the literature remains unclear as to the motivations or tendency for presidents to respond in their public comments to the Court's core role: deciding cases.

Given the difficulty that presidents have had using their speeches to lead Congress, the public, and others, a growing body of literature examines the tendency for presidents to respond to outside actors in their public speeches (e.g., Canes-Wrone 2006; Eshbaugh-Soha and Peake 2011; Rottinghaus 2006).

The literature has not undertaken a serious examination of presidential responsiveness to the Supreme Court, however. In an effort to rectify this, we present our theoretical expectations for why presidents go public on the Court's decisions and subject those expectations to empirical scrutiny using our original database of every presidential comment on decided Supreme Court cases from 1953 to 2017.

WHY DO PRESIDENTS COMMENT ON DECIDED CASES?

Because presidents overwhelmingly reference cases after the Court has handed down its decisions, our theoretical expectations are based on the idea that presidents discuss decided Supreme Court cases not to influence case outcomes, but to promote their reelection, enhance their historical legacies, and develop good public policy (Canes-Wrone 2001; Light 1999; Moe 1985). Much as the political environment motivates presidents to speak about domestic policy (Cohen 1997), the economy (Ragsdale 1984), or foreign affairs (Canes-Wrone 2006, Chapter 4), it should also influence the president's public commentary on Court cases. As strategic actors with limited time and resources, we argue that presidents will comment on cases when it is most optimal for them to do so.

The Presidents' Goals

Presidents have three primary goals: reelection, good public policy, and historical achievement. As Light (1999, 64) notes, the relative weight of each goal depends on the potential benefits of a certain set of actions. That is, a president's choice to act is based on a strategic calculation as to whether that action will help achieve these goals. Presidents can choose whether to prioritize an issue, go public on a legislative proposal, praise the bureaucracy, or hold a press conference depending on whether they think these actions will assist in their goal achievement. Based on the large body of literature demonstrating that these goals influence presidential behavior (e.g. Canes-Wrone 2006; Light 1999), we believe these goals are also central to the president's decision to respond to Supreme Court decisions.

Concerning reelection, all presidents pursue this goal, and they frequently make decisions to further it. Light (1999, 65) references "critical promise theory" in his discussion of this goal. The idea of critical promise theory is that presidents see specific issues as being particularly important to their electoral coalitions. Thus, whether it relates to building their agendas or responding to Supreme Court cases, the reelection goal of presidents will shape the president's choice to act. If the president thinks that referencing a Supreme Court case will be of interest to an electoral coalition, this enhances the potential electoral benefit to the president of speaking about that case, increasing the likelihood of a comment. By definition, reelection is a first-term goal, even though the electoral benefits to the president's party may carry over into the president's second-term choices (Eshbaugh-Soha and Nicholson-Crotty 2009).

The president's goal of good policy is driven by a similar set of calculations. Presidents wish to affect policy change to satisfy personal policy goals and, in so doing, satisfy key constituencies in Congress required to pass good policy. Presidents make campaign promises to prioritize certain policies and offer support for some congressional priorities in exchange for legislative support for their own. Presidents do not only pursue their policy goals in Congress, however. Often, presidents will employ an "administrative presidency" strategy (Nathan 1983) to direct the implementation of public policy. The same factors that have motivated presidents to seek public support for their legislative agenda also drive the strategy to lead the implementation of public policy in the bureaucracy: congressional gridlock and divided government. Naturally, the president's ideological beliefs dictate the specific policies that presidents pursue. For example, a Republican president would tend to support tax cuts, and a Democratic president would tend to support more government spending. Referencing Supreme Court decisions in their public rhetoric is also related to pursing good public policy, as we will show.

Finally, historical achievement relates to the president's ultimate desire to be considered a "great" president. This guides the president's thinking and even shapes a president's public responses to other actors (Light 1999). It is not uncommon for presidents who engage in unpopular actions to defer to history's judgment as a way to rationalize the president's controversial decisions. This was a common refrain of George W. Bush, whose popularity plummeted as the war in Iraq dragged on.[3] What is more, news commentary surrounding a president's waning days in office hover over the issue of historical greatness. Even Donald Trump's early policy goals tended to be framed as dismantling President Obama's historical legacy (Baker 2017). We believe that it follows that presidents would consider their references to Supreme Court cases as related to their goal of historical achievement, especially during their second terms in office.

Although we treat them distinctly for purposes of clarity, these three goals invariably intersect, as presidents who pursue good policy in their first term of office understand that the long-term viability of these efforts will influence the president's historical recognition. Moreover, the president's success in enacting good policy is likely to be one feature of the president's reelection campaign. The president's reelection goal also relates to historical achievement in that presidents who are reelected are often seen as historically more relevant than one-term presidents. Although some may place the goal of policy as second to a politician's desire for reelection (Mayhew 1974), we remain ambivalent as to which goal is most important to the president. Instead, we argue that each of these goals comes into focus at different times and informs the president's decision calculus when they are most relevant.

A Typology of Presidential Responses to Supreme Court Decisions

Although our theory seeks to explain presidential comments on Supreme Court decisions generally, we recognize that presidents may have different motivations for speaking publicly or issuing a written statement about a Court case. We also acknowledge that presidents' motivations for discussing cases decided during their terms in office may be different from their motivations for referencing historical cases. This creates a typology of cases that vary by the timing of the case and the president's means of referencing the case.

The differences between spoken and written discussions of Supreme Court decisions are similar to differences between what explains spoken and written comments more generally. On the one hand, spoken discussions of Supreme Court cases, such as remarks and question-and-answer sessions, should be affected by the larger political environment, which tends to influence presidential speeches on any topic (Brace and Hinckley 1993; Hager and Sullivan 1994). Speeches are designed to affect news coverage, public opinion, and the congressional agenda, and their use should fluctuate according to whether or not the president expects to benefit politically from giving speeches. On the other hand, written statements are much less public in nature, and are geared toward addressing more mundane or technical aspects of governance. Although presidents may use written statements for other reasons, one of the primary intentions of a written presidential statement, such as an executive order, is to guide the implementation of public policy (Mayer 2001). In response to Supreme Court cases, this relates primarily to the president's goal of achieving good public policy.

We also suspect that presidents will respond to different stimuli when referencing historic cases or cases decided during their tenure in office. Presidential responses to recently decided cases are the type of commentary that should follow from previous research on presidential responsiveness. That is, when an issue – or in this case, a decision – is salient to the news media and the public, presidents are likely to respond to these cases. Presidents are clearly motivated to discuss recently decided cases to promote their reelection goals and historical legacies. In some instances, presidents may also use the opportunity of a Supreme Court decision to ask Congress to act (which we explore in Chapter 5), thereby furthering their goal of good public policy. This likely means that presidents will be concerned with contemporary factors when discussing recent cases.

References to historic cases should not be affected by all of the same factors as recently decided cases. Presidential comments on these cases, such as *Marbury* v. *Madison* (1803), are unlikely to be affected by features like contemporary media coverage of a case or conditions of divided government, since these factors are unrelated to the historical significance of a case. Instead, references to historical cases are likely to be more symbolic and driven by other events, such as marking the anniversary of a particularly important decision, like *Brown* v. *Board of Education* (1954). By discussing seminal decisions, presidents can tie themselves to the principles these decisions stand for in an effort to cast themselves in a favorable light, thus potentially increasing their reelection prospects and historical legacies.

Understanding Presidential Responses to Supreme Court Decisions

Our theoretical motivation to explain presidential comments on Supreme Court decisions centers on the intersection of presidential goals with the timing of a decision and the president's style in addressing it. The president's desire to achieve the three primary goals of good public policy, reelection, and historical achievement should apply to and guide presidential responsiveness to Supreme Court decisions, much as they help to explain other presidential actions. Moreover, the motivation for presidential goal achievement should vary by the timing of the decision (recent versus historical), coupled with the president's choice on how to address the Court's decision (spoken versus written). With this framework in mind, there are several guiding principles that should influence presidential references to Supreme Court cases in their public commentary.

First, and consistent with the reelection goal, we think presidents will consider their reelection campaign in their strategic calculus to comment on Supreme Court cases. The desire for reelection shapes the president's incentive to address Supreme Court cases in very clear ways. Supreme Court decisions tend to be an important topic for the president's political base.[4] To mobilize core constituents, the president will likely discuss more Supreme Court cases during reelection years, when voters are most attentive to presidential politics. In speaking about Court decisions, the president attaches himself to specific policies that the Court has adjudicated. For those decisions with which the president agrees, he may praise those cases and the principles they stand for, and pledge to carry out the decisions if reelected. For those decisions a president opposes, he can criticize the Court's opinions and make assurances on the campaign trail to redress the damage done by the Court's decisions. Either way, reelection years should increase the president's attention to Supreme Court cases, but only for spoken remarks given the president's target audience – the American voter – is only likely to hear the president's spoken words during a reelection campaign. We believe this finding should pertain to both recent and historic cases, since presidents can align themselves with or oppose both types of cases in an effort to enhance their reelection prospects. Given this, we expect that presidents will speak more about Supreme Court cases during reelection years.

A second presidential goal is to promote a historical legacy. Supreme Court decisions tend to be durable, meaning that they are rarely overruled (Spaeth et al. 2018). The president's historical legacy may therefore be tied to the Supreme Court and its decisions about his policy agenda. As Light (1999) notes, presidents tend to be more concerned about their historical legacies during their second term in office. Given this, presidents may be more inclined to tie their legacies to Supreme Court decisions during their second terms. This should be especially true for recent cases in that these are the cases that relate most closely to the president's policy agenda. Moreover, we expect that presidents will speak, as opposed to write, about more cases since their public speeches provide a powerful forum to shape a favorable image about themselves in the eyes of the public. Thus, we hypothesize that presidents will speak more about recent Supreme Court cases during their second terms in office to influence their historical legacies in relationship to the Court.

Both of these motivations to speak about Supreme Court cases should be enhanced by a case's salience. As strategic actors, presidents speak publicly when they think it will benefit them and seek to maximize their public exposure when they issue public statements. Presidents will therefore want to comment on Supreme Court cases when the media – and therefore, the public – already has its attention turned to the Supreme Court. Because presidents are often responsive to media attention on a number of foreign and domestic policy issues (Edwards and Wood 1999; Eshbaugh-Soha and Peake 2005), and because Supreme Court decisions influence news coverage (Flemming, Bohte, and Wood 1997), it follows that presidents will more frequently respond to Supreme Court decisions when they are covered in the news. In so doing, presidents are enabled to share their opinions on the most pressing of the Court's decisions, potentially using those decisions to promote their electoral goals and historical legacies. Speaking on high profile cases allows presidents to augment or diminish public acceptance of the decision, which might be particularly useful for enhancing their reelection prospects or affecting the implementation of those decisions via written statements. In addition, attaching themselves to the Court's most salient decisions can promote their historical legacies by highlighting their positions on these important Court cases. Because we think that presidential attention to salient cases will be shaped by contemporaneous media coverage of the cases, we expect that presidents will make more spoken and written references to recently decided Supreme Court cases when media coverage of those cases is high.[5]

Our final hypothesis is based on presidents' desire for good public policy. As we have demonstrated, presidents do not typically comment on pending cases to influence Court decisions. Instead, presidents overwhelmingly comment on decided cases. One way to achieve good policy when commenting on decided Supreme Court cases is by referencing them with the implementation or legitimization of their policy goals in mind. Although presidents can speak to affect the implementation of decisions by calling on Congress or the bureaucracy to take action on Supreme Court decisions, or to shape future Court decisions, a more direct power that the president has to affect the implementation of Court cases is through written statements. Written statements that invoke Supreme Court cases, such as signing statements and messages to Congress, are more likely than spoken comments to address legal interpretations of bills the president has signed, and are thus most appropriately considered to be "constitutional" statements that are not intended to generate a public response (Kelley and Marshall 2010). Instead, written comments are designed to direct the implementation of the decision by the bureaucracy or to motivate Congress to act on the decision.

Of course, the president is not the only branch of government that can influence the implementation of policy. As co-principal of the federal bureaucracy, Congress may also affect the implementation of a Supreme Court decision, whether by holding oversight hearings or writing more detailed legislation. Congress is more likely to wish to direct the implementation of policy differently than the president when the majority party in Congress differs from the president's party affiliation (Ringquist, Worsham, and Eisner 2003). Therefore, presidents may be more compelled to issue written statements to guide the implementation of policy goals that relate to Supreme Court cases under divided government. By doing so, presidents can direct the bureaucracy in the face of a hostile Congress on significant matters of public policy that have been adjudicated by the Supreme Court. Because this concerns the president's relationship with a sitting Congress, we believe concerns about divided government will primarily influence presidential directives relating to recent cases. Accordingly, we expect that presidents will write more about recently decided Supreme Court cases during divided government to promote their policy goals.

DATA AND METHODOLOGY

Our dependent variables are based on the collection of presidential mentions of Supreme Court decisions discussed in Chapter 1 between January 1953 and January 2017. The unit of analysis is the month.[6] We counted the number of times presidents mentioned Supreme Court decisions per month. Cases are counted only once per speech. That is, if the president mentioned the same case multiple times in a single speech or statement, that mention is counted once in terms of the dependent variables. However, if the president mentioned the same case in multiple speeches or statements in a month, that case is counted multiple times in that month.[7] For example, in September 1957, President Eisenhower mentioned *Brown* v. *Board of Education* in four separate speeches. Because Eisenhower did not mention any other case that month, the monthly count for September 1957 is four.

Figure 3.1 illustrates the monthly counts of presidential comments from 1953 to 2017. This measure averages 1.15 cases per month, and ranges from zero (which is the modal category) to a high of 19 cases mentioned by Bill Clinton in November of 2000. Clinton referenced a number of cases in interviews and targeted campaign events for the Democratic Party's presidential nominee, Al Gore. Because we think the timing of a decision (recent versus historical) and the president's style in discussing the decision (spoken versus written) matter, we use four dependent variables in our empirical models: spoken remarks on recent cases, written remarks on recent cases, spoken remarks on historic cases, and written remarks on historic cases.

We separately analyze spoken and written references to Supreme Court cases, since written comments may be responsive to different political stimuli (e.g., Kelley and Marshall 2010) and should be driven primarily by the president's desire to affect policy implementation. Presidents have spoken more than they have written about Court decisions. Of the 884 total comments on decided Supreme Court decisions, 63 percent of public comments (556 statements) came in the form of spoken remarks, while the remaining 37 percent were written (328 statements). Spoken and written remarks average 0.72 and 0.43 cases per month, respectively.

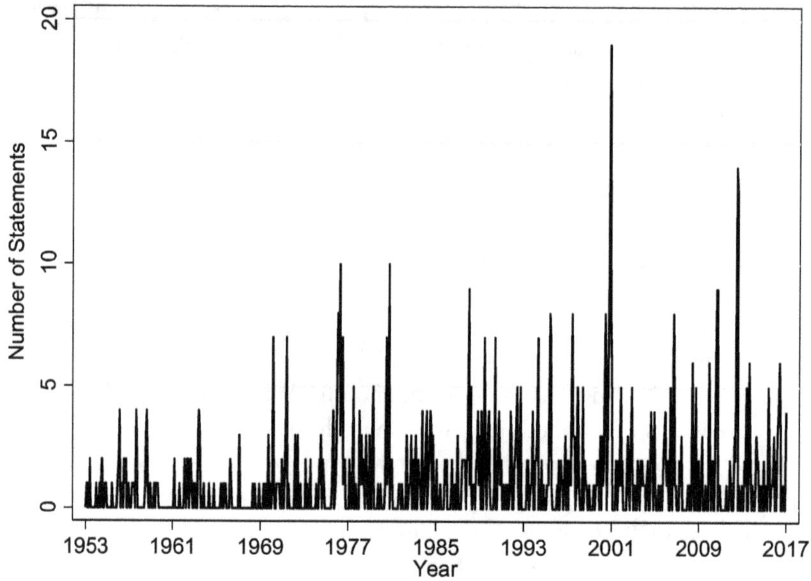

FIGURE 3.1. The number of presidential statements on Supreme Court decisions per month, 1953–2017

We divide these cases further into recently decided and historical cases. Recently decided cases are defined as those cases handed down during the incumbent president's tenure in office. Historic cases are those that were decided before the president entered office. Figure 3.2 summarizes total mentions of historical and recent decisions by presidential term and according to whether these comments were written or spoken. Overall, presidents spoke more about historic (458 mentions) than recently decided (425) cases and mention historic and recent cases, on average, 0.61 and 0.55 times per month, respectively. Historical references are driven by a handful of cases: *Brown* v. *Board of Education* (77 mentions); *Roe* v. *Wade* (72 mentions); *Engel* v. *Vitale* (31 mentions); and *INS* v. *Chadha* (1983) (62 mentions, all written). Although President Eisenhower mentioned *Brown* 27 times during his term in office, President Kennedy mentioned *Engel* only once, and incumbent President Nixon ignored *Roe* in his public commentary. Among rhetoric about historic cases, 251 are spoken and 207 are written. Recently decided cases are also more heavily weighted toward spoken remarks (303) than written statements (120).

To test our hypotheses, we have operationalized our key independent variables as follows. *Reelection Year* is coded 1 for the months of January

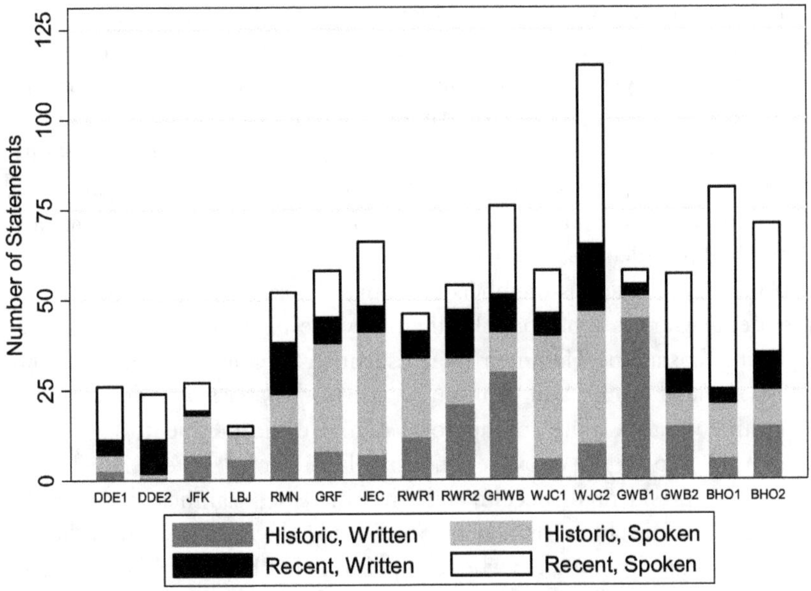

FIGURE 3.2. The number of written and spoken presidential statements on Supreme Court decisions, 1953–2017

through October during the year corresponding to the president's reelection campaign, and 0 otherwise. We expect this variable will be positively signed in the models corresponding to recent, spoken remarks and historical, spoken remarks, indicating an increase in the monthly volume of presidential statements on Supreme Court decisions. Because we do not have expectations for the sign of this variable in the written remarks models, we exclude it from these models. *Second Term* is scored 1 for each month during the president's second term in office, and 0 during a president's first term. We expect this variable will be positively signed in the recent, spoken remarks model. (It does not appear in the other models.) *SC Media Coverage* is the percentage of Supreme Court decisions handed down each month that appeared as the lead case in a story on the front page of the *New York Times* on the day after the decision was rendered (Epstein and Segal 2000, updated by the authors). We expect this variable will be positively signed in the recent, spoken remarks and recent, written remarks models. (It does not appear in the historic models.) *Divided Government* is coded 1 when at least one chamber of Congress is not controlled by the president's party, and 0 otherwise. We expect this variable will be positively signed in the recent, written remarks model. (It does not appear in the other models.)

In explaining the volume of presidential comments about Supreme Court decisions, we also account for two variables that have been instrumental in explaining other presidential public activities: the president's approval ratings and the era in which presidents serve. First, lower approval ratings encourage presidents to speak more frequently with the intent of improving their political situation (Eshbaugh-Soha 2010). When approval ratings are low, presidents may wish to speak about the decisions of a federal institution that is typically more well-regarded than either the presidency or Congress (Kelleher and Wolak 2007),[8] much as members of Congress may wish to campaign with presidents who are more popular than they are in their legislative districts (Cohen, Krassa, and Hamman 1991; Eshbaugh-Soha and Nicholson-Crotty 2009; Keele, Fogarty, and Stimson 2004). *Job Approval t-1* comprises the monthly average Gallup job approval rating of the president, lagged one month (Gallup 2017). We expect this variable will be negatively signed.[9]

Second, presidential speechmaking has increased significantly since the Reagan Administration (Eshbaugh-Soha 2010; Hager and Sullivan 1994). Reagan was the first president who went public to bolster his legislative success (Kernell 1997), and subsequent presidents have built upon Reagan's strategy to speak frequently to achieve their policy goals, especially as part of the "permanent campaign" to win reelection (Doherty 2012). Thus, it is likely that the president will reference more Supreme Court cases since January of 1981 than before. *Post-Carter Presidencies* is coded 1 from January of 1981 through January 2017 (the end of our time series), and 0 before these dates. We expect this variable will be positively signed. Our expectations for these variables pertain to the models that include only spoken remarks as job approval and timing pertain to presidential strategies for improving their image in the eyes of the public, and thus relate to speechmaking. Because presidents can reference both recent and historic cases in such speeches in their efforts to improve their public standing, we believe that these variables will be influential in both the recently decided and historic case models. As we do not have expectations for these variables in the written remarks models, they are excluded from those models.

We also include variables that capture aspects of the Supreme Court and individual presidents. Since the Court tends to fall out of the spotlight when it recesses for the summer, presidents may discuss more judicial decisions during the Supreme Court's traditional session. *Court in Session* is coded 1 for the months of October through June, and 0 otherwise.[10] We expect this variable will be positively signed. In addition, monthly attention to cases may be driven by the number of cases the Court decides in a given month. In months where the Court releases a large number of opinions, there are more

TABLE 3.1. *The expected direction of the independent variables predicting presidential speeches on Supreme Court decisions*

	Recent Spoken	Recent Written	Historic Spoken	Historic Written
Reelection Year	+	none	+	none
Second Term	+	none	none	none
SC Media Coverage	+	+	none	none
Divided Government	none	+	none	none
Job Approval t-1	−	none	−	none
Post-Carter Presidencies	+	none	+	none
Court in Session	+	+	+	+
Court Decisions	+	+	+	+
Lawyer	+	+	+	+
Cases Mentioned t-1	+	+	+	+

cases on which the president may comment, compared with months in which the Court hands down a smaller volume of opinions. *Court Decisions* represents the number of Supreme Court decisions rendered each month, based on information in the *Supreme Court Database* (Spaeth et al. 2018). We expect this variable will be positively signed. Presidents who were attorneys prior to assuming the presidency may be more interested in the Court than non-lawyer presidents, since they have chosen a career path in the law (Blackstone and Goelzhauser 2014). *Lawyer* is coded 1 for the Nixon, Ford, Clinton, and Obama administrations, and 0 for other administrations.[11] We expect this variable will be positively signed. Finally, we include a one-month lag of our dependent variables, *Cases Mentioned t-1*, to account for the possibility of autocorrelation.[12]

The expected signs of the independent variables for each model appear in Table 3.1. Although our core hypotheses do not relate to historic, written decisions, we do have expectations for this model with regard to the control variables. Therefore, we include these presidential statements in our empirical analyses for the sake of comprehensiveness.

Since our dependent variables are count measures, and there is evidence of overdispersion in our data, we use negative binomial regression models to estimate the number of decided Court cases mentioned by presidents per month, along with robust standard errors to account for any heteroskedasticity in the data.[13] Although this is a somewhat sophisticated estimation technique, it is not necessary to understand the complexities of this model in order to comprehend the substance of our results. The reason for this is that, instead of the traditional approach of presenting the statistical findings in a table format containing coefficients, standard errors, and significance levels, we have opted to present our statistical results in an easy-to-understand graphical format (e.g., Kastellec and Leoni 2007).

EMPIRICAL RESULTS

Our findings for the four categories of presidential speeches appear in Figure 3.3. These graphs represent the predicted change in the number of monthly presidential statements regarding Supreme Court decisions given a one-unit change in the independent variable of interest, holding all other variables at their mean or modal values. The circles represent the point estimate of the marginal effects and the horizontal lines coming off the circles are 90 percent confidence intervals.[14] Variables are statistically significant if the 90 percent confidence intervals do not cross the solid line at zero.[15]

For example, in the model of recent, spoken presidential remarks (the top left graph in Figure 3.3) the *Reelection Year* variable indicates the following: during a reelection year, presidents make about 0.6 more statements on recently decided Supreme Court cases each month, compared with non-reelection years. This results in an increase of about seven speeches per year in reelection years. Because the mean of the dependent variable for speeches about recent cases is 0.4, this is a substantively large effect, more than doubling the average number of speeches per month on recently decided cases.

As a whole, Figure 3.3 supports our theoretical expectations, and shows that the president's strategic calculus varies by his choice of communication and the proximity of the Court's decisions. First, consistent with our primary hypothesis, presidents mention more recently decided Supreme Court decisions in their public speeches during reelection years. As noted above, the results of the spoken model of recently decided cases indicate that during the months of a presidential reelection campaign, presidents make about 0.6 more speeches per month, compared with other months. The spoken model of historic cases also indicates that presidents focus more attention on Supreme Court decisions during reelection years. Substantively, we can expect presidents to make about 0.5 more speeches per month about historic cases during reelection years, an increase of about six speeches per year. These findings indicate that presidents discuss both recent (e.g., *National Federation of Independent Business* v. *Sebelius*) and historically significant cases (e.g., *Roe* v. *Wade*) to excite their political bases and bolster their reelection prospects.

This is not surprising. The Supreme Court is often a salient topic in presidential election campaigns. Although a good portion of the presidents'

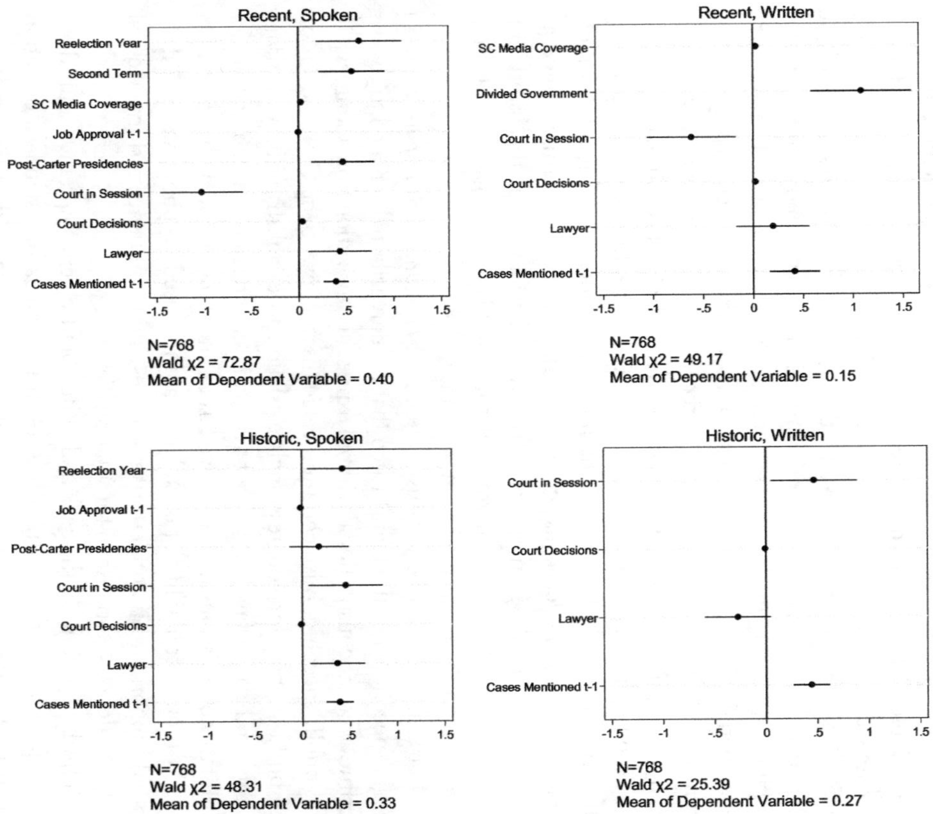

FIGURE 3.3. Influences on the number of monthly mentions of US Supreme Court cases, 1953–2017

rhetoric may center on the type of justices they would like to appoint if given the opportunity, presidents reference Supreme Court cases as a way to underscore their thinking on key issues. For example, President Reagan continued to highlight his support for prayer in public schools by expressing his opposition to *Engle* v. *Vitale* during his 1984 reelection campaign. This appealed directly to evangelical voters, a key constituency. President Obama repeatedly cited the Supreme Court's decision to uphold his signature achievement, the Affordable Care Act, during his reelection campaign as a means to demonstrate a campaign promise kept. And President Carter referenced *Fullilove* v. *Klutznick* (1980) several times after the Court upheld Congress's authority to spend money to redress past discrimination. Such support for affirmative action was important to the Democratic Party, as referenced in the 1980 Democratic Party platform. Each of these efforts, whether highlighting a historical decision or responding to recent cases, illustrates how presidents can use Supreme Court cases to appeal to key electoral constituencies.

Second, presidents devote more speeches to recently decided cases during their second terms in office. Substantively, presidents give about 0.6 more speeches on recent decisions per month during their second terms in office, an increase of about seven speeches per year. This indicates that presidents consider recent cases most relevant to their historical legacies and focus attention on them during their final terms in office.

For example, George W. Bush referenced *Hamdan* v. *Rumsfeld* (2006) in eight speeches after the Court ruled that military tribunals created to try war crimes were unconstitutional without express authorization from Congress. In his public speeches, Bush communicated his response to the Court's decision to build support for congressional legislation to establish military commissions, and spoke favorably about receiving congressional authorization for military commissions that he viewed as essential to his policy for combating the War on Terror. Thus, it is evident that Bush used his public statements to build support for his anti-terrorism policies and to influence history's view of his presidency's response to the War on Terror.

Third, presidents both speak and write about recent Supreme Court decisions featured in the media. For spoken remarks, a one standard deviation increase in the percentage of the Court's docket featured in the media (an increase of about 11 percent) results in an increase of about 0.2 speeches per month, or about three speeches per year. For written remarks, a one standard deviation increase results in an increase of about 0.06 speeches per month, or about one speech per year. Given that the mean number of written remarks on recent cases is 0.15, this is a relatively strong effect.[16] This suggests that presidents can strategically promote their reelection and historical legacy goals through their public comments on high profile, recently decided Supreme Court cases. In short, these findings demonstrate that presidents can use their public speeches to demonstrate their responsiveness to contemporary issues that are salient to the media and the American people.

Fourth, we find that presidents write about more recently decided Supreme Court cases during periods of divided government as a way to counter congressional influence over the implementation of public policy. During periods of divided government, presidential written statements regarding recent cases increase by about 1.1 per month (about 13 per year), as compared with periods of unified government. This finding is consistent with our expectation that presidents want to direct the implementation of Court cases, primarily when Congress – the president's co-principal in the implementation of policy – is controlled by the other party.[17] Gerald Ford was particularly adamant about a Democratically controlled Congress responding quickly to the Court's ruling in *Buckley* v. *Valeo* (1976) and he wrote to Congress extolling them to reconstitute the Federal Election Commission within the 30-day window offered by the Court.[18]

Turning now to the control variables, several of them perform as expected. First, in the post-Carter era, presidents mention significantly more recent Court cases every month than their predecessors in their public speeches. Substantively, presidents since Reagan have given about 0.5 more speeches per month on recent cases (about six speeches per year) than their predecessors. Second, presidents trained as lawyers speak (but do not write) more frequently about Supreme Court cases than non-lawyers. More precisely, lawyers give about 0.4 more speeches per month (about five speeches per year) on recent and historic cases, compared with their non-lawyer counterparts. This suggests that presidents who were lawyers, such as Presidents Clinton and Obama, may be more comfortable than non-lawyers in speaking extemporaneously about Supreme Court decisions due to their background training, familiarity with cases, and heightened interest in the law.

Third, both the number of cases decided and whether or not the Court is in session affect presidential comments. As the number of cases decided each month increases, the number of monthly spoken and written remarks of recent decisions increases. This makes sense in that, when there is a relatively large volume of recently decided cases, this provides presidents with a wealth of decisions to draw from in pursuit of their policy goals. Interestingly though, presidents speak and write more about historic cases when the Court is in session (October through June), but offer fewer remarks on recent cases during this same time frame. At first glance, this seems counter-intuitive. But it may follow from the general tendency of presidents not to interfere with the active business of the Court. Just as we show that presidents do not often speak about cases pending before the Court, this suggests that presidents may wait until after the Court is in session to comment on recent cases.

Indeed, another way to interpret this finding is that presidents discuss recent cases more often when the Court is out of session. We find support for this claim from an example during the Obama Administration. On the last day of the Court's session in June 2012, the Supreme Court handed down a decision which upheld a central feature of the Affordable Care Act, the individual mandate. Although President Obama was sharply criticized for mentioning the pending case in April 2012, he nonetheless responded to the Court's decision in several dozen remarks during his reelection campaign. This fits with our overall argument that one reason why presidents comment on decided cases more frequently than pending cases is to comment publicly on issues that are important to the American people. Given that the Court often waits until the very end of its term to issue the landmark opinions of its term (Epstein, Landes, and Posner 2014), it follows that presidents are most likely to be able to demonstrate democratic responsiveness on the Court's most important decisions only after the Court is out of session.[19]

In all, we find support for our key hypotheses. Presidents speak more frequently about recently decided cases during reelection years to generate support for their reelection. They also speak about more recent decisions during their second terms in office in an effort to build a favorable historical legacy. Presidents discuss more cases in their spoken rhetoric when recent Supreme Court cases are in the media spotlight, which allows presidents to leverage public attention to those cases in pursuit of their electoral goals, primarily. That presidents write about more recently decided cases during divided government lends support to our argument that presidents consider the implementation of judicial decisions in their public commentary on Supreme Court cases. Taken as a whole, these results indicate that the monthly volume of presidential remarks on Court cases is shaped to varying degrees by presidents' desires to bolster their reelections, policy goals, and historical legacies. Further, these findings speak to the rationale behind why presidents emphasize discussing decided cases over pending decisions in their public rhetoric by demonstrating that presidents desire to comment on issues important to the American people, and are not actively attempting to undermine the independence of the judiciary when they discuss Supreme Court decisions.

WHICH DECISIONS?

Having established presidential motivations for going public on the Court's decided cases, we now turn to discussing which cases presidents address in their public commentary. Our purpose here is to shed light on exactly which of the Court's decided cases presidents deem salient enough to discuss in their public commentary. This information is provided in Table 3.2, which presents the fourteen cases that presidents discussed ten or more times in their public statements. The cases are listed in the first column and the initials of each president who discussed the case appears in column two. The third column indicates the number of speeches that referred to each case.

First, with a few exceptions, these cases are among the most notable Supreme Court decisions, dealing with issues including racial segregation (*Brown* and *Plessy*), abortion (*Roe*), campaign finance regulations (*Citizens*

TABLE 3.2. *The most frequently addressed Supreme Court decisions, 1953–2017*

Case (Year)	President(s)[a]	Number of Speeches
Brown v. *Board of Education* (1954)	DDE, JFK, LBJ, RMN, GRF JEC, RWR, WJC, GWB, BHO	104
Roe v. *Wade* (1973)	GRF, JEC, RWR, GHWB, WJC GWB, BHO	72
INS v. *Chadha* (1983)	RWR, GHWB, WJC, GWB	62
NFIB v. *Sebelius* (2012)	BHO	40
Citizens United v. *FEC* (2010)	BHO	36
Engel v. *Vitale* (1962)	JFK, GRF, JEC, RWR, WJC	32
Buckley v. *Valeo* (1976)	GRF, JEC, RWR, GHWB, WJC	27
Plessy v. *Ferguson* (1896)	DDE, JEC, RWR, WJC, GWB, BHO	14
Department of the Navy v. *Egan* (1988)	RWR, GHWB, GWB	13
Swann v. *Charlotte-Mecklenburg* (1971)	RMN, GRF, RWR	12
Hamdan v. *Rumsfeld* (2006)	GWB, BHO	11
Printz v. *United States* (1997)	WJC, GWB	11
Olmstead v. *L.C.* (1999)	WJC, GWB, BHO	10
Texas v. *Johnson* (1989)	GHWB	10

[a] Initials represent the following presidents: Eisenhower (DDE), Kennedy (JFK), Johnson (LBJ), Nixon (RMN), Ford (GRF), Carter (JEC), Reagan (RWR), Bush (GHWB), Clinton (WJC), George W. Bush (GWB), Obama (BHO).

United), prayer in schools (*Engel*), and flag burning (*Texas*). Indeed, save for two decisions, all of these cases are identified by Congressional Quarterly (2018) as key cases, indicating that they were recognized by experts as decisions that had the largest amount of impact on legislation and society. Thus, this table suggests that presidents are quite responsive to discussing Supreme Court decisions involving many of the most pressing issues in American politics in this era.

The two exceptions are *Department of the Navy* v. *Egan* (1988) and *Olmstead* v. *L.C.* (1999). *Egan* involved whether the Merit Systems Protection Board, a quasi-judicial federal executive agency, was authorized to review a security clearance determination made by the Navy. Although a seemingly obscure case, Fisher (2009, 1) notes that "*Egan* is often cited by those who argue that the President has broad and exclusive powers under Article II of the Constitution to control access to national security information, especially classified documents." Thus, it should not be surprising that Presidents Reagan, George H. W. Bush, and George W. Bush took interest in this decision, interpreting it as giving broad powers to the president regarding classifying national security information. *Olmstead* implicated discrimination against individuals with mental disabilities under the Americans with Disabilities Act. Presidents Clinton, George W. Bush, and Obama all spoke favorably about this decision, assuring the country of their administrations' commitment to implementing and enforcing the decision.

Second, all but three of these cases involve civil rights and liberties issues. This provides further evidence that presidents are responsive to the public in their statements about the Court's decisions as civil rights and liberties cases are those most salient to the American public and the media (Epstein and Segal 2000). The three exceptions are *INS* v. *Chadha*, involving the constitutionality of a one-chamber veto; *Printz* v. *United States*, implicating provisions in the Brady Handgun Violence Prevention Act that required local law enforcement officials to conduct background checks; and *NFIB* v. *Sebelius*, involving the constitutionality of the Patient Protection and Affordable Care Act.

Third, most decisions appearing in Table 3.2 were discussed by multiple presidents. This suggests that these decisions have substantial longevity as their relevance to the American political system lasts beyond a single president's term. Perhaps most notably are *Brown* and *Roe*. *Brown* was discussed by every president since it was decided, with the exception of George H. W. Bush. President Nixon, who was in office at the time it was decided, did not discuss *Roe*, but every subsequent president did speak on the decision. Only three decisions were discussed by a single president. President Obama gave numerous statements on the decision involving his signature domestic policy achievement, the Patient Protection and Affordable Care Act, as well as *Citizens United*. President George H. W. Bush was the only president to address the flag burning case of *Texas* v. *Johnson* in a public statement.

Finally, it is evident that the most frequently discussed Supreme Court decisions involve both recently decided and historical cases. Only two decisions appearing in Table 3.2 were not discussed by the incumbent president when they were handed down: *Roe* (Nixon) and *Plessy* (Cleveland). Incumbent presidents discussed all of the other decisions and, with the exceptions of *Sebelius*, *Citizens United*, and *Texas* v. *Johnson*, these cases were discussed by subsequent presidents. This provides further evidence for the longevity of these cases, in addition to highlighting their contemporary relevance.

CONCLUSIONS

Given our foundational observation in Chapter 1 that presidents comment most frequently about decisions already rendered by the Supreme Court, the purpose of this chapter was to explain why they do this. We argued that presidents speak primarily with an eye toward achieving their three primary goals of reelection, good public policy, and historical recognition. Instead of actively attempting to influence the Court as the president may try to lead Congress, presidents strategically target cases to help achieve their goals more indirectly. This provides them with the opportunity to address issues of national importance, without being susceptible to claims that they are violating the norm of judicial independence for taking positions on pending Court cases.

As we demonstrate, most of the president's comments are spoken and thus geared to appeal to a public audience. This is supported by the fact that presidents speak most frequently about recently decided cases during reelection years to help achieve their electoral goals, and by the reality that they repeatedly discuss many of the Court's most recognizable precedents. Presidents also prefer to comment on recent cases when they are salient to the media and the American people, perhaps to maximize their public exposure – and address issues of obvious public concern – when they discuss Supreme Court cases.

We provide evidence in support of two other expectations. First, presidents speak more about recent Court cases in their second terms to further their historical legacy. Second, they write more often about recent Supreme Court cases to guide the implementation of those decisions under periods of divided government. Coupling the latter finding with the predominance of presidential comments on Supreme Court cases after they have been decided provides support for the president's goal of policy implementation in evoking recent court cases since good policy is a goal of presidents when they reference Court cases.

Although presidents both criticize and praise decisions made by the Court – a topic we turn to in the chapter that follows – unearthing why presidents predominately discuss decided cases is important because it reinforces our contention that presidents are not actively seeking to undermine the norm of judicial independence when they reference Court decisions. Instead, presidents seek to reference cases to help achieve their broader goals, which is consistent with their strategic actions concerning nearly all other aspects of presidential governance and in line with the coordinate construction view of constitutional interpretation. This view holds that all three branches of government play an important and legitimate role in interpreting America's most significant founding document.

APPENDIX TABLE 3.1. *Influences on the number of monthly mentions of US Supreme Court cases, 1953–2017*

	Recent		Historic	
	Spoken	Written	Spoken	Written
Reelection Year	0.64[a]		0.43[a]	
	(0.27)		(0.23)	
Second Term	0.56[a]			
	(0.21)			
SC Media Coverage	0.02[a]	0.03[a]		
	(0.01)	(0.01)		
Divided Government		1.08[a]		
		(0.30)		
Job Approval t-1	−0.003		−0.02[a]	
	(0.01)		(0.01)	
Post-Carter Presidencies	0.46[a]		0.18	
	(0.20)		(0.19)	
Court in Session	−1.02[a]	−0.62[a]	0.46[a]	0.47[a]
	(0.26)	(0.27)	(0.24)	(0.25)
Court Decisions	0.04[a]	0.02[a]	−0.01	−0.01
	(0.01)	(0.01)	(0.01)	(0.01)
Lawyer	0.43[a]	0.20	0.37[a]	−0.27
	(0.20)	(0.22)	(0.17)	(0.19)
Cases Mentioned t-1	0.39[a]	0.41[a]	0.39[a]	0.44[a]
	(0.08)	(0.15)	(0.09)	(0.11)
Constant	−1.82	−3.00[a]	−1.03[a]	−1.70[a]
	(0.58)	(0.35)	(0.49)	(0.21)
Wald χ^2	72.87[a]	49.17[a]	48.31[a]	23.39[a]
N	768	768	768	768

Note: Entries are negative binomial regression coefficients. The dependent variable is the number of decided Supreme Court cases presidents mentioned in a month. The N represents the number of months over our time series, which is the unit of analysis. Robust standard errors are reported in parentheses. [a]$p \leq .05$ (one-tailed tests).

4

The Tone of Presidential Rhetoric on Supreme Court Decisions

On January 27, 2010, President Obama boldly used his inaugural State of the Union Address to attack the Supreme Court's decision in *Citizens United v. FEC* (2010). In that case, the Court further strengthened the principle that campaign contributions are a form of political speech protected by the First Amendment by striking down regulations limiting the amount of money corporations and other entities can independently spend supporting or opposing candidates for office. In a sharp criticism of the decision, Obama said:

> With all due deference to separation of powers, last week, the Supreme Court reversed a century of law that I believe will open the floodgates for special interests, including foreign corporations, to spend without limit in our elections. I don't think American elections should be bankrolled by America's most powerful interests, or worse, by foreign entities. They should be decided by the American people. And I'd urge Democrats and Republicans to pass a bill that helps correct some of these problems.[1]

This pointed critique led Justice Samuel Alito, sitting in the front row of the House chamber just feet away from the president, to shake his head and mutter "not true" (Barnes 2010; Greenhouse 2010).

The press's response to the president's remarks was one of surprise. The *Washington Post* described it as a "rare and unvarnished showdown between two political branches" (Barnes 2010); the *New York Times* referred to it as a "rare rebuke" (Liptak 2010); and *Newsday* wrote it was an "extraordinary moment" (Broder 2010). Obama's comments sent legal bloggers "in overdrive" regarding the appropriateness and veracity of the president's comments (Globe and Mail 2010). Political reaction was mixed, depending largely on whether one opposed or supported the president. For example, Republican Senator Orrin Hatch of Utah referred to the president's gesture as "rude" (Barnes 2010), while People for the American Way, a liberal interest group, praised the president, echoing Obama in criticizing *Citizens United* (Targeted News Service 2010).

That President Obama's comments garnered so much attention is not entirely surprising. They were made at the State of the Union Address, a highly significant setting. They pitted the president against the Court, which makes for a great storyline in the media, highlighting conflict between the two branches. Further, because there had been virtually no research on presidential rhetoric on Supreme Court decisions prior to the president's speech, it was difficult to situate Obama's criticism in a historical context. This led some to believe that Obama's actions were unprecedented (Barnes 2010). Even so, the president had a clear goal in mind: to put public pressure on others to adjust campaign finance laws consistent with his own preferences.

The purpose of this chapter is to shed theoretical and empirical light on the tone of the public positions that presidents take on Supreme Court decisions. To do this, we examine all Supreme Court decisions in which sitting presidents take positive, negative, or neutral positions during the Eisenhower through Obama administrations. We find that a variety of factors influence presidential rhetoric toward the Court. Perhaps most notably, we demonstrate that presidents criticize decisions with which they disagree, often calling on Congress to take steps to modify or reverse the Court's decision (a topic we return to in Chapter 5). In addition, presidents praise decisions that are consistent with their ideological preferences in an effort to direct the implementation of those decisions in the bureaucracy and garner support for those decisions among the public (a topic we address in Chapter 7). Thus, this chapter shows how presidents can use their public rhetoric on Court decisions to play a role in directing our understanding of the Constitution and federal law more generally, making them a key player in the coordinate construction of the Constitution (e.g., Meese 1987; Paulsen 1994; Whittington 2001). In so doing, we demonstrate how presidents can frame their rhetoric on the Court's decisions to pursue their policy, reelection, and historical achievement goals.

UNDERSTANDING THE TONE OF PRESIDENTIAL RHETORIC

Scholars have been slow to examine the tone of presidential rhetoric. Instead, most research that has examined presidential rhetoric centers on describing and explaining the volume of presidential remarks and the potential impact those remarks may have on essential features of governance, such as news coverage and the agendas of the public and Congress (Cohen 1997; Edwards and Wood 1999; Hager and Sullivan 1994; McGauvran and Eshbaugh-Soha 2017; Powell 1999; Ragsdale 2014). This line of research touches on the idea of tone, including presidential appeals in support of bills before Congress, which are designed to increase the likelihood of presidential success in Congress (Barrett 2004; Canes-Wrone 2006). However, prior work has not specifically examined these remarks with regard to their tone, per se, and therefore cannot account for whether presidents preferred a carrot (positive rhetoric) or a stick (negative rhetoric) in calling on Congress to support their policies. Traditionally, the expectation was that presidents called for legislative support in an effort to be coercive, and compel a recalcitrant Congress to act. For example, Kernell's (1997) seminal examination of going public hinges on presidential speeches as coercive tools to pressure legislators to support the president's position, although Kernell does not explicitly examine the tone of presidential remarks.

Perhaps sensing an opportunity to learn even more about presidential rhetoric, a separate line of scholarship has undertaken a more direct examination of tone. Defining tone as "a tool people use . . . to create distinct social impressions via word choice," Hart, Childers, and Lind (2013, 9) conceive of tone as having multiple dimensions: activity, optimism, certainty, realism, and commonality. Conceptualizing tone in this way allows the authors to conclude, for example, that presidents are highly optimistic in their Saturday radio addresses. This contrasts with campaign rhetoric, in which presidents tend to be more certain and direct in tone (Hart, Childers, and Lind 2013, 121). Heith (2013) builds on this research to examine broad trends in presidential tone across three presidencies (Clinton, George W. Bush, and Obama). Although she hypothesizes that there will be much consistency across and within presidencies, her analysis of presidential tone reveals much more nuance. For instance, even though Presidents Bush and Clinton exhibited similar tone in their national addresses, their speeches to local audiences differed considerably.

Other studies center on whether the tone of presidential rhetoric is positive or negative and what impact, if any, it may have on other actors. This is examined most easily when the president takes a clear position in favor of or against a policy, an action, or an institution (as is the case in presidential rhetoric on Supreme Court decisions). For instance, Eshbaugh-Soha (2006) explores statements of support or opposition to civil rights, clean air, and farm policies to ascertain the type of signals presidents sent to federal agencies. The idea is that presidents who support a policy, or who speak positively about a policy, are more likely to motivate the actions of bureaucrats. He finds that positive public statements tend to improve the implementation of policy, but only for policies that tend to be salient and uncomplicated, such as civil rights. Extending this line of research to the aggregate turnover of federal agencies,

Eshbaugh-Soha (2017) shows that presidential support for government reduces personnel turnover in agencies that implement salient policies, such as the Environmental Protection Agency and the Department of Education. Thus, it is evident that the tone of presidential rhetoric can affect the implementation of public policies in the bureaucracy.

Other research has begun to examine how the tone of presidential remarks influences the news media. With the advent of text analysis software and comprehensive dictionaries of tone (e.g., Young and Soroka 2012), it has become much easier to examine tone systematically. Using this technique, Eshbaugh-Soha (2018) examines the partisan slant of presidential news coverage and shows that President Obama, for example, enjoyed more positive coverage on MSNBC when he spoke more positively about the unemployment rate. That this relationship does not extend to George W. Bush provides evidence of a liberal slant to MSNBC's news coverage and a biased opportunity for presidential leadership of news tone. In addition, Eshbaugh-Soha and McGauvran (2018) use text analysis software to examine the president's tone concerning income inequality, but show limited impact of presidential tone on news coverage of that topic.

Research concerning presidential tone and its impact on other branches of government is quite sparse. Aside from Heith's (2013) study, there is virtually no research on whether the tone of presidential comments influences Congress, with most research focusing on agenda-setting instead (Edwards and Wood 1999; Fett 1994). Moreover, despite the sizeable literature on senatorial confirmation of the president's judicial nominations, no scholarship examines the tone of the president's remarks on nominations. Without a doubt, the president would be supportive of his own nominee, but a clever analysis of these comments could reveal what kind of rhetoric is most likely to improve the president's success of his nominations. In contrast, Blackstone and Goelzhauser (2014) examine all public statements presidents made about the Court, including the tone of those remarks. They find that presidents are more negative than positive in their public references to the Supreme Court, but this varies considerably by presidential administration. The two key factors that explain more negative rhetoric is whether a president was trained as a lawyer and whether it was a presidential election year (Blackstone and Goelzhauser 2014, 187), both of which we consider in this chapter.

EXPLAINING THE TONE OF PRESIDENTIAL RHETORIC ON SUPREME COURT CASES

The chief goal of this chapter is to explain the tone of the president's remarks concerning Supreme Court decisions. Our primary theoretical framework is based on the notion that presidents praise or criticize Supreme Court decisions to affect support for, or opposition to, the decisions by Congress, the bureaucracy, and the public, thus contributing to constitutional and policy development. What's more, we posit that, by taking public positions on Court decisions, presidents can pursue goals related to reelection and historical achievement. We begin by proposing why we think presidents will praise or criticize decisions affecting the implementation and acceptance of the Court's decisions. We then turn to presenting our specific theoretical expectations about the tone of presidential remarks on Supreme Court decisions, followed by a discussion of our data and the empirical results.

Our focus in this chapter is limited to explaining the tone of presidential remarks, and not whether those remarks are effective at generating a reaction by other actors. We address the effectiveness of presidents' rhetorical strategies in subsequent chapters by investigating how presidential remarks on Supreme Court cases are related to congressional and media activities, as well as public attitudes toward the Court and its decisions. In this chapter, we argue that presidents can use their speeches to help to achieve their goals, though we do not posit that presidents are necessarily successful in these efforts, nor that they believe they are always capable of motivating responses through their public speeches. Rather, our position is that presidents can use their public speeches to praise or criticize the Court's decisions and this, in turn, might generate responses by primarily three other actors: Congress, the bureaucracy, and the public.

The President's Targets

Congress is a common target of the president's rhetoric, whether as a way to garner support for the president's legislative policies (Barrett 2004) or to set the legislative agenda (Light 1999). Although presidential comments on Supreme Court cases do not always call for congressional actions, many do, as we show in Chapter 5. When presidents reference Supreme Court cases in commentary directed at Congress, they are likely doing so in an attempt to bring Congress on board with their efforts to help implement – or impede the execution of – policies related to the Court's decisions.

Although we often think of Congress as being a primary actor in the adoption of policy, Congress also plays a primary role in the implementation of policy in several ways (Anderson 2015). For example, Congress can use its oversight authority to direct federal agencies to carry out policies consistent with legislative wishes. The Court's cases can facilitate congressional oversight by prompting Congress to hold oversight hearings regarding the enactment of those cases, possibly at the behest of the president's comments (Eskridge 1991). Congress may also write legislation more specifically to direct an agency in how it carries out a policy. In response to a Court decision, therefore, the president may encourage Congress to write more detailed legislation to facilitate the implementation of the Court's decisions (Canon and Johnson 1999). If a president disagrees with a decision, he may call upon Congress to overturn decisions through legislative statutes or constitutional amendments (Epstein and Knight 1998; Eskridge 1991). Finally, Congress plays a dominant role in passing the federal budget. The absence of adequate appropriations may undermine the successful implementation of Supreme Court decisions and serve as a signal to the Court that Congress is unhappy with its decisions (Rosenberg 1991; Toma 1991).

Presidents may also use their public statements to influence the enforcement of the Court's decisions by the bureaucracy (Bullock and Lamb 1984; Spriggs 1996). Perhaps most obviously, presidents have two major tools at their disposal to direct policy implementation: executive orders and signing statements. Executive orders have the force of law and enable presidents to compel the bureaucracy to enforce laws and judicial decisions consistent with the content of the orders (Mayer 2001). Lesser known than executive orders, signing statements can perform a similar function by directing federal agencies regarding how to administer a law, in addition to allowing presidents to address their view of the constitutionality of a law, which has obvious implications for the Supreme Court (Dellinger 1993; Rush 2018).

Whether in conjunction with these written directives or not, presidents may signal their support (or opposition) for Supreme Court decisions through their public speeches as a means of directing bureaucratic implementation. This support (or opposition) may signal to the bureaucracy that presidents prioritize a policy (Whitford and Yates 2009) or support or oppose a specific bureaucratic action (Eshbaugh-Soha 2006). Although presidents tend to have the greatest impact over the federal bureaucracy through strategic appointments and targeted budget increases or decreases (Wood and Waterman 1994), presidential speeches are short-term mechanisms that presidents may use to lead the bureaucracy to implement a Court decision in line with their own preferences.

Presidents also may appeal to the public to promote the acceptance of, or opposition to, the Court's decisions. As Canon and Johnson (1999) explain, the public is at the center of the "consumer population" of Court decisions, and one way that presidents can motivate the public to accept or oppose the Court's decisions is through their public commentary. Presidential speeches "can do much to encourage people to cooperate with or resist judicial policies" (Canon and Johnson 1999, 128), after all. Thus, public speeches provide presidents with forums to openly express their opinions of Supreme Court decisions, which may influence how the public views those decisions. Besides, speeches on Court decisions may afford presidents electoral benefits by appealing to their base through the tone of their public remarks on cases, potentially affecting their reelections and historical legacies. Further, by speaking about Court decisions, presidents can enhance their historical legacies by linking themselves to the Court's decisions in ways that enhance their image in the eyes of the public.

In addition to these three primary targets, presidents may also use their public statements on the Court's decisions to influence the media, and perhaps the Court itself. Presidential efforts to reach the public are, of course, centered in part on leading the news media (Eshbaugh-Soha and Peake 2011). We save an analysis of the tone of presidential remarks on news coverage of Supreme Court cases for Chapter 6. Here we contend that presidents are motivated to reach the public by supporting or opposing Supreme Court decisions due to the public's impact on presidents' ability to secure reelection, good public policy through the implementation of Court decisions, and a positive historical legacy. This can be accomplished by generating favorable news coverage.

Presidents can also use their remarks to influence the Court. As we demonstrated in Chapter 2, presidents rarely take public positions on the Court's pending decisions in an attempt to influence the justices' decision-making. However, presidents may support or oppose the Court's cases in an effort to affect the Court's future decisions in similar policy areas. For example, President Obama's public opposition to California's Proposition 8,[2] addressed by the Court in *Hollingsworth* v. *Perry* (2013), may have signaled to the Court his support for same-sex marriage, providing justices with evidence of likely presidential support on related cases yet to be heard by the Court. Although we do not test this proposition directly – nor do we provide any evidence that President's Obama's comments influenced the *Obergefell* v. *Hodges* (2015) decision – we recognize that it is possible for presidents to attempt to influence future Court decisions with the tone they take on prior rulings. The Court's ruling in *McCutcheon* v. *FEC* (2014) highlights the limits of such a strategy. In that case, the Court struck down legislation that limited the amount of money contributors can donate to candidates for federal office and other political entities, despite President Obama's public criticism of the related campaign finance case of *Citizen's United*. As we discussed in Chapter 2, the Office of Solicitor General provides presidents with a formal mechanism for relaying their preferences to the justices, obviating the need to use public speeches to communicate with the Court.

Explaining the Tone of Presidential Remarks

Based on this theoretical framework, we think that several key factors motivate the president to use a particular tone to describe Supreme Court decisions in their public rhetoric. First, the president's ideological alignment with the Court's decision should influence the tone of the president's rhetoric on that decision. Like Supreme Court justices (Segal and Spaeth 2002), presidents are ideological actors whose behavior is in part driven by their policy preferences (Bond and Fleisher 1990). Given this, we hypothesize that presidential responses to Supreme Court decisions will be shaped by their ideological agreement with a Court decision. If the president disagrees with the ideological outcome of a case, the president will issue more negative comments about the decision. If, however, the president agrees with the ideological direction of the decision, we expect the president will make more favorable comments about the decision to promote the acceptance of the decision by the public, Congress, and the executive branch.

Presidents who publicly disagree with the Court's decisions likely do so to decrease support for the decisions, which can occur in several ways. First, by taking a negative tone, presidents can communicate that they intend to ignore, undermine, or indifferently enforce the implementation of a decision. For example, George W. Bush was critical of the Supreme Court's ruling in *Massachusetts* v. *Environmental Protection Agency* (2007), in which the Court held that federal law allows the Environmental Protection Agency to regulate greenhouse gas emissions. Bush criticized the implications of such a ruling, noting that it could create a "glorious mess" of regulations, and maintained that the Court overstepped its bounds on a decision that should be "made by the elected representatives of the people they affect."[3] In so doing, he signaled that implementing such regulations would not be a key priority for his administration. Second, critical statements may be made for future benefits, to move the Court ideologically closer to the president's preferred policy preferences, as was the case with Roosevelt's disdain for the Court's New Deal decisions that led to his infamous Court-packing plan (Leuchtenburg 1966). Third, by admonishing the Court for making decisions that the president views unfavorably, the president may motivate public support behind efforts to legislatively overrule the decision. President Eisenhower employed this strategy in response to *Kent* v. *Dulles* (1958), in which the Court limited the Secretary of State's authority to deny passports for reasons related to national security. In his Special Message to Congress about the case, Eisenhower outlined his plans for legislation to amend the decision, noting that "Each day and week that passes without it exposes us to great danger. I hope the Congress will move promptly toward its enactment."[4] Thus, we expect that presidents will speak less favorably about decisions that run counter to their ideological preferences.

Conversely, by publicly applauding decisions with which he agrees, the president can attempt to strengthen support for the Court's decisions in a number of ways. First, the president can make it clear to Congress and federal agencies that he will back efforts to ensure the faithful implementation of the decision. Consider, for example, President Obama's response to *United States* v. *Windsor* (2013), which struck down part of the Defense of Marriage Act that defined marriage to apply only to opposite-sex unions. Praising the decision, Obama indicated that he "directed the Attorney General to work with other members of [his] Cabinet to review all relevant federal statutes to ensure this decision, including its implications for federal benefits and obligations, is implemented swiftly and smoothly."[5] Second, by speaking favorably about decisions with which he agrees, the president can help legitimize the rulings in the eyes of the American public. By using the bully pulpit to express approval of the Court's opinions, the decisions made by a politically unaccountable Court can gain democratic legitimacy, which may promote their acceptance by the public (Blackstone and Goelzhauser 2014). Thus, we expect that presidents will speak more favorably about decisions that mesh with their ideological preferences.

Second, we hypothesize that presidents will consider whether the Court declares a law unconstitutional, criticizing decisions that do and praising those that do not. Debates about whether the Court should engage in judicial review date to the founding era and have gained a renewed sense of importance since the 1950s as allegations of judicial overreach have routinely been lobbed at the Court (e.g., Bickel 1962). When the Court declares a law unconstitutional, it substitutes the will of an unelected institution for that of its duly elected counterparts in the executive and legislative branches. This is potentially troubling from a normative perspective as it demonstrates judicial superiority over the democratic process. This view was articulated by George H. W. Bush in one of his attacks on *Texas* v. *Johnson* (1989), in which the Court determined that burning an American flag is protected by the First Amendment: "Forty-eight States had laws protecting the flag against desecration. Forty-eight States. And those laws were effectively struck down when the Supreme Court ruled that flag-burning is protected by the Constitution."[6]

Moreover, the American public appears to view declarations of unconstitutionality negatively. For example, Caldeira (1986, 1222) finds that public confidence in the Court decreases when it engages in high levels of judicial activism, concluding that "the Supreme Court treads on thin ice in the act of invalidating large numbers of statutes." This may enable presidents to leverage declarations of unconstitutionality to motivate public opposition to such decisions. Further, in criticizing the Court's decisions that declare a law unconstitutional, presidents can call on Congress to remedy this activity, or direct the bureaucracy to take actions to limit the scope of the Court's decisions. When the Court engages in this form of countermajoritarian behavior, therefore, we expect presidents to speak more negatively about Court decisions. On the contrary, we hypothesize that presidents will praise decisions that do not involve declarations of unconstitutionality since the negative connotations associated with judicial activism are absent.

Third, we posit that presidents are likely to criticize cases that were decided by minimum winning coalitions. When the Supreme Court hands down a decision with a bare majority of justices in support of it, this signals to the president and the public that the Court is fractured. One consequence of this division is that the decision can be altered by a single vote. Indeed, Hansford and Spriggs (2006) demonstrate that cases decided by minimum winning coalitions are more likely to be subsequently overruled by a future Court. Because minimum winning coalitions make support for the decision appear weak among the justices, these cases make for easy targets of presidential (and public) attacks, enabling presidents (and the public) to stand by the dissenters in the case and urge the Court to reconsider the issue.[7] In addition, presidents can leverage such delicate decisions to increase public support for their attempts to promote legislative or constitutional efforts to overrule the Court, or to gain public support for their Supreme Court nominees (who might later vote to overturn the decisions). For example, President Obama highlighted *Citizens United*'s narrow majority in stating his remedy to what he saw were the negative effects of the decision: "By a 5-4 vote, the Court overturned more than a century of law . . . . When this ruling came down, I instructed my administration to get to work immediately with Members of Congress willing to fight for the American people to develop a forceful, bipartisan response to this decision."[8] What is more, presidents can use the logic of the dissenting opinion(s) in such cases to criticize the majority opinion, thus reducing the amount of effort that White House staff need to expend to justify the president's criticism of the decision. Thus, we expect that presidents will speak less favorably about decisions decided by minimum winning coalitions.

Fourth, we hypothesize that presidents will criticize decisions in which the Court rules against the federal government. The relationship between the executive branch and the Supreme Court is particularly close in many regards, with the Solicitor General – the chief attorney for the executive in the Court –

traditionally receiving a substantial amount of deference from the Court (Black and Owens 2012; Nicholson and Collins 2008; Pacelle 2003). Examples of this abound, and include the Solicitor General's very high success rates related to certiorari and merits decisions, as well as the Solicitor General's ability to substantially shape the content of the Court's opinions (Black and Owens 2012; Collins, Corley, Hamner 2015). Thus, when the justices render a decision that is unfavorable to the executive branch, that decision will be particularly notable to presidents for three reasons. First, the executive branch has taken a clear, public position on the dispute through the Office of Solicitor General, and has exhausted a great deal of resources litigating the case in the Supreme Court and in lower courts. Second, loses are relatively rare. For example, during the time period under analysis here (1953–2017), the federal government won approximately 65 percent of cases in which it appeared as a litigant (Spaeth et al. 2018). Third, losses stand out more than wins, and are thus harder to accept (Kahneman, Knetsch, and Thaler 1991). By criticizing decisions that are unfavorable to the executive branch, presidents are enabled to motivate public opposition to the decisions, and can limit the impact of negative decisions by discussing bureaucratic guidelines or by proposing congressional actions to alter or override decisions. Therefore, we expect that presidents will speak less favorably about decisions that the federal government loses.

DATA AND METHODOLOGY

The data that we analyze in this chapter is based on the same data collection used throughout this book and discussed in Chapter 1. Since our focus here is to explain the tone of presidential rhetoric on the Court's decided cases, we focus solely on those cases in which the Court rendered decisions. Thus, this chapter does not include pending cases. The unit of analysis in our data is the Supreme Court case[9] and our time period runs from 1953 to the end of the Obama Administration on January 19, 2017.

Because we are interested in the tone of presidential discussions of Supreme Court decisions, we create three dependent variables: 1) the number of negative mentions of a decision; 2) the number of positive mentions of a decision; and 3) the number of neutral mentions of a decision. To operationalize the dependent variables, we determined whether the case discussed was rendered during the incumbent president's tenure based on the date of the Court's decision and the date of the president's speech. Thus, our dependent variables are limited to discussions of decisions made by sitting presidents and do not include mentions of Supreme Court cases by presidents who, for example, served decades after a decision was rendered. Such mentions are largely ceremonial, pro forma, or used for comparative purposes, and typically include speeches commemorating the anniversaries of particularly salient cases;[10] references to cases in presidential signing statements as a means of justifying the president's interpretation of statutory provisions signed into law;[11] or instances in which the president compares a recently decided case to an existing decision.[12] As a result, they generally do not implicate presidential efforts to affect support for or opposition to the Court's decisions.[13] Further, each case mentioned in a speech is counted only once per speech, since presidents may make multiple references to a case in a single speech. If a case was mentioned in multiple speeches, however, it is counted multiple times (once for each speech in which it was discussed), indicating that the president engaged in substantial efforts to target the case in his public rhetoric.[14]

We examined the language in presidential speeches to code the tone of presidential remarks regarding Supreme Court decisions. Negative mentions include those comments that are critical of, or offer disagreement with, the Court's decisions. President George W. Bush's reaction to *Boumediene* v. *Bush* (2008), in which the Court declared his administration's policy related to holding suspected terrorists in Guantanamo Bay, Cuba unconstitutional, illustrates this nicely: "We'll abide by the Court's decision. That doesn't mean I have to agree with it. It's a deeply divided Court, and I strongly agree with those who dissented[.] And their dissent was based upon their serious concerns about U.S. national security."[15]

We code as positive those comments in which the president expresses praise, confidence in, or agreement with the Court's decisions. For example, President Ford discussed the Court's decision in *Gregg* v. *Georgia* (1976) in positive terms, explaining that "I have stated on a number of occasions I support the death penalty at the Federal level for espionage, treason, et cetera. I support the death penalty for the kind of crimes that involve murder, et cetera. I support the direction in which the Supreme Court is going."[16]

Neutral comments include discussions of recently decided cases in which presidents do not take a clear negative or positive position on the outcome of the case or the means by which it is carried out. President Nixon's discussion of *Flood* v. *Kuhn* (1972), which upheld Major League Baseball's anti-trust exemption, illustrates this. In response to a reporter's question about the case, Nixon stated: "In any event, as an old baseball fan, and the rest, I have no present thoughts on that. I would like, perhaps, to talk to Bowie Kuhn [Commissioner of Baseball], who is a good lawyer and also interested in baseball."[17]

To examine the reliability of the coding of the dependent variable, we extracted a random sample of 10 percent of speeches and had an independent coder determine whether the speeches made negative, positive, or neural references to Supreme Court decisions. The inter-coder agreement level was 94.7 percent and the kappa value was 0.92, which is considered "almost perfect" by one commonly used metric (Landis and Koch 1977). Thus, the coding of the dependent variable is very reliable. Given this, we do not use the more sophisticated analysis of tone that we reserve for the tone of news coverage examined in Chapter 6. This coding decision is consistent with past research that has examined the tone of the president's remarks in relation to the Supreme Court (Blackstone and Goelzhauer 2014). Moreover, the level of intercoder agreement as to what constitutes a positive, negative, or neutral comment is so high that we are very confident in our use of human coding (e.g., Eshbaugh-Soha 2006), as opposed to computer-assisted coding (Hart, Childers, and Lind 2013).

Figure 4.1 displays the number of negative, positive, and neutral comments made by sitting presidents on Supreme Court decisions. Negative comments are identified by black portions of the bars, positive comments by the white portions, and neutral comments by the gray portions. Overall, incumbent presidents made 119 negative, 176 positive, and 99 neutral mentions of cases. President Obama made the most negative mentions of cases, followed by Presidents Clinton and George H. W. Bush. Of those negative references, two cases stand out. Obama criticized *Citizens United* v. *Federal Election Commission* on 35 separate occasions, and Bush condemned the Court's decision in *Texas* v. *Johnson* (1989) in 10 speeches. President Obama made the most positive references to decisions, followed by Presidents Reagan, Clinton, George W. Bush, and Eisenhower. The most commonly praised decision is *National Federation of Independent Business* v. *Sebelius*, which Obama extolled 37 times, followed by *Brown* v. *Board of Education* (1954), which was lauded by Eisenhower in 16 speeches. President Reagan made the most neutral references, followed by Presidents Eisenhower and Ford. Reagan made 10 neutral comments about *INS* v. *Chadha*; Eisenhower made 10 neutral reference to *Brown*; and Ford made 9 neutral references to *Buckley* v. *Valeo* (1976).

To test our hypotheses, we have coded our independent variables as follows. *Ideological Distance* represents the ideological congruence between the president's ideology and the ideological direction of the Supreme Court's decision, and is adapted from existing work on executive-judicial interactions (Bailey, Kamoie, and Maltzman 2005; Nicholson and Collins 2008). If the Court rendered a conservative decision (as reported in Spaeth et al. 2018), this

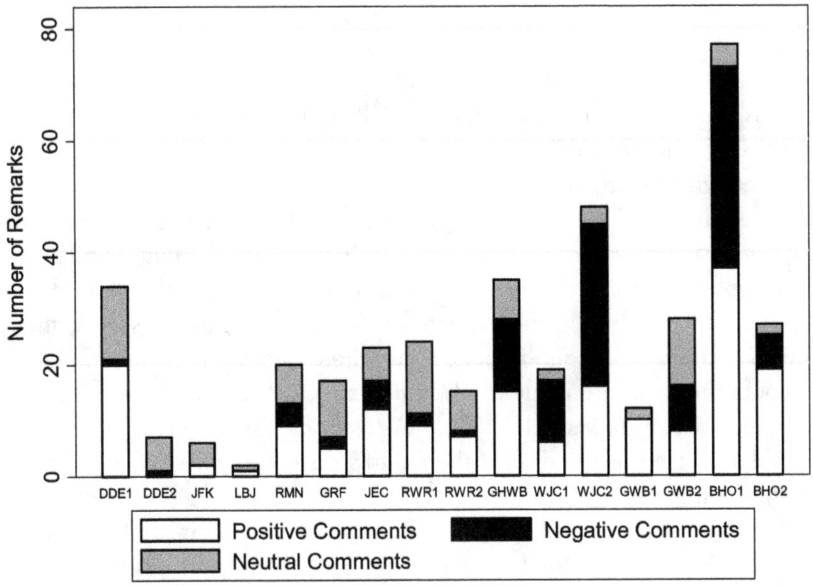

FIGURE 4.1. The number of negative, positive, and neutral remarks made by presidents on Supreme Court decisions, 1953–2017

variable represents the president's Common Space score (as calculated by Poole 2015) multiplied by −1. If the Court rendered a liberal decision, this variable is the president's Common Space score multiplied by +1. Because higher Common Space scores designate more conservative presidents, positive values of this variable indicate that the Court's decision is ideologically distant from the president. We expect this variable will be positively signed in the model predicting negative mentions of decisions and negatively signed in the model capturing positive mentions of decisions. We exclude this variable from the neutral rhetoric model because ideological distance should have no impact on the likelihood of neutral comments.

Our *Unconstitutional* variable is scored 1 if the Supreme Court's declared a federal or state law unconstitutional in its opinion, and 0 otherwise (Spaeth et al. 2018). We expect this variable will be positively signed in the negative model, and negatively signed in the positive model. (It does not appear in the neutral model.) We code *Minimum Winning Coalition* as a 1 if the decision was decided by a one vote margin (i.e., 5-4 or 4-3), and 0 otherwise (Spaeth et al. 2018). We expect this variable will be positively signed in the model predicting negative references. (It does not appear in the positive and neutral models.) The *US Loss* variable captures whether presidents make more negative references to cases in which the federal government received an unfavorable result. This variable is coded 1 if the federal government was the losing party in the case, and 0 otherwise (Spaeth et al. 2018). We expect it will be positively signed in the negative model. (It does not appear in either the positive or neutral models.)

Although our primary theoretical framework in this chapter is focused on the idea that presidents can use their public speeches to generate support for or opposition to decisions by the executive branch, legislature, and public, we recognize that presidents have multiple goals when speaking publicly, including those related to their reelection prospects, their ability to make good public policy, and their capacity to generate public support for their presidencies (Edwards 2003). Accordingly, we include a variety of control variables that allow us to capture other influences on presidents' decisions to discuss the Court's cases, regardless of the tone of those comments.

As demonstrated in Chapter 3, presidents can use their public remarks on the Court's decisions to enhance their reelection prospects. Such is the case because mentioning the Court's decisions during reelection years allows presidents to take on salient matters of public concern. Because presidents can use judicial decisions to rally support for their reelection by both praising and criticizing decisions, depending on which is electorally advantageous (Blackstone and Goelzhauser 2014), we expect that presidents will make more positive, negative, and neutral comments about judicial decisions during reelection years. *Reelection Year* is coded 1 if the president's remarks occurred during a presidential reelection year (January through November), and 0 otherwise. We expect this variable will be positively signed in all models, indicating that presidents discuss Supreme Court decisions during reelection years to motivate public support behind their reelection campaigns (Blackstone and Goelzhauser 2014).

Presidents may also more frequently take positions on Supreme Court decisions during their second terms in an effort to attach themselves to those decisions for the purpose of enhancing their historical legacies. For example, if the Court handed the president a major victory, such as with Obama and the Affordable Care Act, the president can praise that decision as a way of tying his historical legacy to the Court's decision. Conversely, if the Court ruled against the president's position in an important case, the president can criticize that decision as a way of reminding the public of the president's position. This appears to have been the case with President Clinton and *Printz* v. *United States* (1997), in which the Court struck down provisions related to preventing handgun violence that the president supported. *Second Term* is coded 1 for the president's second term in office, and 0 during a president's first term. We expect this variable will be positively signed in all models, indicating that presidents discuss more Supreme Court cases during their second terms to enhance their historical legacies.

Presidents may also discuss more frequently the Court's decisions during periods of divided government. In so doing, presidents can use their public rhetoric to direct the bureaucracy regarding the implementation of the Court's decision in the face of a hostile Congress who might not act consistently with the president's desires. *Divided Government* is coded 1 when at least one chamber of Congress is not controlled by the president's party, and 0 otherwise. We expect this variable will be positively signed in all three models, indicating presidents discuss more decisions during periods of divided government.[18]

It is also plausible that presidents take more positions on Court decisions in response to their public approval ratings. As we argued in Chapter 3, presidents may more frequently take positions on Court decisions when their approval ratings are low to draw attention away from their lack of public support. *Job Approval t-1* comprises the monthly average Gallup job approval rating of the president, lagged one month (Gallup 2017). We expect this variable will be negatively signed in all models, indicating that presidents discuss more decisions as their job approval ratings decrease.

As demonstrated in Chapter 3, presidential speechmaking has increased since the Reagan Administration as presidents have followed Reagan's strategy of going public as part of their permanent campaign to win reelection. Because many of the Court's decisions are salient to this rhetorical strategy, we believe that presidents beginning with Reagan will reference more Supreme Court cases than earlier presidents. Post-Carter Presidencies is coded 1 from January of 1981 through January 2017, and 0 before these dates. We expect this variable will be positively signed in all models.

As head of the executive branch of the federal government, we expect that presidents will pay closer attention to cases in which the Court reviewed the constitutionality of federal policies than those cases in which the Court examined state and local policies (e.g., Nicholson and Collins 2008). Accordingly, we include a *Federal Review* variable, scored 1 if the Supreme Court reviewed the constitutionality of the actions of a federal official (most commonly Congress), and 0 otherwise (Spaeth et al. 2018). We expect this variable will be positively signed in all models.

We also include a variable that captures media attention to the case. *Case Salience* is scored 1 if the case appeared as the lead case in a story on the front page of the *New York Times* on the day after the decision, and 0 otherwise (Epstein and Segal 2000). As presidents are responsive to the issues covered in the media, and because the media are capable of shaping the issues discussed by the president (Edwards and Wood 1999; Eshbaugh-Soha and Peake 2005), we expect this variable will be positively signed in all models.

Finally, we include a *Lawyer* variable, scored 1 for Presidents Nixon, Ford, Clinton, and Obama, and 0 otherwise. Because they have chosen a career in the law, we believe that presidents who are attorneys will be more interested in the business of the Court than other presidents and will thus be more likely to take positions on the Court's decisions (Blackstone and Goelzhauser 2014). This variable should be positively signed in all models.

The expected signs of the independent variables for each model appear in Table 4.1. As with Chapter 3, our dependent variables are count measures and there is evidence of overdispersion in our data. Accordingly, we use negative binomial regression models to estimate the number of negative, positive, and neutral comments incumbent presidents made on each case, along with robust standard errors to account for heteroscedasticity. And, like Chapter 3, we report our results in an easy-to-understand graphical format.

TABLE 4.1. *The expected direction of the independent variables predicting the tone of presidential remarks on Supreme Court decisions*

	Negative	Positive	Neutral
Ideological Distance	+	–	none
Unconstitutional	+	–	none
Minimum Winning Coalition	+	none	none
US Loss	+	none	none
Reelection Year	+	+	+
Second Term	+	+	+
Divided Government	+	+	+
Job Approval t-1	–	–	–
Post-Carter Presidencies	+	+	+
Federal Review	+	+	+
Case Salience	+	+	+
Lawyer	+	+	+

EMPIRICAL RESULTS

Our findings appear in Figure 4.2. These graphs represent the predicted change in the number of negative, positive, and neutral presidential statements regarding Supreme Court decisions given a one-unit change in the independent variable of interest, holding all other variables at their mean or modal values. Negative remarks appear in the upper left graph, positive remarks in the upper right figure, and neutral remarks in the bottom left graph. The circles represent the point estimate of the marginal effects and the horizontal lines coming off the circles are 90 percent confidence intervals. Variables are statistically significant if the 90 percent confidence intervals do not cross the solid line at zero.[19]

Beginning with our main variable of interest – the president's ideological agreement with the Court's decision – we find support for our theoretical expectations in both the negative and positive rhetoric models. As the ideological distance between the president and the Court's decision increases, so too does the number of negative comments presidents make about those decisions. In other words, presidents attack decisions with which they disagree. In substantive terms, a one standard deviation increase in the ideological distance variable, moving the president further from the Court's decision, results in an increase of about two negative presidential statements about the decision. The opposite holds true in the positive rhetoric model, such that the negative coefficient indicates that presidents tend to praise decisions with which they agree. Substantively, a one standard deviation decrease in this variable, moving the president closer to the Court's decision, results in an increase of about 0.6 positive statements about the decision. Given that the mean of these variables are 0.02 (negative remarks) and 0.03 (positive remarks), these are substantively very large increases, thus indicating that the president's ideological disagreement or agreement with the Court's decisions dictates much of their criticism or praise of those decisions.

In light of our theoretical framework, this is evidence that presidents take positions on the Court's decisions to shape their implementation and acceptance by other actors, and to generate support for their presidency. By criticizing the Court's cases, presidents can weaken public support for those decisions, while calling on Congress and the bureaucracy to take actions to alter the Court's decision. Conversely, by praising the Court's decisions, presidents may increase public support for the Court's decisions, at the same time encouraging Congress and the federal bureaucracy to faithfully implement the decision. Thus, this type of position taking can help presidents achieve their goals of creating good public policy, which may affect their

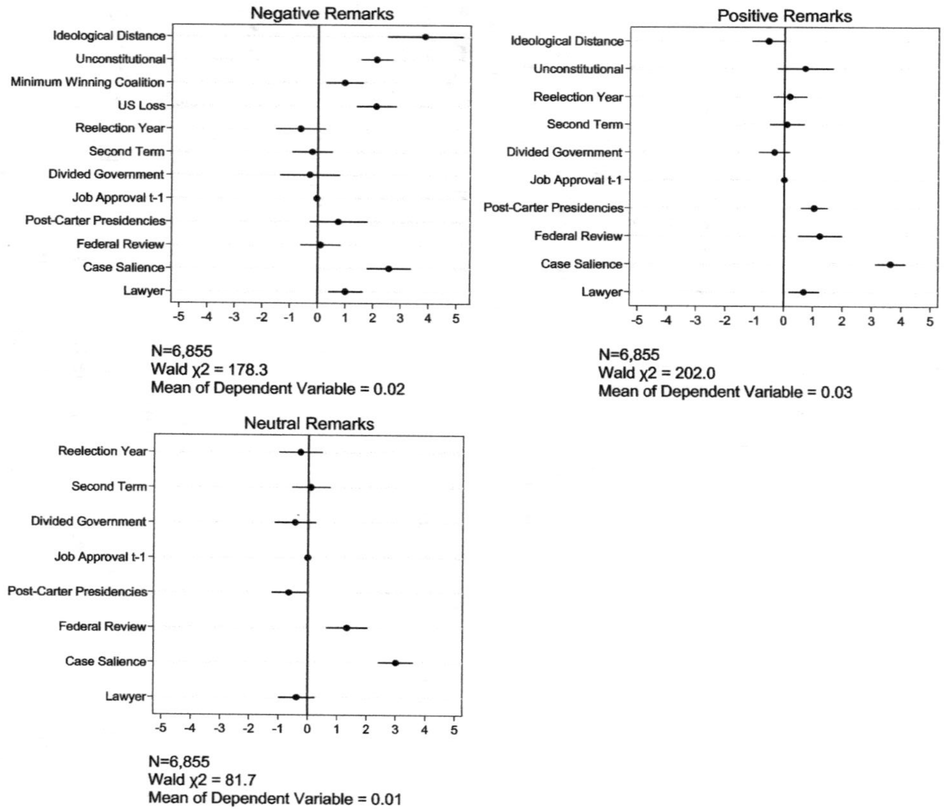

FIGURE 4.2. Influences on the number of negative, positive, and neutral remarks made by presidents on Supreme Court decisions, 1953–2017

historical legacies. In addition, by criticizing or praising decisions with which they disagree or agree, presidents are enabled to take firm positions on issues important to their electoral bases, thus potentially enhancing their standing in the electorate.

The negative remarks model also reveals that presidents criticize Supreme Court decisions that declare laws unconstitutional. Substantively, presidents make about two more negative statements about decisions that involve declarations of unconstitutionality, relative to those without. This suggests that decisions in which the Court declares a law unconstitutional provide easy ammunition for presidents, enabling them to frame their criticism of cases in the language of judicial activism and overreach, terms often viewed as having negative connotations (e.g., Caldeira 1986). This might help build support against the decision in the public, and potentially the bureaucracy and Congress, who might see the Court as behaving in an overly activist manner by striking down laws duly passed by elected representatives. If they are successful at motivating a response to these decisions, presidents can benefit electorally by claiming credit, or they can help their policy goals by moving the policy closer to their ideological viewpoints. Doing either can enhance their historical legacies.

The negative rhetoric model also reveals that presidents target cases decided by minimum winning coalitions. Compared with cases decided by broader coalitions, presidents make about one more negative remark regarding cases decided by minimum winning coalitions. By targeting these cases, the president can remind the public of the importance of Supreme Court appointments and how a single justice occasionally has the power to mold the direction of public policy, which may motivate electoral support for the president. In addition, presidents can use these cases to demonstrate the frailty of the precedent and to suggest the case be overruled in the future, or that the bureaucracy or Congress take steps to modify the decisions. Indeed, there is evidence that the Court itself is more likely to invite further action by Congress to alter the Court's decisions in cases decided by minimum winning coalitions (Rice n.d.). Thus, presidents can secure electoral and policy goals by attacking cases decided by a bare majority of justices.

Figure 4.2 also shows that presidents tend to attack decisions in which the Court hands the federal government an unfavorable judgment. Substantively, presidents make about two more negative comments on decisions that the United States lost, compared with other types of cases. Our results suggest that such decisions stand out in the president's mind, in part because losses are relatively rare for the Solicitor General and because the federal government has expended a great deal of time and resources litigating the case (Black and Owens 2012). By attacking decisions that are unfavorable to the federal government, the president can attempt to weaken public support for them and suggest ways in which the executive and legislative branches might work around the Court's dictates, thus enabling presidents to pursue their policy goals.

Turning now to the control variables, our results indicate that presidents do not address more Supreme Court decisions during reelection years, during their second terms, or during periods of divided government. Recall that our findings in Chapter 3 showed that presidents comment more often on Supreme Court decisions under certain circumstances related to these conditions. This difference is attributable to two factors. First, Chapter 3 disaggregated the data by whether presidents discussed recent or historical cases, and by whether they delivered written or spoken remarks. Second, that chapter focused on all mentions of Supreme Court decisions and did not disaggregate the data on the basis of whether the president's remark was critical, positive, or neutral toward the case. Nonetheless, these findings somewhat undermine our argument that presidents focus the tone of their public remarks on judicial decisions to build support among their electoral constituencies. However, we do find that presidents increasingly criticize the Court's decisions when their approval ratings are low. A one standard deviation decrease in approval ratings results in presidents making about 0.3 more negative speeches about a decision, the weakest substantive effect in the negative remarks model. Given this, while there is evidence that low approval ratings motivate one type of presidential response to the Court's decisions, the models reveal that the variables associated with our key hypotheses offer more explanatory power than the aforementioned factors.

We do, however, find fairly strong support for the remaining control variables. Presidents in the post-Carter era issue more positive remarks on Supreme Court decisions (about one more speech in the post-Carter era), though they make neutral remarks less frequently (about 0.8 fewer remarks). Presidents also make about one more positive and neutral remark about cases involving the review of federal laws, compared with other types of cases. Case salience also exerts a very powerful effect in all of the models. Compared with non-salient cases, presidents make about 2.5 more negative remarks, 3.5 more positive remarks, and 3 more neutral remarks about salient cases. Thus, even after controlling for presidents' ideological alignment with the decision, presidents more frequently single out high-profile cases in their public rhetoric, indicating they are responsive to salient matters of public concern. Finally, the negative and positive remark models indicate that presidents who were attorneys make about one more speech about Court decisions than their non-lawyer counterparts.

CONCLUSIONS

This chapter further illustrates that presidents view the Court's decisions as fair game in their public rhetoric, using their public appeals to participate in the shared process of constitutional lawmaking by staking out positions on important matters of constitutional law (e.g., Friedman 1993). Most notably, we find that when presidents are in ideological agreement with the Court's decision, they are more likely to praise the decision. By speaking favorably about the case, presidents may build public support for the decision and signal that they intend to implement the Court's dictates. However, when presidents disagree with the Court's decision, they make more negative comments about the case. This enables presidents to attempt to build public opposition to the decision, and may motivate congressional action to legislatively alter the rulings or dissuade active bureaucratic implementation of the Court's ruling, thus making the president a key player in constitutional lawmaking. In addition to potentially providing presidents with policy gains, taking positions on Supreme Court decisions in their public rhetoric can also help presidents motivate public support for their presidencies by demonstrating to the public that they have firm positions on important matters of public policy.

We also find that presidents make more negative remarks about cases that declare laws unconstitutional and those cases decided by minimum winning coalitions. By criticizing judicial decisions that declare laws unconstitutional, presidents can highlight the decisions' non-democratic nature. Since the public tends to view declarations of unconstitutionality negatively (Caldeira 1986), this might motivate public support to amend the decision. Similarly, presidents can highlight to the American public the fragile nature of cases decided by minimum winning coalitions to generate public support to overrule the decision, or as a means to garner public support for their nominees (who might cast the deciding vote to overturn the decision in a future case). Thus, these attributes might be thought of as easily discernible heuristics that presidents can employ to determine which of the Court's decisions to target in their public criticism.

Our negative rhetoric model reveals two other important findings. First, presidents speak more negatively about decisions that the federal government lost. Such cases are likely to be particularly memorable for presidents because these losses are rare and indicate a negative return on the substantial investment of resources that went into litigating the case in the lower courts and the Supreme Court. By criticizing these decisions, presidents are provided with opportunities to attempt to weaken public support for the decisions, in addition to limiting affirmative congressional or bureaucratic reactions to what presidents see as negative features of the decisions. Second, presidents attack decisions for instrumental reasons, particularly when their approval ratings are low. Though the substantive impact of this finding is not as strong as other effects, it reveals nonetheless that unpopular presidents attempt to draw attention away from themselves by criticizing the Court's decisions. This denotes that multiple factors motivate the volume and tone of presidential speeches, including attempts to generate short-term political benefits. In the chapters that follow, we examine the extent to which these statements generate responses by Congress, the media, and the public.

APPENDIX TABLE 4.1. *Influences on the number of negative, positive, and neutral remarks made by presidents on Supreme Court decisions, 1953–2017*

	Negative	Positive	Neutral
Ideological Distance	3.86[a]	−0.55[a]	
	(0.82)	(0.34)	
Unconstitutional	2.13[a]	0.72	
	(0.35)	(0.58)	
Minimum Winning Coalition	0.96[a]		
	(0.40)		
US Loss	2.10[a]		
	(0.43)		
Reelection Year	−0.62	0.20	−0.27
	(0.54)	(0.35)	(0.45)
Second Term	−0.20	0.10	0.09
	(0.44)	(0.36)	(0.39)
Divided Government	−0.28	−0.33	−0.44
	(0.65)	(0.32)	(0.43)
Job Approval, t-1	−0.03[a]	0.01	−0.01
	(0.02)	(0.01)	(0.01)
Post-Carter Presidencies	0.75	1.04[a]	−0.65[a]
	(0.63)	(0.27)	(0.35)
Federal Review	0.10	1.24[a]	1.32[a]
	(0.43)	(0.45)	(0.42)
Case Salience	2.58[a]	3.64[a]	3.00[a]
	(0.48)	(0.31)	(0.36)
Lawyer	1.01[a]	0.69[a]	−0.38
	(0.37)	(0.31)	(0.37)
Constant	−7.64[a]	−7.40[a]	−5.02[a]
	(1.37)	(0.92)	(0.91)
Wald χ^2	178.3[a]	202.0[a]	81.7[a]
N	6,855	6,855	6,855

Note: Entries are negative binomial regression coefficients. The dependent variables are the number of decided Supreme Court cases presidents remarked on in a negative, positive, or neutral manner. Robust standard errors are reported in parentheses. [a]$p < .05$ (one-tailed tests).

5

Presidential Calls to Congress

On June 21, 1989, the Supreme Court announced its decision in *Texas v. Johnson.* By a 5-4 vote, the Court's majority held that burning the American flag in a political protest was a form of expressive political speech protected by the First Amendment. The Court's majority opinion recognized the special place of the flag in American society, but noted that the country's reverence for the flag does not outweigh individuals' free speech rights. As Justice Brennan wrote, "If there is a bedrock principle underlying the First Amendment, it is that the government may not prohibit the expression of an idea simply because society finds the idea itself offensive or disagreeable" (491 U.S. 397, at 414).

Brennan was correct in stating that in 1989 many Americans found burning the American flag offensive and disagreeable. This is perhaps no more evident than in President George H. W. Bush's reaction to the decision. The day after the Court announced its ruling, Bush provided guests at a luncheon with his personal opinion about the case, stating that, "Flag-burning is wrong – dead wrong – and the flag of the United States is very, very special."[1] Subsequently, President Bush discussed the case in a series of speeches over the course of the next year, criticizing the decision and calling on Congress to pass a constitutional amendment to overturn the decision. This is perhaps best exemplified in the prepared marks Bush provided in opening a routine news conference less than a week after the decision:

> On Wednesday morning, the Supreme Court issued a decision which held that a person could not be convicted for desecration of our flag, the American flag, because to do so would infringe upon the right to political protest. Now, we've got to be very careful in our society to preserve the right to protest government action. However, I believe that the flag of the United States

> should never be the object of desecration. Flag burning is wrong. Protection of the flag, a unique national symbol, will in no way limit the opportunity nor the breadth of protest available in the exercise of free speech rights.
>
> And I have the greatest respect for the Supreme Court and, indeed, for the Justices who interpreted the Constitution, as they saw fit. But I believe the importance of this issue compels me to call for a constitutional amendment. Support for the first amendment need not extend to desecration of the American flag. And we are reviewing proposed language for a constitutional amendment. We are beginning consultation with Members of the United States Congress who hold similar views. And as President, I will uphold our precious right to dissent. But burning the flag goes too far, and I want to see that matter remedied.[2]

Congress reacted swiftly.[3] Many rank-and-file members of Congress sought to ratify President Bush's call for a constitutional amendment to protect the flag, recognizing public outrage over the Court's decision (Jacoby, McDaniel, and McKillop 1989; Tiefer 1992). However, congressional leadership preferred a legislative response over a constitutional amendment, fearing that a constitutional amendment might go too far. Congressional leaders proposed amending the Flag Protection Act of 1989 to focus on protecting the physical integrity of the flag, which they believed could withstand further Supreme Court review in light of *Texas* v. *Johnson* (Tiefer 1992). The leadership prevailed, and the Flag Protection Act of 1989 became law on October 28, 1989, without the signature of President Bush, who stuck to his position that a constitutional amendment was necessary to protect the flag (Luckey 2009).

On June 11, 1990, in *United States* v. *Eichman*, the same five-justice majority struck down the Flag Protection Act of 1989 as inconsistent with the First Amendment's right to free expression. In response to that decision, President Bush once again called for a constitutional amendment to protect the flag:

> Accordingly, I want to take the chance today to renew my commitment to the surest, safest way to guarantee that, while speech remains free, flag desecration is unacceptable and must carry a price, and, yes, a constitutional amendment to protect the truly unique symbol of all that we are and that we believe. Our constitutional amendment will preserve the widest conceivable range of options for free expression. It applies only to the flag. Its language is simple but eloquent: The Congress and the States shall have power to prohibit the physical desecration of the flag of the United States.
>
> Our forefathers, with remarkable foresight, provided a mechanism for amending the Constitution. And they wished it to be used sparingly and wisely, and it has been, and it must today. Just as the Constitution is a unique symbol of America, so is our flag.[4]

The constitutional amendment to protect the flag was introduced in Congress on June 21, 1990. By this time, support for the amendment had weakened from the previous year, as some members of Congress worried about enacting a constitutional amendment that would limit freedom of expression. In a vote taken the same day that the amendment was introduced, the amendment failed by a 254-177 (58.9 percent) margin, garnering less than the two-thirds of the House necessary to adopt a constitutional amendment. The Senate also defeated the amendment by a vote of 58-42 (58 percent), short of the two-thirds majority necessary to adopt an amendment (Tiefer 1992, 377–378). Subsequently, flag protection amendments have been introduced into Congress more than half a dozen times, though the amendments have never garnered the necessary two-thirds support to pass (Luckey 2009, 3). Thus, despite President Bush's best efforts, flag burning remains constitutionally protected as a form of political speech.

The story of flag burning legislation and proposed constitutional amendments illustrates how presidents can respond to Supreme Court decisions in a very specific way: by calling on Congress to take action to oppose a Supreme Court ruling. In this chapter, we describe not only these instances where presidents call for Congress to oppose a Court decision, but also when presidents ask Congress to implement Supreme Court decisions, including passing legislation and proposing constitutional amendments. Our evidence indicates that presidents call on Congress in 19 percent of their speeches regarding the Court's decided cases. We also find that presidents more often call for congressional action to reverse or alter the Court's decisions, rather than request legislation to assist with the implementation of a decision. We further show that presidents call for congressional action regarding Court decisions that involve some of the most controversial constitutional issues in American society. In our examination of how Congress responds to these presidential calls, we demonstrate that, after the president called for a congressional response, Congress took some form of action on 54 percent of cases and passed legislation in 31 percent of cases.

Our motivation in this chapter is to contribute to our understanding of how the executive, legislative, and judicial branches do and do not coordinate to interpret the constitution (e.g., Epstein and Knight 1998; Murphy 1986; Paulsen 1994). In Chapter 4, we established that presidents are willing to contribute to constitutional dialogue by expressing their support for, or opposition to, the Court's decisions. Here, we look at how presidents bring Congress into the picture by calling for legislative action to support or oppose the Court's decisions.

In addition, by investigating this topic, we bring new evidence to bear on the president's role in the implementation of judicial decisions, which speaks directly to the ability of the president to engage in constitutional construction by attempting to influence how Congress understands the Constitution and its agenda in relation to constitutional interpretation (Cohen 1995; Edwards and Barrett 2000; Edwards and Wood 1999; Gant 1997; Whitford and Yates 2009; Whittington 1999, 2001). Indeed, although presidents are often seen as the primary movers of the national policy debate (Baumgartner and Jones 1993; Kingdon 1995), it remains unclear how presidential remarks on Supreme Court cases shape the national debate on the issues considered in those cases or whether these remarks are used by presidents as a tool for agenda-setting in Congress. Although we find in Chapter 3 that presidents issue more written statements to guide the implementation of recent Court decisions by the bureaucracy under divided government, President Bush's reaction to *Texas* v. *Johnson* shows that presidents also call on Congress to act in response to Court decisions through their public speeches. Thus, it is also important to examine presidential leadership of Congress in response to Court decisions.

In the next section, we discuss why presidents call for legislative in action in Congress, building on the literature that focuses on executive-legislative interactions. Then, we turn to the specific focus of this chapter: presidential calls on Congress to react to Supreme Court decisions. Here, we discuss the positive and negative motivations presidents have to engage in this type of coordinate construction of the Constitution. Following this, we present the data used to examine these topics and the empirical results. We conclude by discussing what these results mean for our understanding of the rhetorical presidency and constitutional interpretation more generally.

WHY DO PRESIDENTS CALL ON CONGRESS?

Presidents have multiple audiences and motivations when they issue public remarks, often doing so for the purpose of shaping news coverage, informing the public, or directing the implementation of public policy. Each of these efforts align with the president's broader goals of reelection, the pursuit of good public policy, and historical achievement. Of course, since legislative accomplishments provide the clearest path to significant goal achievement, presidents often target Congress through both public speeches and written statements.

Perhaps the most accepted model of presidential leadership of Congress through a public relations strategy is that offered by Canes-Wrone (2006). In essence, the president's efforts to increase legislative success are tied to increasing the salience of issues before legislators, rather than building public support and moving the public to action, which is extraordinarily difficult (Edwards 2003).[5] Just as Canes-Wrone (2006) finds that more public appeals increase the president's success in Congress, she also finds that public appeals tend to work indirectly through existing public support. That is, presidents target issues that are already popular with the public and, by speaking frequently about them, they increase the relevance of the issue to legislators. With heightened salience, legislators have a strong electoral incentive to support issues that the public already supports.

Given the strong, positive relationship that Canes-Wrone (2006) finds between public appeals and legislative success, one might assume that direct presidential calls for congressional action are common. They are not. Barrett (2005) has catalogued the number of appeals on important legislation for the Carter, Reagan, and Bush Administrations. This database, built from Mayhew's (1991) list of important legislation that passed Congress, and Edwards, Barrett, and Peake's (1997) list of important legislation that failed to pass Congress, comprises 253 bills. Categories of public appeals include general appeals, appeals for public action, and appeals for congressional action.

Barrett's analysis reveals a number of important findings. First, presidents target few bills before Congress. Among all types of appeals, presidents are most likely to make general (or vague) appeals, issuing at least one appeal on 67 percent of important legislation. Demanding congressional action is uncommon, as presidents have called directly on Congress to act on only 35 percent of important bills. It is even less likely for presidents to request public action or to appeal publicly on television. In all, the modal category of the number of presidential appeals on important legislation is zero.

Second, when presidents do target Congress, they are more likely to do so when they support legislation. Whereas Presidents Carter, Reagan, and George H. W. Bush issued at least some direct appeals to Congress on legislation they supported, averaging 1.4 appeals per bill overall, they virtually ignored invoking Congress when they opposed a piece of legislation. Presidents were much more likely to oppose legislation in general appeals, although this, too, was quite rare at 1.5 appeals per bill.

Third, individual presidents behave differently in their calls for legislative action. Barrett (2005) shows that Reagan issued more appeals for congressional action than did Carter, and Bush called on Congress more than Reagan. This holds overall and specifically for appeals in support of legislation. Whereas Carter failed to average even one legislative appeal per bill and Reagan barely surpassed this mark, Bush averaged nearly three legislative appeals per important bill before Congress. These numbers held for Carter and Reagan's supportive appeals. Yet, Bush's average supportive remarks to Congress rose to nearly five appeals per important bill. This is somewhat surprising given Reagan's famous calls for legislative support as summarized by Kernell (1997, Chapter 5). Clearly, Bush learned from Reagan as Vice President and chose to issue more public calls on congressional action, despite his less successful presidency (Ragsdale 2014).

The increasing tendency for presidents from Carter through Bush to call on Congress raises the possibility that even more recent presidents would continue this strategy. Heith (2013) helps to answer this question by examining the presidencies of Clinton, George W. Bush, and Obama. Reporting on presidential calls to Congress during a time of increasingly fragmented media and amplified reliance on targeting local media, she finds considerable variation in each president's strategies for going public. Although President Clinton appealed to Congress in speeches that targeted national audiences, he did not attempt to motivate it to act. Only rarely did Clinton ask the public to contact their legislators and he was more likely to argue that Congress was part of a policy solution, not the problem (Heith 2013, 56). President George W. Bush targeted local, rather than national, audiences more frequently than Clinton and aimed his messages at supportive audiences. Even so, and similarly to Clinton, he did not ask the public to contact their legislators nor was he overly critical of Congress when he appealed to them in his public rhetoric (Heith 2013, 81). Perhaps surprising, President Obama never called on citizens to contact their legislators on his top legislative priorities (although he did employ this strategy occasionally on other issues like deficit reduction). Moreover, he rarely criticized Congress, instead using his direct appeals to Congress to argue how Congress could be part of a policy solution (Heith 2013, 103).

Although neither of these lines of research examines presidencies earlier than Carter, it is not likely that we would witness many calls for legislative action prior to the Carter Administration. After all, overall speechmaking – except for Gerald Ford who gave several hundred campaign speeches in 1976 – had not yet increased substantially until the Carter Administration for two reasons. First, the Office of Communications was not institutionalized, and so it could not provide the president with the necessary and reliable resources to be able to address the public frequently. Second, the conditions that Kernell (1997) identified as being essential to the rise of going public as a governing strategy had not fully materialized until the Reagan Administration. Thus, we think the absence of research on public appeals for legislative action prior to Carter is evidence of a lack of presidential effort to do so. Whether we find something different on presidential calls for congressional action in response to Supreme Court decisions is something this chapter will determine.

CALLS FOR CONGRESSIONAL ACTION IN RESPONSE TO SUPREME COURT DECISIONS

President George H. W. Bush's call for a constitutional amendment to overturn *Texas* v. *Johnson* generated a substantial amount of interest on both sides of the debate. On the one hand, the clear majority of the American public, 71 percent, supported passing a constitutional amendment making flag burning illegal (Kiefer 2005), allowing Bush to harness public support for this already popular proposal. The pro-flag rhetoric burned especially bright in Republican circles on Capitol Hill, with Representative Ron Marlenee (R-MT) invoking the famous Marine Corp Memorial featuring marines raising the flag over Iwo Jima in stating that, "Yesterday, those six brave soldiers were symbolically shot in the back" (Gailey 1989). On the other hand, the president's efforts were met with substantial resistance on a wide array of fronts. Some criticized the president for exaggerating the importance of the flag burning issue, particularly as the country was facing more pressing problems, such as increasing human rights violations in China (Lewis 1989) and growing concern over civil rights abuses at home (Evans 1989). Others suggested that the president's efforts were a form of nationalism, offensive to some of the country's core values (St. Louis Post-Dispatch 1989). Still others argued that the president was using the flag burning issue as a political prop to generate support for his reelection among his political base (Goodman 1989). Others pointed out that the amendment strategy was unwise and politically risky, given how difficult it is to pass a constitutional amendment (Mauro 1989).

When presidents call on Congress to oppose or support the Court's decisions, they participate in a form of constitutional reasoning referred to as the coordinate construction of the constitution, or departmentalism (Whittington 2001, 368). That is, because presidents are an independent constitutional authority, they can engage in constitutional interpretation that may put them in conflict with the other branches of government (Chemerinsky 1997). This view of constitutional interpretation is perhaps less familiar than the judicial supremacy view, which holds that the Supreme Court is the primary institution charged with the final interpretation of the Constitution, but it is nonetheless consistent with the separation of powers system in which each branch of government has authority to interpret the Constitution (Burgess 1992; Gant 1997; Murphy 1986).

What we examine in this chapter is a particular form of the coordinate construction of the Constitution: one branch of government (the president) criticizing or supporting a second branch of government (the Supreme Court) and calling on a third branch of government (Congress) to react to the second branch's perspective on constitutional interpretation. Scholars interested in the coordinate construction of the Constitution have generally focused on communication between only two branches of government. For example, a vast body of research has examined congressional attempts to alter Supreme Court decisions (e.g., Blackstone 2013; Eskridge 1991; Ignagni and Meernik 1994; Nelson and Uribe-McGuire 2017; Pickerill 2004; Rice 2018; Uribe, Spriggs, and Hansford 2014; Whittington 2003), or efforts by Congress to curb the Court's jurisdiction (e.g., Clark 2009, 2011; Devins 2006; Harvey and Friedman 2006; Hettinger and Zorn 2005; Mark and Zillis 2018; Nagel 1964). In addition, there is an extensive vein of scholarship on the interactions between the president and the Court, in the form of judicial appointments (Abraham 2008; Cameron and Park 2011; Holmes 2007, 2008; Johnson and Roberts 2004; Maltese 1995a, 1995b; Nemacheck 2007; Yalof 1999) and the role of the Office of Solicitor General (Black and Owens 2012; Caplan 1987; Nicholson and Collins 2008; Pacelle 2003). Here, we break new ground by providing an exploratory look at how presidents engage in this form of constitutional discourse by calling on Congress to react to the Court's decisions.

The fervor surrounding George H. W. Bush's call for a legislative response to *Texas* v. *Johnson* may lead one to think that presidents regularly call on Congress in response to key Supreme Court decisions. Certainly, there are reasons why presidents would want to involve Congress. If the president disagrees with a Court decision, then one vehicle to undermine the Court's conclusion would be to call on Congress to pass legislation that would withstand judicial scrutiny or to begin the process of amending the Constitution. In this sense, presidents might be able to leverage or even mobilize public support on an issue, via the bully pulpit, to convince Congress to correct judicial decisions they disagree with. Alternatively, if the president agrees with a Court decision, the president may need to enlist Congress to codify into statute provisions necessary for the federal government to follow or implement the Court's opinion. Court rulings are far from self-executing, after all (Canon and Johnson 1999; Epstein and Knight 1998). Engaging in such rhetoric also sends a strong signal to the American public that two branches of government agree with the decision, potentially increasing compliance.

In addition to these specific reasons for calling on Congress to take action on Supreme Court decisions, there are more general principles involved that might motivate presidents to engage in this form of the coordinate construction of the Constitution. For example, Burgess (1992, 19) argues departmentalism enables more collegial constitutional conversations, limits institutional attacks on the judiciary, and enhances public awareness of constitutional issues (see also Gant 1997). One can argue that all three of these functions were evident in Bush's call for a constitutional amendment to overturn *Texas* v. *Johnson*. For example, the president engaged in a dialogue with Congress and the public regarding the benefits of the constitutional amendment route, as compared with the legislative course, to protect the flag. In addition, Bush criticized the Court's decision, as opposed to the institution itself. In fact, he frequently did so using language similar to that found in the Court's majority opinion that recognized the special place of the flag in American society, recalling the patriotic fervor of his campaign (Sullivan, Fried, and Dietz 1992). Finally, by publicly speaking to the flag burning amendment for over a year, President Bush was able to keep the issue on the public's agenda, promoting public debate about the balance between protecting the flag and free speech rights (Jacoby, McDaniel, and McKillop 1989; Pollitt 1992; Tiefer 1990).

Despite these reasons for why presidents may choose to call on Congress to react to the Court's decisions, it is nonetheless likely that they will use their public rhetoric only sparingly to lead Congress after a Court decision. First, there are risks involved in this strategy. As noted above, Bush faced substantial criticism from a wide array of quarters for his role in the flag burning debate. Among other things, he was criticized for politicizing the issue, engaging in a form of hyper-nationalism, and putting the issue at the top of an agenda when the country had more pressing problems. Thus, presidents must weigh the risks and benefits of calling on Congress and may err toward refraining from doing so to limit criticism.

Second, it is evident that presidents rarely call for congressional action in general. For example, Barrett (2005) demonstrates that presidential appeals to Congress involving legislative (and not judicial) priorities are rare, and typically involve the president's own legislative priorities. If these findings apply to the Court's decisions, it suggests that presidents may be reluctant to spend their political capital on public calls to Congress to react to the Court's decisions.

Finally, there are more general hazards to engaging in the coordinate construction of the Constitution that may discourage presidents from calling on Congress to react to Supreme Court decisions. For example, presidents may be accused of politicizing constitutional issues, failing to safeguard rights and liberties, exerting a type of executive authority over the judicial branch, constitutionalizing personal animosity toward the Court, and confusing the country's ability to arrive at settled constitutional meanings (Burgess 1992; Gant 1997; Whittington 1999).

Our goal in this chapter is to explore the extent to which presidents engage in this particular form of constitutional interpretation. Doing so will provide three primary insights into how presidents conceptualize their role in constitutional interpretation and change with respect to the Court and Congress. First, our investigation offers leverage over the extent to which presidents view constitutional interpretation as a role played by all three branches of government. Second, it highlights those issues where presidents and the Court disagree over the meaning of the Constitution, helping us better understand areas of constitutional contestation. Finally, in examining whether Congress responds to presidents' calls for action, we contribute to our understanding of how presidents can shape the congressional agenda on matters of constitutional concern. Because we can contribute to our understanding of these three areas through descriptive analyses, we proceed using a descriptive, rather than an inferential, approach.

DATA

From our list of all decided cases on which the president made a public remark, we examined each speech to determine if the president called for Congress to react to the Supreme Court decision. To do this, we searched each speech for the following terms: congress, legislat, constitution, amend, statut, and bill. If one of these terms was identified, we read the relevant portion of the speech to determine if the president called for some type of action by Congress – such as passing a bill or initiating the constitutional amendment process – in reaction to the Court's decision. If the president made such a call to Congress, we included that speech in the data used in this chapter.

We also identified the type of action called on by the president. Negative actions involve calling on Congress to alter, ignore, override, modify, undo, or correct the Supreme Court decision (Uribe, Spriggs, and Hansford 2014). This is exemplified in President Bush's actions with respect to *Texas* v. *Johnson* that opened the chapter. President George W. Bush's response to *Clinton* v. *City of New York* (1998), in which the Court struck down the presidential line-item veto, also demonstrates a negative action:

> In 1996, the Congress gave the President a line item veto – an important tool to limit wasteful spending – but the Supreme Court struck down that version of the law in 1998.

> My proposed legislation, the "'Legislative Line Item Veto Act of 2006," would provide a fast-track procedure to require the Congress to vote up-or-down on rescissions proposed by the President.[6]

Positive actions involve calling on Congress to take action to ensure the Court's decision is followed, implemented, or expanded upon in a manner consistent with the decision. For example, President Clinton praised the Court's decision in *Nixon* v. *Shrink Missouri Government PAC* (2000), which upheld the ability of states to set campaign contribution limits, and called for Congress to pass additional campaign finance legislation consistent with the decision:

> The Court's opinion is a victory for democracy. The American people know that our political system needs to be fixed, and today's decision sets the stage for further reform. For years, I've challenged Congress to pass legislation that would ban the raising of unregulated soft money, address backdoor spending by outside organizations, and strengthen public discourse. Now I am again asking Congress to restore the American people's faith in their democracy and pass real reform this year.[7]

Finally, we code as mixed those actions in which the president's message to Congress is neither entirely negative nor entirely positive, but rather it calls for the implementation of parts of the decision and the alteration of other parts of the decision. For example, President Nixon asked Congress to pass two separate pieces of legislation in the wake of *Brown* v. *Board of Education* (1954) and *Swann* v. *Charlotte-Mecklenburg Board of Education* (1971):

> First, I shall propose legislation that would call an immediate halt to all new busing orders by Federal courts – a moratorium on new busing. Next, I shall propose a companion measure – the Equal Educational Opportunities Act of 1972. This act would require that every State or locality grant equal educational opportunity to every person, regardless of race, color, or national origin. For the first time in our history, the cherished American ideal of equality of educational opportunity would be affirmed in the law of the land by the elected representatives of the people in Congress.[8]

Thus, the first measure called for stripping lower courts of the ability to order busing, thus overriding the spirt of *Brown* and *Swann*. Yet, the second measure is consistent with both cases. Accordingly, we code proposals such as these as mixed requests from the president.

Existing work on congressional responses to Supreme Court decisions has used a variety of thresholds to identify a congressional response. For example, Blackstone (2013) includes all bills and amendments introduced; Eskridge (1991) includes only bills that received committee hearings; Ignagni and

Meernik (1994) include only bills that were reported out of committee; and Uribe, Spriggs, and Hansford (2014) limit their analysis to bills that passed both chambers of Congress. While these scholars had their own reasons for creating these thresholds, we follow the expansive approach used by Blackstone (2013; see also Clark 2011) and include all bills introduced into Congress that responded to the president's call for action on a Supreme Court decision. In addition, we identify the fate of these bills by including information on the final action taken on each bill. Thus, ours is a broad investigation into whether and how Congress responds to presidents' calls for action on the Court's decisions.

To identify these congressional actions, we used a two-pronged approach. First, we searched for the name of each case that presidents called for legislative action on in Westlaw's Legislative History database. This online database provides the legislative history of public laws from the US Code Congressional and Administrative News (USCCAN) from 1948 through 1989 and all congressional committee reports (including bills that were introduced, but did not become law) from 1990 to the present (e.g., Eskridge 1991; Uribe, Spriggs, and Hansford 2014). In most instances, we were able to determine whether or not Congress responded to a president's call for legislation in response to a Supreme Court case using this database. For example, President Ford issued ten separate calls to Congress in 1976 asking it to pass legislation to comply with the decision in *Buckley* v. *Valeo* (1976). Westlaw identified the Federal Election Campaign Act Amendments of 1976 as a legislative response to *Buckley*, which is included in our data.

Second, to verify the accuracy of what we found in Westlaw and to ensure Westlaw did not produce incomplete results, we checked each presidential call for legislative response with the yearly volumes of *Congressional Quarterly Almanac* and the online database of *Congressional Weekly Reports*. These sources provide very specific information about presidential calls for legislation and the essence of congressional responses. For example, Richard Nixon asked Congress to pass legislation to curb mailings of sexually explicit materials.[9] Although we had determined that Nixon responded to *Ginsberg* v. *New York* (1968) in these calls for action, Westlaw did not associate this case with the Postal Revenue and Offensive Intrusion of Sexually Oriented Mail Act of 1969. After reviewing the legislative history provided in the *Congressional Quarterly Almanac*, we were able to determine that Congress responded to Nixon's call for legislative action by passing a bill out of committee.

For each of the president's calls on Congress, we determined the president's success in generating a legislative response. To do this, we coded the final action taken on each piece of legislation that was introduced into Congress according to whether the bill: 1) was introduced, but never received a committee hearing; 2) was supported by a congressional committee; 3) received a floor vote in at least one chamber of Congress; 4) was passed by the House and Senate and signed into law; or 5) was passed by the House and Senate and was vetoed by the president. This enables us to take a detailed look at the extent to which Congress acts upon presidential calls for congressional action.

EMPIRICAL RESULTS

We examine our data in two ways. First, we report the number of calls for congressional action and describe the types of cases that presidents reference most frequently in conjunction with calls for legislative action. Second, we detail congressional responses to each of the president's remarks by following congressional responses through the legislative process, thus shedding light on the extent to which Congress follows through on the president's calls for action. Our data provide clear evidence that presidents are willing to call upon their legislative counterparts to react to Supreme Court decisions and that Congress frequently responds to these calls for action, thus bringing all three branches of government into the process of constitutional interpretation.

Presidential Calls for Congressional Action

Figure 5.1 reports the number of calls for congressional action in presidential speeches about Supreme Court decisions from the Eisenhower (1953) to Obama administrations (2017). Negative comments are identified by the black portion of the bars, positive comments by the white portions, and mixed comments by the grey portions. Several notable patterns emerge. First, this is not an uncommon rhetorical strategy. Of the 883 speeches presidents have given on decided Supreme Court cases, they have called for congressional action in 167 of these speeches, discussing 84 unique cases. That presidents call for congressional action in one out of every five of their speeches on Court decisions demonstrates that they believe all three branches of government play a role in constitutional law making.

Second, presidents call for congressional action with differing frequency. Reagan made the most calls for congressional action (32), followed by Ford (24), and George H. W. Bush (23). Johnson made the fewest calls to Congress (4), followed by Eisenhower (5), and Kennedy (5). Looking at the temporal trends, it is evident that this did not become a relatively common rhetorical

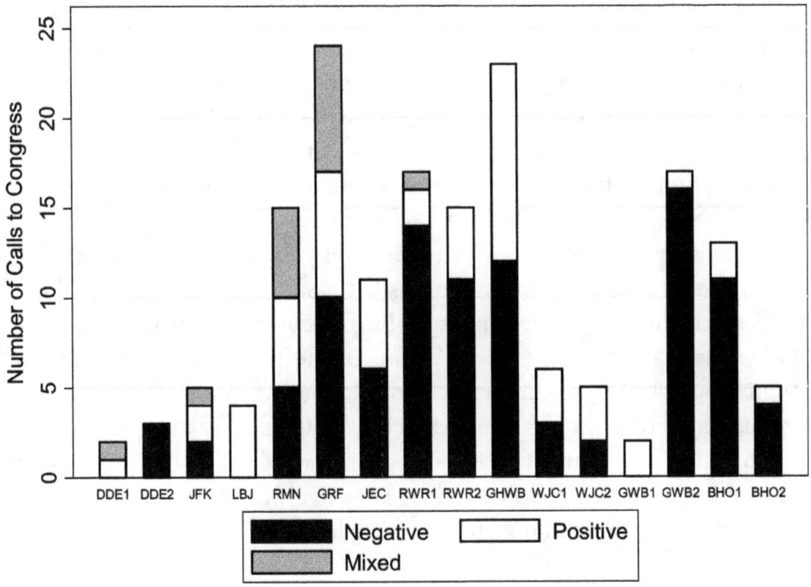

FIGURE 5.1. The number and type of calls to Congress, 1953–2017

strategy until the Nixon Administration. It hit its peak during the Reagan Administration, and then decreased during the Clinton Administration, but gradually increased through the presidencies of George W. Bush and Barack Obama. These trends are generally consistent with Barrett's (2005) and Heith's (2013) findings with respect to individual variation on the frequency with which presidents call for congressional action on legislation more generally. However, these trends also reveal that presidents prior to Jimmy Carter were more willing to call on Congress to take action on the Court's decisions, indicating that this rhetorical strategy predates what scholars generally conceive of as the contemporary era of going public (e.g., Barrett 2005; Heith 2013). Moreover, these specific calls do not follow the upward trajectory of all presidential speeches noted by others (Hager and Sullivan 1994; Powell 1999).

Finally, and as a whole, presidents most frequently call for negative congressional action to alter the Court's decisions. Almost 60 percent of calls for congressional action were negative, compared with 32 percent of positive calls for the implementation of the decision, and 9 percent of mixed calls that request both positive and negative action in response to the decision. This is interesting considering the findings of Barrett (2005) and Heith (2013) that presidents seldom call on Congress when they oppose legislation. At least for our subset of calls for legislation, presidents seem quite willing to call for congressional action when they oppose Court decisions. President Reagan made the most negative calls for congressional action about decisions, followed by George W. Bush and Obama, while President George H. W. Bush made the most positive calls for congressional action, followed by Ford. Mixed calls for action are the rarest and were most frequently invoked by Presidents Ford and Nixon involving *Brown* v. *Board of Education*.

Table 5.1 lists the nine cases that presidents called for Congress to act on four or more times. The first column is the case name, the second column represents the number of comments calling for congressional action, and the third column contains the abbreviations of the presidents who called for congressional action on each case. Perhaps not surprisingly, many of these cases are immediately recognizable and almost all of the cases represent areas of historically (and contemporarily in some cases) deep political division in the country, including abortion rights, campaign finance, prayer in schools, racial segregation, the war on terror, and flag burning. Indeed, *Clinton* v. *City*

TABLE 5.1. *The most frequently addressed Supreme Court decisions in presidential calls to Congress, 1953–2017*

Decision (Year)	Number of Comments[a]	Presidents[b]
Roe v. *Wade* (1973)	17	GRF, JEC, RWR, GHWB, WJC
Buckley v. *Valeo* (1976)	16	GRF, JEC, GHWB, WJC
Engel v. *Vitale* (1962)	15	JFK, GRF, RWR
Citizens United v. *Federal Election Commission* (2010)	12	BHO
Brown v. *Board of Education* (1954)	9	JFK, LBJ, RMN, GRF, JEC
Hamdan v. *Rumsfeld* (2006)	8	GWB
Texas v. *Johnson* (1989)	6	GHWB
Communications Workers of America v. *Beck* (1988)	4	GHWB
Clinton v. *City of New York* (1998)	4	GWB

[a] The Number of Comments is the total number of statements involving an individual decision. Presidents are represented by the abbreviations of the presidents who called for congressional actions on each case.

[b] Initials represent the following presidents: Eisenhower (DDE), Kennedy (JFK), Johnson (LBJ), Nixon (RMN), Ford (GRF), Carter (JEC), Reagan (RWR), Bush (GHWB), Clinton (WJC), George W. Bush (GWB), Obama (BHO).

of New York (1998), which involved the line-item veto, is the only case that did not touch on one of these highly salient issues. Perhaps presidents find it more useful to gain the attention of Congress by referencing landmark, salient cases when they frame their requests as a way to enhance their legislative success.

Roe v. *Wade*, which established that the right to privacy protects a woman's decision to have an abortion, is both the most frequently addressed case in which presidents call for legislative action and the one addressed by the most presidents. President Ford first called for action on this case, requesting that Congress pass a constitutional amendment to allow states to ban abortions. Subsequently, Carter called to end federal funding for abortions, Reagan called for both legislative action and a constitutional amendment to overrule *Roe*, and George H. W. Bush called for a constitutional amendment to ban abortions. Only Clinton called for congressional action to ensure the decision was implemented by requesting an amendment to an abortion bill to ensure that abortions are available to protect the life and health of the mother. Unlike Graber (1993), who argues that political parties may prefer to use the courts as the primary venue for policy making on issues like abortion, our data show that presidents have not been shy about asking Congress to respond to their views on *Roe* v. *Wade* specifically, and on the issue of abortion more generally.

The next most frequently addressed decision is *Buckley* v. *Valeo*, in which the Court upheld certain campaign finance restrictions, while striking down others. President Ford repeatedly called for congressional action to comply with the decision in its immediate aftermath and reconstitute the Federal Election Commission, while Carter called for Congress to pass legislation allowing for the public financing of congressional election campaigns. Both George H. W. Bush and Bill Clinton used the decision to push for their preferred legislation involving campaign finance regulations.

Engel v. *Vitale*, which prohibited prayer in public schools, received uniformly negative reactions from Presidents Kennedy, Ford, and Reagan. That is, all of these presidents called for some type of congressional action to modify the decision. Kennedy used a discussion of the decision to ask Congress to pass legislation that allowed for the related issue of public aid to religious colleges and universities, although he did indicate the importance of supporting Supreme Court decisions, even when they are unpopular. Presidents Ford and Regan went much further by calling on Congress to pass a constitutional amendment allowing for prayer in public schools.

Brown v. *Board of Education* (1954), which ruled unconstitutional racial segregation in public elementary schools, was invoked by Presidents Kennedy, Johnson, Nixon, Ford, and Carter in calls for congressional responses. Kennedy, Johnson, and Carter all made positive calls on Congress to implement the decision. For example, Kennedy proposed amendments to the Civil Rights Act of 1963, "In order to achieve a more orderly and consistent compliance"[10] with *Brown*, and Carter called for amending the Fair Housing Act to ensure "the educational benefits of the *Brown* decision" are available to the northern poor who are victims of housing discrimination.[11] Nixon and Ford sent mixed messages to Congress. As noted above, Nixon spoke in favor of enforcing the decision, but also fought hard against certain remedies authorized by *Brown*, such as busing. Ford made similar calls on Congress, such as when he committed to carrying out *Brown*, but also asked Congress to pass legislation to limit busing and ensure that school districts are not under federal court supervision for extended periods of time.

The remaining five most frequently addressed decisions in calls to Congress were only invoked by a single president each. President Obama repeatedly criticized the Court's *Citizens United* decision, which authorized interest groups, corporations, and other entities to engage in unlimited campaign communication expenditures so long as they are independent of the campaign. Obama pushed Congress to take action to limit the reach of *Citizens United* by advocating support for transparency in campaign disclosures, more generally, and support for the Disclose Act, specifically. George W. Bush frequently criticized the Court's *Hamdan* decision, which rejected his administration's ability to set up military tribunals on Guantanamo Bay, Cuba, by calling on Congress to pass legislation authorizing the tribunals. As noted above, George H. W. Bush repeatedly called on Congress to begin the constitutional amendment process in response to *Texas* v. *Johnson*. George H. W. Bush also asked Congress four times to pass additional campaign finance reform legislation to help implement the Court's *Communications Workers of America v. Beck* decision. This case limited the ability of unions to use membership dues for political purposes. Finally, George W. Bush asked Congress to pass legislation overriding *Clinton* v. *City of New York*, which ruled the line-item veto unconstitutional, by authorizing a presidential line-item veto that would meet the Court's standards.

Congressional Responses to Presidential Calls for Action

Just because the president calls on Congress to respond to a Supreme Court case through legislation or a constitutional amendment, does not mean that Congress will take action. It may ignore the president entirely, or even when a member of Congress introduces a bill, the bill may not be voted out of committee or receive a floor vote. Table 5.2 reveals the distribution of final actions taken by Congress in response to a presidential call related to a Supreme Court case. To count as an action, a legislator simply needs to introduce a bill in response to the president's call. Of the 167 individual calls

TABLE 5.2. *Congressional responses to calls for action by presidents, 1953–2017*

President	Total Calls	Unique Calls	Action Taken	Final Action Taken				
				Introduced	Committee Support	Floor Vote	Passed	Veto
Eisenhower	5	3	2	0	0	0	2	0
Kennedy	5	4	1	1	0	0	0	0
Johnson	4	3	2	0	0	1	1	0
Nixon	15	12	8	0	3	1	4	0
Ford	24	11	5	0	0	1	4	0
Carter	11	9	5	1	1	0	3	0
Reagan	32	14	8	0	0	2	5	1
Bush	23	13	9	0	1	4	0	4
Clinton	11	8	5	0	0	4	0	1
Bush	19	6	4	0	0	2	2	0
Obama	18	7	3	0	1	2	0	0
Total	**167**	**90**	**52**	**2**	**6**	**17**	**21**	**6**

Total Calls = the total number of times presidents called for congressional action. Unique Calls = the number of unique calls for congressional action. Action Taken = Congress took some action on the case. Introduced = bill was introduced, but never made it to committee. Committee Support = bill was supported by congressional committee, but never received a floor vote. Floor Vote = bill received a floor vote in at least one chamber of Congress. Passed = bill passed both chambers of Congress. Veto = president vetoed the congressional legislation.

for a legislative response, Congress took action 52 times, or 31 percent of the time. Among these, the total count of 167 includes instances where multiple presidents referenced a case in a call for congressional action or when the president made repeated calls for the same bill in response to the same case. For example, three presidents referenced *Engle* v. *Vitale* while invoking the need for a congressional response, with Reagan discussing it 11 times in his calls for a constitutional amendment to overturn that decision.

Eliminating from our total count instances where a president made multiple calls for the same congressional action in response to the same case, our database reveals 90 unique calls for a congressional response. Among these unique calls, Congress took some form of action in response to 52 calls, or 58 percent of the president's requests. Of these, the president's overall success in signing legislation is 24 percent, as presidents signed 21 laws in response to their 90 unique calls for Congress to take action. Even though this is a relatively low percentage, when Congress responds to a presidential call, our numbers reveal that signing a bill is the most common outcome for the president. A public law occurs more frequently than a bill being introduced, but not making it to committee (two times); a bill being voted out of committee, but not garnering a floor vote (six times); or a bill receiving an unfavorable vote in either chamber of Congress (17 times). There were six instances of presidential vetoes, with Congress overriding President Reagan's veto of the Civil Rights Restoration Act of 1987. This legislation was a response to *Grove City College* v. *Bell* (1984), a statutory interpretation case in which the Court held that Title IX of the Education Amendments of 1972 applies to private colleges whose students receive federal financial aid scholarships.

The distinction between the total and unique calls on Congress is interesting, as the difference between the two counts is in the number of times a president called on Congress to act on a single piece of legislation and in response to a specific case. Thus, this speaks to the volume of presidential calls for action on each case. Overall, there are 77 instances where presidents made more than one call for a congressional response to the same Court decision and 90 instances of presidents making a single call for action. Consider the following three examples of repeat calls. First, Gerald Ford issued ten remarks that implored Congress to respond to *Buckley* v. *Valeo*. In turn, the president signed the Federal Election Campaign Act Amendments of 1976 in May of 1976. George W. Bush issued eight calls on Congress in response to *Hamdan* v. *Rumsfeld*. The president's efforts led to the Military Commissions Act of 2006. Reagan was also successful in his calls to limit the reach of *Roe* v. *Wade*. Although his three pleas for a constitutional amendment failed in the Senate, his five remarks in 1988 led to portions of his proposed "Pro-life Act" passing in a Health and Human Services Appropriations bill (PL 100-436) in September of that year.

While more presidential attention to an issue indicates the president's level of commitment to a congressional action, the amount of attention alone is insufficient to generate a successful outcome in Congress. George H. W. Bush's call for a constitutional amendment to ban flag burning is one example. Bush made six such calls overall without securing passage in the Senate or House. Reagan also called on Congress nine times to pass a constitutional amendment concerning school prayer, but this was defeated on the Senate floor in 1984. Obama asked Congress 11 times in 2010 to respond to *Citizens United*, but the Disclose Act failed its Senate cloture vote in May of 2010. Of the 21 bills signed into law, presidents made a single call for action on 10 of these cases (48 percent), and made multiple calls for action on 11 cases (52 percent). Thus, presidents are slightly more successful when they issue multiple calls for congressional responses, although the small sample size makes it difficult to draw firm conclusions.[12] That being said, these findings do correspond to those of Canes-Wrone (2006), who demonstrates that presidential success in Congress is enhanced when presidents make multiple calls for action.[13]

CONCLUSIONS

Our purpose in this chapter was to explore the extent to which presidents engage in a particular form of the coordinate construction of the Constitution: by calling on Congress to react to Supreme Court decisions, both positively and negatively, with legislation or a constitutional amendment. We find that presidents call for congressional action in about 20 percent of the speeches in which they discuss Court cases. When presidents participate in this form of constitutional discourse, they overwhelmingly ask Congress to alter Court decisions with which they disagree, either by legislation or constitutional amendment. These calls for action tend to involve many of the most controversial constitutional issues of the era in which presidents speak, including abortion, campaign finance regulation, prayer in public schools, and flag burning. Thus, it is evident that presidents see themselves as playing a key role in the development of our understanding of these highly significant constitutional issues.

This chapter provides further evidence that presidents are comfortable engaging in the coordinate construction of the Constitution with the Court and Congress (e.g., Gant 1997; Paulsen 1994; Whittington 1999, 2001). This chapter's primary contribution to this debate demonstrates a three-way interaction in constitutional discourse: the Court speaks, and the president calls on Congress to act to alter or support the Court's decisions. Most of the time, Congress responds, and about 25 percent of these responses lead to a final legislative outcome that supports the president's initial call.[14] As our empirical results demonstrate, this type of dialogue often puts the president in conflict with the Court, with the hope that Congress will take the executive's side in the dispute. The chapter therefore augments Sager's (2004) idea of constitutional interpretation as being a partnership between the legislative and judicial branches, by adding the executive branch as a key agenda-setter in Congress.

Further, this chapter shows that referencing Court cases in conjunction with presidents' policy agendas may help to legitimize presidential calls for legislation by tying their policy agendas to the Court's cases. Although this is not the same thing as presidents actively supporting judicial review (Whittington 2005), or inviting the judiciary to resolve concerns that remain unaddressed by elected officials (Graber 1993), it illustrates another way that presidents can benefit from judicial review. Simply put, the Court's decisions can provide presidents with additional justification for calling for legislative action. Taken as a whole, it is evident from this chapter that constitutional interpretation is a three-way partnership between the executive, legislative, and judicial branches, with the chief executive not infrequently reacting to the judicial branch by attempting to mobilize the legislative branch in public rhetoric.

6

Presidential Leadership of News Coverage

One common perspective of presidential statements on Supreme Court cases is that presidents are motivated to discuss pending disputes to influence the outcomes of the Court's decisions (e.g., Fabian 2015; Ferris 2015; Wallsten and Barnes 2012). This view follows from classic models of presidential leadership, which posit that presidents make speeches to influence the decisions of others, such as the public or Congress (e.g., Kernell 1997). As we have demonstrated in Chapters 1 and 2, presidents do not tend to follow this rhetorical strategy very frequently. Instead, they speak much more often about cases the Court has already decided. As we have argued in Chapter 3, one reason why presidents do this is to demonstrate democratic responsiveness by addressing issues of public concern.

What Chapter 3 left unresolved was whether presidents are successful at using their public comments on Supreme Court cases to exhibit democratic responsiveness. One of the primary means by which presidents can show they are responsive to issues that are important to the American people is by generating news coverage of their public commentary (Eshbaugh-Soha and Peake 2011). Moreover, there is reason to believe that presidents can be successful influencing news coverage of the public comments they make on Supreme Court cases. After all, presidents engage actively in managing the news and, especially when it comes to influencing the news agenda, have had some success in this role (Cohen 2010). Presidents speak about issues that are potentially important to the public and news media. They issue public remarks about myriad topics – including the Supreme Court – strategically so as not to oversaturate their presence in the news. Further, the profit incentive of the news business and norms of professional journalism afford presidents numerous opportunities to lead news coverage of their remarks on Supreme Court cases.

Determining whether, how often, and under what conditions presidents lead news coverage of Supreme Court cases by speaking about those cases is the primary purpose of this chapter. To do this, we explore the ability of presidents to shape both news coverage of their speeches on the Court's cases and the tone of that coverage. We find that presidential statements on Supreme Court cases do increase news coverage, especially when presidents devote a substantial amount of attention to the case, criticize the Court's decisions, use press conferences and national addresses to talk about decided cases, and focus on recently decided cases. However, there is minimal evidence that presidents are capable of shaping the tone of media coverage of speeches involving Supreme Court cases.

This chapter adds to our understanding of the president's ability to shape public debate and understandings of legal and constitutional issues by generating media coverage of their remarks on the Court's decisions. That is significant because the news media represent one of the primary intermediaries by which presidents' messages are filtered to the public (e.g., Eshbaugh-Soha and Peake 2011), a particularly important role given the limited attention the public pays to the Supreme Court (Dost 2015; Hoekstra 2003). By influencing media coverage of Court cases, presidents can put important constitutional issues on the public's agenda, thus providing presidents and the public with a means to contribute to the shared process of constitutional meaning (e.g., Chemerinsky 1997; Kramer 2004; Tushnet 1999). Further, it enables presidents to demonstrate that they are responsive to constitutional issues that are important to the public, thus potentially helping them secure their reelection, policy, and legacy goals. More broadly, this chapter provides additional evidence that presidents can lead the news media in their public remarks.

PRESIDENTIAL LEADERSHIP OF THE NEWS MEDIA

As the center of American government, presidents are seen as having ample power to lead the news media and the national policy agenda (Baumgartner and Jones 1993; Kingdon 1995). Despite the many resources presidents have to influence news coverage (Kumar 2007), however, media are not always responsive to the president's message. Typically, presidents respond to the news in their speeches when they react to the decisions of others, events covered by the media, or salient issues in the news (Edwards and Wood 1999). For example, as coverage of a poor economy floods the news agenda, presidents are obliged to respond to this news coverage and remind the American people that they have policies designed to improve economic and job growth (Eshbaugh-Soha and Peake 2005). Presidents are most limited in their ability to lead news coverage when it is a foreign policy issue long on the systemic agenda (Wood and Peake 1998). Their chances for leadership of the news are greater when they prioritize an issue that is absent from the current news agenda. This happened, for example, when President Clinton prioritized health care reform at a time when it was on neither the congressional nor the media agendas (Edwards and Wood 1999). In other words, issues that are not previously salient afford presidents greater opportunity to affect news coverage (Peake 2001).

Other research tackles presidential leadership of the news from a news management perspective. This work underscores presidential strategies for leading the news, suggesting two primary means by which presidents can influence the media. First, a strategy of focused attention helps the president lead the news media. Specifically, national addresses provide presidents with the opportunity to captivate news coverage in the short-term (Bradshaw, Coe, and Neumann 2014; Peake and Eshbaugh-Soha 2008; Wanta et al. 1989). Second, presidents can endeavor to saturate the news agenda through a series of speeches in an effort to lead the news, referred to as a strategy of continuous attention (Eshbaugh-Soha and Peake 2011). Cohen (2010) shows that the volume of presidential speeches on a topic increases the number of newspaper stories on the president. In addition, presidents may be capable of shaping the tone of media coverage. For example, negative coverage of the president is associated with a larger number of presidential speeches overall, although the probability of a positive tone increases as soon as presidents deliver seven speeches in a day (Cohen 2010, 165).

A subset of the strategy of continuous attention is "going local." Here, presidents travel outside Washington, DC, with the express purpose of building public support for their policies and their presidencies by generating positive local news coverage. The White House likes to choreograph these media events to create at least the appearance of support for presidents and their policies. The White House guides news coverage by providing local reporters, who also tend to be less experienced and less cynical than members of the Washington press corps, with information that supports its perspective. These visits usually generate positive and voluminous coverage, especially in areas of the country that support the president (Barrett and Peake 2007). This contrasts with national news coverage of the same local events, which is more negative (Eshbaugh-Soha and Peake 2006).

The literature presents a smattering of other evidence suggestive of presidential leadership of the news. Although Cohen (2010) shows that press conferences do not increase coverage in local and regional newspapers, Eshbaugh-Soha (2013) reveals that the content of a president's press conference makes up a sizeable portion of an evening news broadcast. Radio addresses also increase newspaper coverage of the president (Cohen 2010), a relationship that has weakened significantly over time (Horvit, Schiffer, and Wright 2008). Further, Boydstun (2013) finds that the number of executive orders issued by presidents influences coverage in the *New York Times*.

Barrett (2007) authored an especially pertinent article on presidential leadership of the news media. Exploring the relationship between presidential commentary on important issues and the extent to which those remarks made the news, Barrett reports a number of findings relevant to our research. First, more presidential attention to an issue influences the volume of coverage in both the *New York Times* and *Washington Post*. This indicates that the more attention the president devotes to an issue, the more important it is and, thus, the more the media cover it. Second, presidents who issues remarks outside Washington, DC, akin to going local, tend to receive more coverage of those remarks. Third, even with these benefits to presidential leadership of the news, the media do not cover most presidential appeals. This is striking given the importance of going public to generate public concern for an issue, which translates into greater legislative success (Canes-Wrone 2001).

We know much about whether presidents affect news coverage on a variety of policy issues and through different speeches and strategies. However, we know very little about how presidents may be able to influence news coverage when it pertains to specific actions of other federal institutions. This is especially the case concerning how the news media fit into the relationship between the president and the Supreme Court. Although presidential news coverage tends to be more negative than positive (Farnsworth and Lichter 2006; Groeling and Kernell 1998), the little research that examines whether presidential tone affects news tone (Cohen 2010) insinuates some opportunity for presidential leadership of the tone of news coverage of Supreme Court cases, as well. After all, if presidents are strategic in their remarks – and say things that are relevant enough to quote – presidents should have some influence over news tone, just as it is all but assured that presidential comments on important issues will generate a fair amount of news coverage (Barrett 2007). In the next section, we present a theory of presidential news management and apply it to news coverage of presidential rhetoric concerning Supreme Court decisions.

THE PRESIDENT, THE COURT, AND THE MEDIA

Two threads of reasoning motivate our expectations for how presidential comments on Court cases will lead to media coverage of those statements.

First, presidents engage in a concerted effort to manage news coverage. In doing so, they take advantage of the media's incentives to cover presidents, which center on profit (because presidents generate viewer interest) and norms of professional journalism (because media cover that which is newsworthy). The primary question that we answer in this chapter is whether a subset of the president's remarks – those that target Supreme Court cases – are capable of generating news coverage. If they are, then this is evidence in favor of our contention that presidents speak publicly about predominately decided cases to demonstrate responsiveness to the American people on issues of public concern. Further, it would show that presidents can successfully engender a national discussion of constitutional issues, thus playing an important role in the coordinate construction of the Constitution. Such is the case because the public cues off the media in terms of which issues garner their attention (Entman 2012). This may benefit presidents in generating public support for their preferred positions on matters of constitutional concern, thus helping them achieve electoral and policy benefits, both of which may enhance their historical reputations.

Second, the factors that shape the news media's tendency to cover the Court are also likely to play a role in whether they cover the president's remarks on Court cases. That is, newspapers are more likely to cover Supreme Court cases that have certain characteristics, such as high levels of interest group engagement and those that declare laws unconstitutional (Collins and Cooper 2012; Maltzman and Wahlbeck 2003). As a result, when presidents comment on cases with such characteristics, media coverage of the president's statements regarding the cases should increase. Conversely, it may follow that media do not respond to the president's remarks at all, but rather respond to case characteristics as they do when they cover the Court more generally.

Why Presidents May Lead the News

The foundation of presidential leadership of the news media centers on the White House's efforts to manage news coverage. Presidential news management is defined by Cohen (2010, 73) as "all activities that presidents engage in to affect the content ... of news coverage." Without question, presidents devote a substantial amount of time and effort to influence the news media, with the primary goal to set the news agenda (Kumar 2007). In addition, they have some impact on leading the news agenda, as noted above. The idea that presidents will be able to manage the news effectively relies on the notion that both the profit incentive of news organizations and professional norms of journalism encourage news media to respond to presidential speeches or other actions taken by the president.

First, much of what is reported in the news is in response to that which generates audience interest and profit (Graber and Dunaway 2015; Leighley 2003). Media have a profit incentive to cover an individual or event that is likely to stimulate audience interest. Since most Americans are interested in presidential news (if they are interested in political news at all) (Hamilton 2004), the media tend to cover the president. The White House knows this, and can appeal to the profit-incentive of journalists by making it easier for journalists to cover the president. It does this by dedicating considerable resources to influencing the news (Cohen 2010) and setting the news agenda (Edwards 2003, 245; Kumar 2007). For example, the White House can hold press conferences (Cohen 2010; Eshbaugh-Soha 2013) and have the president deliver national addresses (Bradshaw, Coe, and Neumann 2014; Peake and Eshbaugh-Soha 2008), each of which are relatively easy to cover. This reduces the costs to producing presidential news, and increases the likelihood that the media will cover the content of the president's speeches.

Second, norms of professional journalism assure coverage of stories that are newsworthy. As defined by Graber and Dunaway (2015, 113–114), newsworthy stories have a substantial impact on viewers or society, involve conflict or scandal, are familiar to viewers, and are proximate, timely, and novel (see also Groeling 2010). Since presidential news will often meet or exceed the standard of what is newsworthy, media are likely to cover the president. News media are also likely to cover the president because they index coverage to the debate and policy process in Washington, DC (Bennett 2016), which usually includes the president. According to Entman's (2012) cascade activation theory, moreover, news flows in a top-down direction, moving from the president to the media, and cascading further down to the public, which promotes presidential influence of the news. Taken together, both the profit incentive and norm of journalistic professionalism encourage news media to respond to the president's speeches.

Leading News Coverage of Presidential Remarks on Supreme Court Decisions

This theory of news management helps to explain news coverage of presidential remarks about Supreme Court cases, both pending and decided. A presidential remark concerning a Supreme Court case adds a newsworthy quality to that case, which may be newsworthy on its own (as we discuss below). Thus, presidential statements on the Court's cases give reporters an extra element of importance to their coverage of the case and the breadth of their stories. When the president comments on a case, a news story becomes more than just a summary of the legal, political, and social implications of a case or the justices' commentary during oral arguments and in opinions. It becomes presidential news, which is more likely to generate public interest, heightening the journalistic incentive to cover the Court case. This is particularly true when presidents allocate substantial attention to discussing a case in their public remarks. In so doing, presidents send a strong and clear signal to the media that an issue is important to their policy priorities and that they have devoted a considerable amount of time and resources to thinking about the case (Cohen 2010). In response to lengthy statements on the Court's cases, we believe the media will devote more attention to covering those speeches. Therefore, we expect that, as the number of paragraphs presidents allocate to discussing a case increases, so too will media coverage of the president's speech.

The tone of presidential remarks regarding decided Supreme Court cases may also influence media coverage. When the president speaks about a case negatively, this creates a conflict between the executive and judicial branches that heightens the importance of the case in the eyes of the media (Groeling 2010). Further, if the president criticizes the Court's decision and calls for Congress to take action to remedy the effects of the Court's decision, such as passing legislation or introducing a constitutional amendment, this expands the scope of the conflict beyond the president and the Court (Schattschneider 1960). Moreover, by speaking negatively about a Court decision, presidents may be criticized for violating the norm of judicial independence (Eshbaugh-Soha and Collins 2015).[1] We believe that these consequences of negative statements about judicial decisions are likely to garner media attention since they all relate to conflict, a central aspect of a newsworthy story (Graber and Dunaway 2015; Groeling 2010). Accordingly, we anticipate that negative discussions of Supreme Court decisions by presidents will increase media coverage of the president's speech.

Conversely, less media coverage is likely when the president speaks positively about a Court decision. In the main, such speeches do not create conflict between the executive and judicial branches. Rather, they signal harmony between the branches, which is less newsworthy given the media's tendency to focus on stories that feature conflict (Groeling 2010). Moreover, when presidents praise the Court's decisions, this typically indicates the president's willingness to implement the decisions which is, in effect, an assurance that that the status quo created by the Court will continue. Because the media tend to focus on legal disruptions to the status quo (Sill,

Metzgar, and Rouse 2013), we believe they will devote less attention to speeches commending the Court's decisions. Therefore, we expect that positive discussions of Supreme Court decisions by presidents will decrease media coverage of the president's speech.

The types of speeches presidents use to discuss cases should also influence whether presidents lead the news. After all, media are more likely to cover some types of speeches than others, whether because they are easier to cover (thereby reducing the costs of news production), or because they are more important or newsworthy. Without question, national addresses, including the State of the Union Address, generate ample coverage. Although the news media may not sustain their attention to the policies presidents discuss in their national addresses (Peake and Eshbaugh-Soha 2008), the norm of professional journalism and the profit incentive both make it likely that the news media will cover the presidents' national addresses. Therefore, we expect that discussions of Supreme Court cases in national addresses will increase news coverage of those remarks.

For similar reasons, we believe that remarks given at press conferences will generate coverage of the president's remarks, since press conferences combine features of news management that assist presidential leadership. First, press conferences are newsworthy events that are relatively easy for journalists to cover. Second, journalists are active participants in the event, making it more likely that they will want to report on it in later news coverage (Cohen 2010). Other research shows that media cover a relatively high percentage of the president's own words delivered in a press conference given the ease with which media may report on this clearly newsworthy event (Eshbaugh-Soha 2013). Thus, we hypothesize that discussions of Supreme Court cases in press conferences will increase news coverage of those remarks.

Whereas national addresses and press conferences may increase the likelihood of news coverage of presidential remarks on Court cases, other types of speeches are unlikely to do so. This is not because these other speeches are less newsworthy, necessarily. After all, the strategy of going local tends to generate ample news coverage of the president's remarks. Rather, the president is unlikely to use going local to target Supreme Court cases. Such is the case because going local is typically reserved for presidential attempts to build local support for presidential policy priorities, which is unlikely to necessitate repeated references to a Supreme Court case. Moreover, fewer and fewer newspapers have court reporters, making coverage of presidential remarks on Supreme Court cases in local papers even less likely (e.g., Magnuson and Walcker 2017). The converse should be correct, however, in that presidential remarks delivered in Washington, DC, are most likely to generate news coverage, particularly as the Supreme Court is a national institution with its home in the nation's capital. Because presidential efforts to lead the news are strategic (Kumar 2007), we anticipate that presidents will utilize speeches given in Washington, DC, to shape national media coverage of their perspectives on Court cases. Therefore, we expect that presidential speeches given in Washington, DC, will generate more news coverage of those remarks.

Presidents can choose to comment on cases under consideration by the Court or those already decided by the Court. Speaking about a case before or after the Court renders its decision presents different challenges to presidents (Eshbaugh-Soha and Collins 2015). Because of these differences, we expect to observe less news coverage of presidential remarks on pending decisions for two reasons. First, since the media cover the Court predominately when it issues rulings (Epstein and Segal 2000), presidents are unlikely to prioritize cases currently pending on the docket in an effort to lead the media. They are more likely to wait until after a case is decided if their goal is to generate news coverage. Second, the media are more likely to focus their limited resources on already decided cases than pending cases, since rendered decisions allow them the opportunity to discuss the vote, opinions, and likely impact of the decision, and to highlight areas of conflict related to the outcome (Slotnick and Segal 1998). On the contrary, reporting on pending cases typically involves sometimes technical speculation as to how the case might be decided, which may be of less interest to an audience made up primarily of legal novices. Thus, we anticipate that there will be more media coverage of presidential speeches on already decided cases.

Why Media Cover Court Cases

The media have a clear incentive to respond to the president's public comments by reporting on them, including presidential statements about Supreme Court cases. Yet, the media's motivation for covering presidential speeches on Court cases is not driven solely by the president. Rather, news coverage of Court cases should also be driven by a series of other factors that make the case worth covering (Collins and Cooper 2012; Epstein and Segal 2000; Maltzman and Wahlbeck 2003; Slotnick and Segal 1998).[2] Among these are several factors that heighten newsworthy elements of a story. Recall that stories are most likely to be considered newsworthy when they involve conflict, are important, and timely. Thus, cases that promote a conflictual frame and are more pertinent to newspaper readers are more likely to be covered (Collins and Cooper 2015).

This is reinforced by the general claim that the relationship between the press and the Court is "marked by tension" (Davis 2014, 6).

Several factors that represent conflict should increase news coverage of a presidential speech on a Supreme Court case. First, if the Court decided a case with a minimum winning coalition, we believe the media will be more likely to cover the case. This is consistent with the idea that media prefer conflict to compromise in its news coverage. In cases with minimum winning coalitions, the media can focus on conflictual aspects of the case, including ideological disagreements among the justices. Thus, it is no surprise that research that seeks to explain news coverage of Court cases shows that cases decided by minimum winning coalitions are more likely to garner news coverage (Maltzman and Wahlbeck 2003). As a result, we expect the media to cover more speeches involving cases decided by minimum winning coalitions.

Second, we believe there will be increased media coverage if the Court rules against the president's position in the case. To be sure, the Solicitor General – the executive branch's chief attorney in the Court – is among the most prolific and successful litigators in the Supreme Court (Black and Owens 2012; Nicholson and Collins 2008; Pacelle 2003). Thus, when the Solicitor General loses, this is newsworthy in its own right. More than this, Chapter 4 reveals that presidents are especially likely to criticize cases in which their positions are unsuccessful, which may be portrayed in the media as a conflict between the Court and the president. Consequently, we expect the media to cover more speeches discussing cases in which the president's position was unsuccessful before the Court.[3]

In addition to this, several factors related to the importance of a case are likely to raise its profile in the media (Sill, Metzgar, and Rouse 2013). First, if the Court's decision involves declaring a law unconstitutional, that speaks to the case's importance since it is a rare event (Maltzman and Wahlbeck 2003). In such cases, the Court is interjecting itself directly into the policy making process and altering the status quo (Sill, Metzgar, and Rouse 2013). Accordingly, we expect to observe more media coverage of speeches involving cases that declare laws unconstitutional. Second, we believe that news coverage will increase for cases that involve certain issue areas. Cases involving the First Amendment and civil rights tend to be most interesting to readers and generate higher levels of newspaper coverage since they touch on issues of importance to the American public (Collins and Cooper 2015; Maltzman and Wahlbeck 2003). Moreover, the Court tends to oppose the executive branch more on civil liberties issues (King and Meernik 1999), providing opportunities for presidents to criticize the Court, which may produce more news coverage. We expect to observe more media coverage of speeches involving First Amendment and civil rights cases. Third, we contend that liberal decisions will increase news coverage (Johnson and Socker 2012). Because liberal decisions tend to expand individual rights and liberties, thus disrupting the status quo, we believe that the media will view these decisions as especially significant because of the large number of people they affect and due to their overall importance (Sill, Metzgar, and Rouse 2013). So, we expect to see more media coverage of speeches about liberal decisions. Fourth, we believe that cases with a relatively large number of amicus curiae briefs will raise a case's importance in the eyes of the media. High levels of amicus participation signal that a case will have broad importance beyond the parties to litigation, as interest groups, governments, and other entities choose to expend their finite resources in an attempt to influence the Court's decision (Collins 2008a). For that reason, we anticipate more media coverage of speeches with relatively high levels of amicus briefs.

We also think that the media will cover speeches that involve timely cases. Although presidents have from time to time discussed cases that are centuries old, they are more likely to discuss relatively contemporary cases in their speeches. For example, the median age (in years) of the cases presidents discuss in their speeches is 4 years. Yet, this age ranges from 2 years (for a pending to case) to 197 years (for a statement on *Marbury* v. *Madison* by President Clinton). Because the news media focus their coverage on timely events (Groeling 2010), we think media will devote more attention to covering speeches that are currently part of national concern. Thus, we expect that media coverage of speeches will decrease as the number of years between the speech and the age of the case discussed increases.

The Tone of Coverage

Many of the same expectations we developed for the volume of news coverage also drive the tone of news coverage, and the president's ability to influence it, albeit for slightly different reasons. Recall that the news media's desire for profit and obligation to follow norms of professional journalism should shape the amount of coverage, and each of the factors discussed above should promote news coverage of the president. However, these motivations for the volume of presidential news coverage may work differently in explaining tone given that both the profit incentive and professional norms encourage negative news coverage of the president, overall (Cohen 2008). Profit encourages negative or conflictual stories, which tend to drive audience interest. Additionally, the norms of professional journalism promote analytical news coverage and, to fulfill their goal of balancing news coverage, this norm should encourage negative coverage even when the president is more positive in his rhetoric. According to this view of presidential leadership of tone, a positive presidential comment on a Supreme Court case may be cancelled out by more analytical and negative news coverage of the story. Logically then, it should be unlikely that presidential tone influences news tone (see Eshbaugh-Soha 2018), even when presidents successfully manage the amount of news coverage (Kumar 2007).

Even so, we want to be clear that there are reasons to expect presidential leadership of the tone of news coverage; expectations that some limited research on the subject supports. Mainly, the president is well positioned to be able to increase favorable coverage. Just as the media's profit incentive encourages negative coverage, it also encourages news media to cover the president's perspective. After all, it is not costly to report on the president's words when the president speaks about an issue. Covering the president's perspective is also consistent with norms of professional journalism. Thus, when the president can increase the accessibility of his own words and increase the importance of a comment, news coverage is more likely to reflect the president's tone (Cohen 2010).

Although scholarship is virtually silent on what drives the tone of news coverage of the Supreme Court (Haider-Markel, Allen, and Johansen 2006), it should follow that, if presidents are capable of shaping the tone of coverage, the subsequent factors will affect presidential leadership of news tone. First, when presidents devote substantial attention to discussing a case, this signals to the media that the president considers the case salient and may serve to convince the media as to the validity of the president's position (e.g., Chaiken 1980). So, we expect to observe more positive tone when the president devotes a relatively large amount of attention to a case. Second, when the president makes a negative remark about a case, the president is creating conflict by pitting himself against the Court. Due to this, the media are likely to highlight this conflict by covering the president's speech in a more critical light, resulting in coverage that is more negative. Third, consistent with Cohen's (2010) findings, a positive remark by the president about a Supreme Court case should generate more positive news coverage of the president's position, since positive comments indicate the president and the Court agree about the outcome of a case. Fourth, when presidents discuss the Court's cases in a national address, in a press conference, and in Washington, DC, we expect to observe more positive tone as the media is more likely to quote the president in such instances. Fifth, we contend that presidential remarks on pending cases will generate negative tone since presidents risk being criticized for violating the norm of judicial independence in making such statements.

In addition, we believe that aspects of the Court's cases that represent conflict are more likely to generate negative coverage of the president's speeches. Cases decided by minimum winning coalitions reveal a higher level of disagreement among the members of the Court and should afford the news media an opportunity to frame their coverage as driven by conflict. Thus, cases decided by minimum winning coalitions should increase the negative tone of coverage. Furthermore, when the Court hands the president a loss by ruling against the Solicitor General, media may frame this as representing ideological disagreement between the two institutions. This may increase the incentive for presidents to criticize the Court and lead to more negative news coverage. Finally, when the Court rules a law unconstitutional, this puts the Court in conflict with the elected branches of government who passed the law. This, in turn, may generate more negative coverage of the presidents' speeches by portraying disagreement between the Court and elected politicians.

Summary

Newspaper coverage of the president's remarks on Supreme Court cases should be guided by the president's efforts to manage the news and the news media's own determinations of which Court cases are newsworthy. Presidents can use specific types of speeches to reduce the costs of news coverage and increase media response to presidential remarks. Moreover, the tone of their remarks toward the Court's decisions should also influence the amount of news coverage. Still, presidents are not the only drivers of news coverage of cases, and so several case-specific factors, such as whether the case was decided by a minimum winning coalition or whether the Court ruled against the president's position in the case, should also affect news coverage. Conflict is especially likely to drive the tone of news coverage, and we are particularly interested in determining whether the tone of presidential speeches on Court decisions influences the tone of newspaper coverage of those speeches. Although this is unlikely, past research on presidential leadership of news tone broadly provides some evidence that presidents may be able to lead the tone of news coverage (e.g., Cohen 2010).

DATA AND METHODOLOGY

To examine the ability of presidents to lead news coverage of their remarks on Supreme Court cases, we use the same data employed throughout this book, with the addition of information on the Court's cases and media coverage of the president's speeches. To obtain information on the Court's decisions, we merged our data with the Spaeth et al. (2018) database, which provides many of the Court-specific variables that we think may affect news coverage of presidential statements on Supreme Court cases. As in earlier chapters, the data cover the Eisenhower through Obama presidencies, during which presidents remarked on 937 cases and among these, 883 cases were decided before the president's remarks.[4] The unit of analysis in this chapter is the speech-case, such that we count a speech multiple times if the president referenced multiple cases in a single speech.

Our first dependent variable relates to the amount of news coverage of the president's remarks. It captures the number of *New York Times* stories about the presidential speech that mentioned a Supreme Court case from the day the speech was given to the day after the speech was given (e.g., Epstein and Segal 2000). We obtained this information from LexisNexis and the *New York Times* archives by searching for "Supreme Court" and "president." We then read each article returned to determine whether the article discussed the president's speech about the Supreme Court case. If so, we included the story in our analyses and incorporated its text into our database to capture its tone (see "Tone of Coverage"). Out of the 937 cases on which presidents commented over this period, the *New York Times* produced at least one story for 224 of these instances (24 percent). In total, the *New York Times* covered the presidents' comments in 378 separate stories. President Eisenhower's August 27, 1958, speech on *Cooper* v. *Aaron* (1958), which required Arkansas officials to enforce the Court's racial desegregation decisions, garnered the most attention, with 10 stories.

We choose to focus on *New York Times* coverage since it is the nation's paper of record (Sill, Metzgar, and Rouse 2013), and it has a general readership across the nation and is less likely than other papers to have a regional bias (Epstein and Segal 2000, 72).[5] Moreover, the *Times* covers the Supreme Court more than other newspapers, with stories dedicated to about 63 percent of cases (Collins and Cooper 2012, 405). Further, television coverage of the Supreme Court is particularly limited, superficial, and often misreported (Slotnick and Segal 1998), making newspaper coverage a better choice. Finally, the length of our analysis requires a news source that has existed throughout our time frame of which the *New York Times* is most prominent. We recognize that limiting our analyses to the *Times* has some drawbacks. For example, it does not reflect all of the types of media that cover presidential speeches on Court decisions (Collins and Cooper 2012), and it does not account for the diversity of news sources available in the post-broadcast era.

Nonetheless, we are confident we can gain substantial insights into presidential leadership of the news through an analysis of *Times* coverage, just as others have (Epstein and Segal 2000; Maltzman and Wahlbeck 2003; Sill, Metzgar, and Rouse 2013).[6]

We code our independent variables in the following ways. *Presidential Attention* is the number of paragraphs presidents devoted to a Supreme Court case in their public remarks (American Presidency Project 2017). We expect this variable will be positively signed, indicating that, when the president devotes more attention to the case in his speeches, this results in increased media coverage of the speech.

Negative and *Positive Tone* for the president's remarks are the same measures as the dependent variables in Chapter 4. That is, *Negative Tone* is coded 1 if the president made a negative statement about a decided case, and 0 otherwise. Negative comments are those in which the president criticizes a case or expresses an opinion contrary to the Court's ruling. *Positive Tone* is coded 1 if the president made a positive statement about a decided case, and 0 otherwise. Positive comments are those in which the president expresses praise, confidence in, or agreement with the Court's decisions. The excluded category for the *Negative Tone* and *Positive Tone* variables are neutral comments made by presidents – those in which presidents do not take a clear negative or positive position on the outcome of the case or the means by which it is carried out – and statements made on pending cases. We expect the *Negative Tone* variable will be positively signed, and the *Positive Tone* variable will be negatively signed.

We include several variables related to aspects of presidential speeches that we expect will affect the volume of news coverage. *National Address* is coded 1 if the president's statement was made to the nation, and 0 otherwise (American Presidency Project 2017). *Press Conference* is coded 1 if the president's address was made during a press conference, and 0 otherwise (American Presidency Project 2017). *Washington, DC*, is coded 1 if the statement was made in the nation's capital, and 0 otherwise (American Presidency Project 2017). We expect these variables will be positively signed. In addition, we include a *Pending Case* variable, coded 1 if the statement was about a pending decision, and 0 if it was made about a decided case. We expect this variable will be negatively signed.

We further expect several case-specific variables to influence the tendency for the *New York Times* to cover presidential speeches on the Court's cases. *Minimum Winning Coalition* is coded 1 if the case was decided by a 5–4 or 4–3 vote, and 0 otherwise (Spaeth et al. 2018). *US Lost* is coded 1 if the Court ruled against the position taken by the United States in the case, either as a litigant or amicus curiae, and 0 otherwise (Collins 2008a; Spaeth et al. 2018). *Unconstitutional* is coded 1 if the Court declared a law unconstitutional, and 0 otherwise (Spaeth et al. 2018). *First Amendment* is coded 1 if the case involved the First Amendment, and 0 otherwise (Spaeth et al. 2018). *Civil Rights* is coded 1 if the case involved civil rights, criminal procedure, or due process (Maltzman and Wahlbeck 2003), and 0 otherwise (Spaeth et al. 2018). *Liberal Decision* is coded 1 if the Court decided the case in the liberal direction, and 0 otherwise (Spaeth et al. 2018). *Amicus Curiae Briefs* represents a count of the number of amicus briefs filed in the case. Data from 1953 to 2001 were obtained from Collins (2008a), and we collected the remaining data using Westlaw, the bound volumes of *US Reports* available on the Court's website, and the Court's official counsel listings. We expect each of these variables will be positively signed. *Years from Case* represents the number of years from the date of the president's speech to the date the case was decided (American Presidency Project 2017; Spaeth et al. 2018). We expect this variable will be negatively signed.

Beyond these key measures, we also control for several factors that could affect news coverage of presidential remarks on Supreme Court cases. First, *Presidential Approval* ratings may influence the amount of presidential news coverage (Cohen 2010). Thus, we model the percentage of the public that approves of the president's job performance on the survey date most proximate to and before the date of the president's remarks. These are Gallup Poll data taken from Ragsdale (2014), updated through January 2017 by using the daily tracking poll results available on the American Presidency Project (2018) webpage. We expect this variable will be positively signed, indicating that, when the president is popular with the American public, the media is more likely to devote attention to the president's speeches. Second, we think that the news media may more frequently cover presidential remarks on Court cases when the president is running for reelection, since the presidents' statements about cases might be made in an effort to enhance their reelection prospects (Eshbaugh-Soha and Collins 2015). We code *Reelection Year* as January through October in a presidential election year when a sitting president is running for office. Finally, we include a *Post-Carter Presidencies* variable, coded 1 from January of 1981 through January 2017, and 0 before these dates. As shown in Chapter 3, presidential speechmaking has increased since the Reagan administration. Given this, we expect that the media will be less likely to cover any given presidential speech in the post-Carter era. Thus, we expect this variable will be negatively signed.

Our second dependent variable captures the tone of news coverage. To determine the tone of news coverage, we relied on Lexicoder, a sentiment analysis software package used to evaluate news coverage of a variety of important topics (Young and Soroka 2012). Lexicoder calculates tone by counting the number of positive and negative words in a text based on the comprehensive list of positive and negative words found in the Lexicoder Sentiment Dictionary (LSD). Our dependent variable for tone is the number of positive words minus the number of negative words, divided by the total number of words in the article pertaining to the president's remarks about the case.[7]

We use Lexicoder for a variety of reasons. Lexicoder, and its associated LSD, has been thoroughly vetted in social science research. It has been used to analyze the sentiment or tone of newspaper text, with resulting articles published in many leading journals (Soroka 2012; Soroka, Stecula, and Wlezien 2015; Soroka and Wlezien 2015). Moreover, Provalis (2017), a leading provider of text analysis software, indicates that LSD is the most appropriate dictionary for the textual analysis of political information and news.

The following are examples of text that exhibits positive, neutral, and negative tone in news coverage of the president's remarks on Supreme Court cases. A mostly positive summary of Ronald Reagan's comments concerning the fifteenth anniversary of *Roe* v. *Wade* (1973)[8] indicates, "An estimated 50,000 people demonstrated here today against abortion on the 15th anniversary of the Supreme Court decision legalizing it. The demonstrators, bearing various banners and signs, marched through the city, moving from the Ellipse near the White House, where they cheered President Reagan's declaration of support for them, to the Supreme Court building" (New York Times 1988).

Relatively balanced remarks include both positive and negative words and register as more neutral in Lexicoder. Many of the more neutral presentations of presidential remarks on Supreme Court cases tended to occur earlier in our dataset and often reflected the president's own words, reprinting an entire transcript of a president's press conference, for example, or excerpts from written or spoken remarks. On August 8, 1956, Chalmers M. Roberts asked the president whether he thought that the Republican Party platform should endorse *Brown* v. *Board of Education* (1954). Eisenhower responded in classic fashion:

> I don't know, Mr. Roberts, how the Republican plank on this particular point is going to be stated, and I haven't given any thought of my own as to whether it should just state it in that way. The only thing I can say is, I am sworn to uphold the Constitution of the United States; but what we are talking about, probably, is procedures rather than principles. Everybody knows I am sworn to uphold the Constitution of the United States. That is my job.[9]

Negative coverage tends to be more analytical in reflecting on a Supreme Court ruling or is critical of the president's remarks. Following Richard

TABLE 6.1. *The expected direction of the independent variables predicting the volume and tone of newspaper coverage of presidential remarks on Supreme Court decisions*

Variable	Coverage	Tone
Presidential Attention	+	+
Negative Tone	+	−
Positive Tone	−	+
National Address	+	+
Press Conference	+	+
Washington, DC	+	+
Pending Case	−	−
Minimum Winning Coalition	+	−
US Lost	+	−
Unconstitutional	+	−
First Amendment	+	none
Civil Rights	+	none
Liberal Decision	+	none
Amicus Curiae Briefs	+	none
Years from Case	−	none
Presidential Approval	+	none
Reelection Year	+	none
Post-Carter Presidencies	−	none

Nixon's supportive comments about the death penalty in reference to *Furman* v. *Georgia* (1972),[10] the *New York Times* placed the president's comments into context by writing, "Last June, the Supreme Court divided 5 to 4 in declaring that the death penalty violated the constitutional prohibition against cruel and unusual punishment when it was imposed infrequently and randomly, killing a criminal in one jurisdiction but sparing a similar one elsewhere" (Weaver 1973).

Our model that seeks to explain the tone of news coverage is similar to our model that explains the amount of news coverage. It includes all the variables discussed above with respect to the volume of news coverage of presidential speeches on Supreme Court decisions relating to the president's speeches, with a few exceptions. Mainly, we exclude presidential approval and reelection year variables and some of the control variables that do not relate to conflict on the Court from the tone model, because we do not have a theoretical expectation for how they might influence the tone of newspaper coverage.[11]

The expected signs of the independent variables for each model appear in Table 6.1. In the model that captures the overall volume of coverage, we use a negative binomial regression model with robust standard errors, since this is a count variable and there is evidence of overdispersion in the data. In the model that captures the tone of coverage, we use an ordinary least squares regression model with robust standard errors, since the dependent variable is a continuous variable that takes on negative and positive values. Like Chapters 3 and 4, we report our results in an easy-to-understand graphical format.

EMPIRICAL RESULTS

Amount of Coverage

We begin by describing the tendency for the *New York Times* to cover presidential remarks on Supreme Court cases. Figure 6.1 reports the number of stories on speeches published by the *Times* by presidential term. The black portions of the bars represent stories on cases that were decided by the Court, and the white portions indicate stories on pending cases. The number of stories per term ranges from a high of 55 during the Nixon administration to a low of less than 10 for Jimmy Carter and George W. Bush's second term. Moreover, this figure reveals that presidents before and including Nixon generally enjoyed much more news coverage of their remarks on Supreme Court cases than more recent presidents. We see an uptick in coverage during Obama's presidency, but otherwise, Presidents Ford through George W. Bush hover in the same range of stories. The clear downward decline over time is very much in line with past research that shows the amount of news coverage of the presidency (Cohen 2008) – and the Supreme Court (Johnson and Socker 2012) – has decreased over time. However, our data reveal an earlier start to this, beginning with the Nixon administration. In contrast, others point to after the Reagan Administration as the main turning point in the decline of presidential news coverage (Cohen 2008) and the mid-1990s as the decline in coverage of the Supreme Court (Johnson and Socker 2012, 441). Finally, Figure 6.1 reveals that newspaper coverage of presidential speeches tends to focus primarily on remarks presidents make related to already decided cases, as opposed to pending cases. This provides initial support for our expectation that presidents will stimulate news coverage when they respond to issues of national concern related to the Court's decisions, rather than trying to lead the national agenda on issues under consideration by the Court.

Although part of the decline in coverage revealed by Figure 6.1 is a function of changes in news coverage of Supreme Court cases and presidential remarks about them, we do not think that this is the only reason. The decline also reflects the changing frequency and intensity of Court decisions, which affects

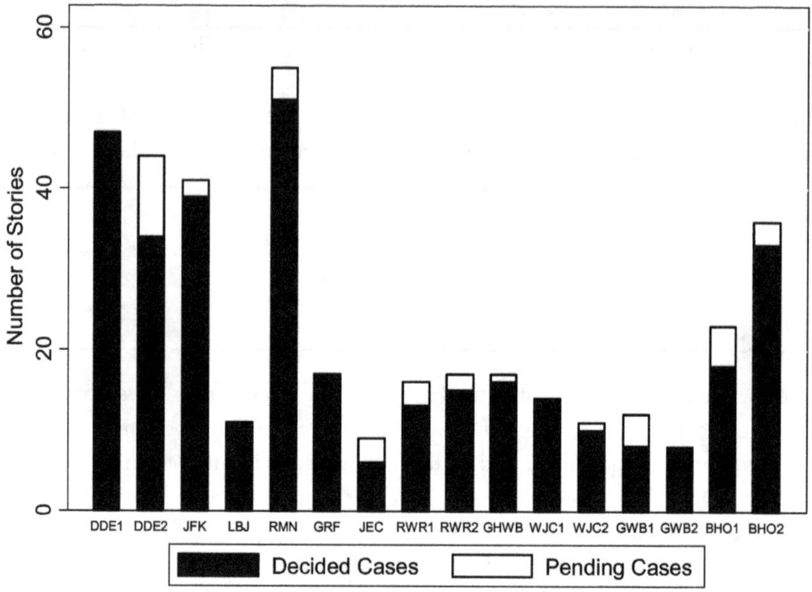

FIGURE 6.1. The number of newspaper stories covering presidential remarks on Supreme Court cases, 1953–2017

opportunities for presidents to respond to issues of national importance. For example, civil rights dominated the national agenda in the 1950s, 1960s, and 1970s, providing these presidents – and Eisenhower and Nixon, in particular – with numerous opportunities to address cases that were particularly salient to the American people. The press asked Eisenhower frequently to comment on important civil rights cases, perhaps most notably *Brown* v. *Board of Education*. Because this decision was highly controversial and difficult to implement (Rosenberg 1991), it is not surprising that the president's comments on this case generated such substantial news coverage. In total, the *Times* covered all but three of Eisenhower's 27 references to *Brown*. This is particularly interesting as Eisenhower did not exactly provide clear leadership on the issue of desegregation, which may have increased the newsworthiness of the president's words. Instead, Eisenhower's comments were often vague and, at times, he attempted to balance the moral justification for *Brown* without overly criticizing those who opposed the ruling. To wit, President Eisenhower reflected that "it is going to take time for them to adjust their thinking and their progress to [accept the decision]," and he "deplore[d] any great extreme action on either side."[12]

President Nixon also commented on issues that were of particular national concern. Like Eisenhower, he spoke often of cases involving desegregation. Whereas *Brown* provided the focus of Eisenhower's comments, Nixon tangled with the more complicated aspects of implementing desegregation, such as those issues covered in *Alexander* v. *Holmes County Board of Education* (1969) and *Swann* v. *Charlotte-Mecklenburg Board of Education* (1971). Nixon also had personal and political interest in several Court cases that implicated the powers of his presidency, including *US* v. *Nixon* (1974). Nixon remarked several times about these cases, often in response to reporters' questions, and his comments made the news given the underlying importance of the Watergate investigation surrounding these cases. In other words, Nixon responded to reporters' questions about these cases to address issues of national concern.

We also see an increase in media coverage during the Obama Administration, even amid declining news coverage of the presidency and the Court overall. President Obama emphasized Court cases frequently in his public rhetoric, fixating much of his attention on *Citizens United* v. *FEC* (2010) and *National Federation of Independent Business* v. *Sebelius* (2012). These national issues surely afforded the president a greater opportunity to generate news coverage than his recent predecessors did, but they did not lead to consistent coverage. The president's State of the Union Address remarks about *Citizens United* generated a firestorm of news coverage, but led to only five *New York Times* stories that referenced the president's remarks directly. Moreover, despite the president's more than two dozen references to Supreme Court support for the Affordable Care Act, the *Times* covered only President Obama's initial remarks that responded more substantively to the Court's decision in July of 2012. The remaining comments noted the case, but were likely drowned out by other newsworthy elements of the president's reelection campaign. Each of these instances shows that presidents have the opportunity to lead news coverage of their remarks so long as they devote sufficient attention to Court cases or otherwise speak about cases of particular salience to contemporaneous political news. This does not mean that the president is always likely to lead news coverage, however.

Figure 6.2 presents counts of news stories regarding decided cases according to the type of remark and the timing of the Court case organized by the president's term in office. The black portions of the bars identify coverage of spoken remarks, and the white portions denote coverage of written statements. The dark gray portions of the bars indicate references to historic cases (defined as those decided before the president's term in office), and the light gray

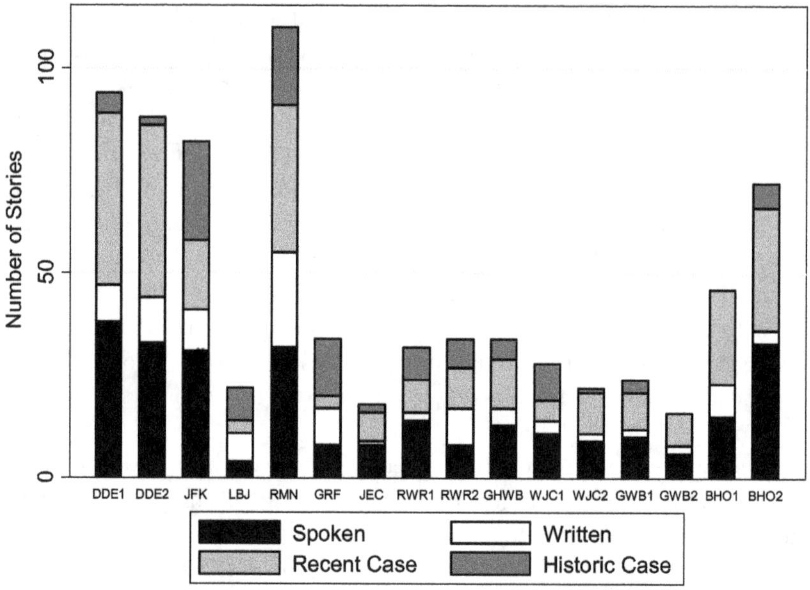

FIGURE 6.2. The number of newspaper stories covering presidential remarks on Supreme Court cases by type and timing, 1953–2017

portions are references to recent cases (defined as cases decided during the president's term in office). As we have previously shown that presidents more frequently speak, rather than write, about Supreme Court cases, it is unsurprising to find that newspaper coverage of the president's spoken remarks is also more common. We expected this given that spoken words are the primary way by which presidents attempt to lead the news media and public. They also more clearly demonstrate democratic responsiveness to issues of public concern than written statements, which tend to speak more to the implementation of public policy. Still, some presidents, such as Nixon, received a greater balance of coverage of written (23 stories) and spoken (32 stories) remarks.

Figure 6.2 also reveals that the media more frequently cover presidential remarks on recent cases, than historic cases. On this comparison, two presidents stand out. First, Kennedy garnered more news coverage of his comments concerning historic cases, driven, as one might expect, by his many references to school desegregation cases as he increased his public attention to civil rights. Second, Obama's comments on recent cases generated much more news coverage than his statements on historic cases. Predictably, his statements on the two cases related to the Patient Protection and Affordable

Care Act drove this coverage. He was especially attentive to *Sebelius* during his 2012 reelection campaign. However, as we just pointed out, he commented much more frequently on these cases than he received news coverage, with news coverage devoted primarily to the president's remarks shortly after the Court's ruling.

Figure 6.3 reports the results of our examination of influences on newspaper coverage of presidential remarks on the Court's decisions. These graphs represent the predicted change in the number of *New York Times* stories regarding presidential speeches on Supreme Court decisions given a one-unit change in the independent variable of interest, holding all other variables at their mean or modal values. The circles represent the point estimate of the marginal effects and the horizontal lines coming off the circles are 90 percent confidence intervals. Variables are statistically significant if the 90 percent confidence intervals do not cross the solid line at zero.[13]

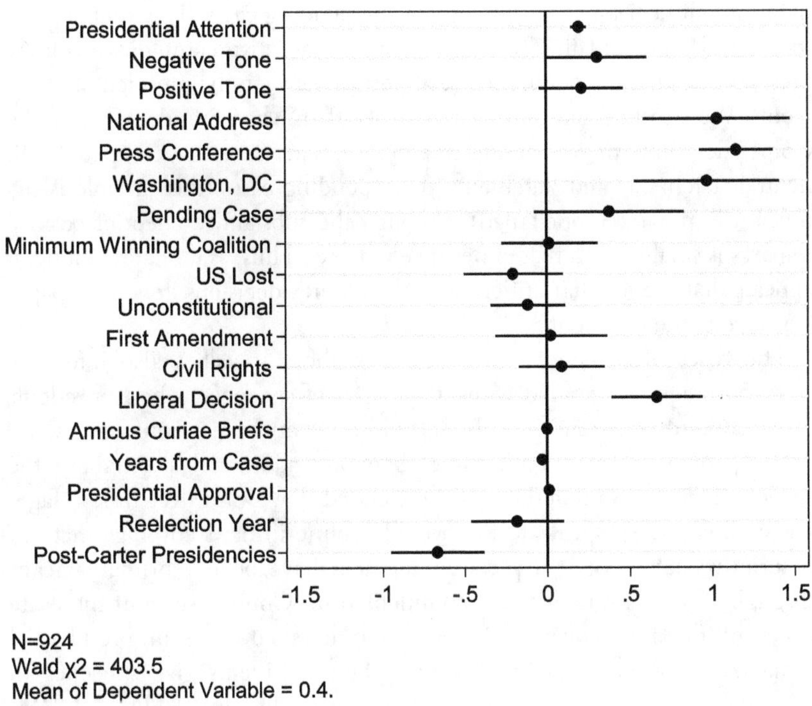

FIGURE 6.3. Influences on the number of newspaper stories covering presidential remarks on Supreme Court cases, 1953–2017

Taken as a whole, this model provides strong evidence that presidents are capable of shaping news coverage of their speeches on Supreme Court decisions. Indeed, most of the variables that exert a statistically significant influence on the volume of coverage of the president's speeches are related to those speeches, rather than attributes of the Court's decisions. First, we find that the volume of attention the president devotes to discussing a case in a speech positively influences the amount of coverage of that speech. For every one additional paragraph dedicated to a case, there is a corresponding approximately 0.2 increase in the number of stories on the president's speech. Thus, compared with a one-paragraph remark on a case, a six-paragraph remark on a case is predicted to result in one additional newspaper story about the case. It is therefore evident that presidents can lead the media by devoting more attention to Court cases in their speeches, which gives the cases an added element of newsworthiness.

In addition, the tone used by presidents is important. When presidents criticize Supreme Court decisions in their speeches, the number of stories about those speeches increases by about 0.3, compared with neutral comments about decisions and those involving pending cases. This supports our theoretical argument that the media can use negative comments made by presidents to frame a conflictual relationship between the president and the Court. We also find some modest evidence that, when presidents praise the Court's decisions, there is an increase in newspaper coverage, compared with neutral statements and statements about pending cases (this variable is significant at $p = 0.08$, one-tailed), although the substantive effect of positive remarks is smaller than that of negative remarks. Thus, as it relates to tone, it appears that presidential criticisms of the Court's decisions drive newspaper coverage of the president.

The types of speeches and location of those speeches also influence news coverage. Compared with other types of speeches, when presidents discuss Court decisions in national addresses and press conferences, we can expect to observe a bit more than one additional story about the speech. That press conferences have trended downward over time (Hager and Sullivan 1994) speaks to the overall decline in news coverage that our descriptive data reveal. If press conferences have been a primary means through which presidents have commented on Court cases, but there are fewer of them to cover, it follows that news coverage of presidential remarks would decline. In addition, when presidents give speeches in Washington, DC, we predict that there will be one additional story about the speech, compared with remarks given in other locations. Given that the mean of the dependent variable is 0.4 stories, these are substantively strong attributes of newspaper coverage. It is thus clear that the choice of speech type and venue plays among the largest roles in influencing presidents' ability to lead media coverage of their speeches about Supreme Court decisions.

Consistent with our descriptive findings, Figure 6.3 also provides modest statistical evidence that newspaper coverage focuses on decided, rather than pending cases. (The *Pending Case* variable is significant at $p = 0.08$, one-tailed.) Presidential discussions of pending cases garner about 0.4 fewer stories than discussions of already decided decisions. This is consistent with our expectations, on the one hand, but contradicts the idea that presidential discussions of pending cases are especially newsworthy, on the other. Given the outcry over presidential remarks about pending cases from the media and politicians for violating norms of judicial independence (e.g., Fabian 2015; Ferris 2015; Wallsten and Barnes 2012), one might have concluded that the media would be likely to report on the president's remarks when a case was under consideration by the Court. Our results show that, in comparison with decided cases, the *New York Times* covers fewer speeches regarding pending cases, as compared with decided cases.

Turning now to the variables relating to the Court's decisions, we find a 0.7 increase in the number of stories devoted to the president's speech if the Court decided the case in the liberal, as opposed to conservative, direction. We also find that, as the number of years between the date the case was decided and the president's speech increases, newspaper coverage decreases. For each one-year increase between the year of the speech and the year the case was decided, there is a corresponding 0.02 decrease in the number of stories about the case, a substantively small effect. The other case-related variables in the model fail to achieve statistical significance.

Finally, our results show a positive, but substantively small, effect of presidential approval on newspaper coverage. For each one-percentage point increase in presidential approval, we can expect to observe a 0.01 increase in the number of stories about the president's remarks. However, we do not find evidence that the *Times* devotes more stories to the president's remarks in reelection years. We do reveal that the *Times* devotes about 0.6 fewer stories to presidential statements on the Court's decisions in the post-Carter era. This is notable in light of our earlier findings that demonstrate an increase in presidential remarks about the Court's decisions since the Carter Administration. It shows that an overall increase in presidential attention to the Court's cases beginning with the Reagan Administration has not translated into more overall coverage of those remarks.

Tone of Coverage

As discussed above, the tone of newspaper coverage of the president's speeches is based on the relative number of positive and negative words in an article. We begin our analysis of tone by examining tone in two ways. First, we explore the tone of the entire article that addressed a Supreme Court case that the president mentions in his rhetoric. Second, we examine the tone of only those paragraphs that referenced the president or the president's words. This can be an important distinction. For example, if the president speaks about a Court case, but the *Times* covers the case without referencing the president's remarks, this is an example of presidential rhetoric being irrelevant to the journalist's take on the case. Fortunately for the president, this occurred only once in our dataset.[14]

Figure 6.4 shows both measures of tone. The black bars indicate the overall tone of a story, and the white bars designate the tone of references to the president's remarks alone. Positive values indicate that the story's tone was positive, while negative values indicate negative tone. In all, tone is more positive than negative, with only President Johnson experiencing decidedly negative coverage, even when the *Times* covered the president's own remarks.

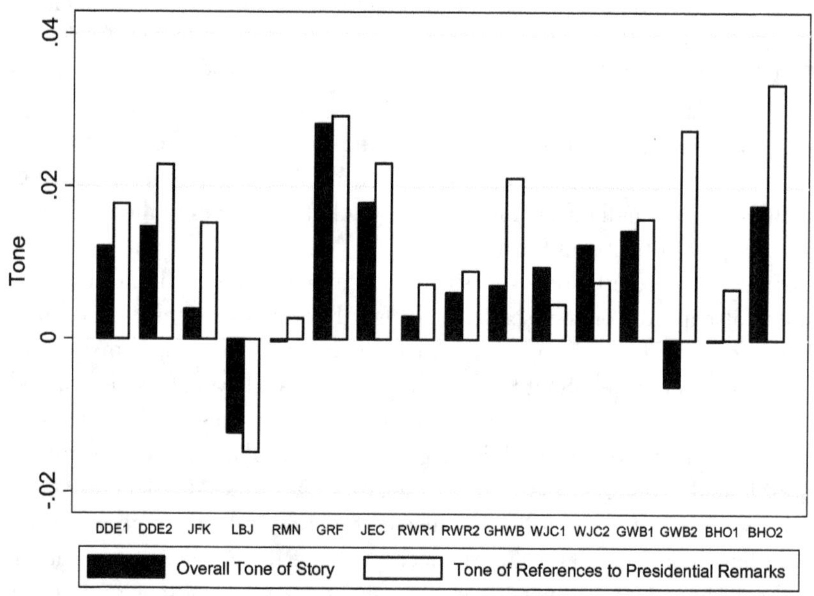

FIGURE 6.4. The tone of newspaper stories covering presidential remarks on Supreme Court cases, 1953–2017

With the exception of Carter, when the *Times* covers the president's remarks, the tone of that coverage is positive. Overall, the difference between our measures of tone is not large: the two variables are correlated at 0.82. The notable exception to this tendency occurred during George W. Bush's second term. The overall tone of stories devoted to his remarks was negative in nature, while the coverage of his specific remarks about the cases was positive in nature. In other words, coverage of the president's words was more positive than overall coverage of those speeches. The bulk of these stories involved cases implicating the president's efforts to fight the war on terrorism.

Figure 6.5 contains our analysis of influences on the tone of newspaper coverage of the presidents' speeches on Supreme Court decisions. Again, the dependent variable is the number of positive words minus the number of negative words, divided by the total number of words in the article pertaining to the president's remarks about the case. This model contains only speeches

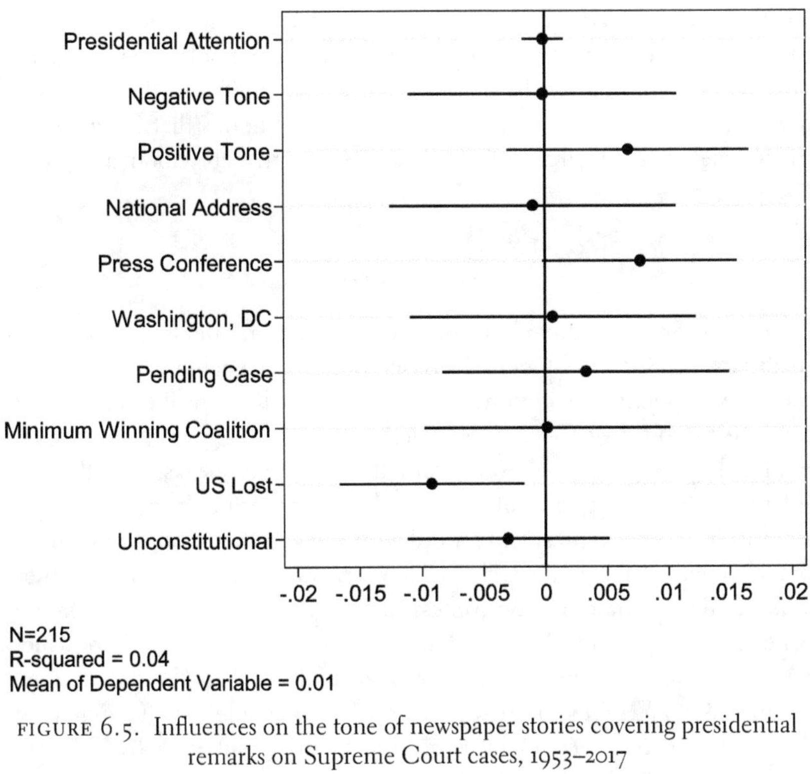

FIGURE 6.5. Influences on the tone of newspaper stories covering presidential remarks on Supreme Court cases, 1953–2017

featured in newspaper stories, because we cannot compute values for the dependent variable in the absence of a story.[15]

Overall, there is minimal evidence that presidents are capable of shaping the tone of newspaper coverage of their speeches about Court cases. Indeed, only two variables appear to influence the tone of coverage. First, presidential remarks given at press conference result in more positive tone, compared with other types of public rhetoric. This supports our theoretical expectations that the media would quote the president more often in press conferences, leading to more positive coverage of the president's remarks. Substantively, statements given at press conferences increase the relative amount of positive tone by almost 80 percent. Second, when the federal government loses a case, newspaper coverage tends to be about twice as negative in tone. Because these are instances in which the president is increasingly likely to criticize the Court, as demonstrated in Chapter 4, it makes sense that the media devotes more negative coverage to the president's remarks since the two branches of government are in conflict with one another with regard to the outcome of these cases. These findings are consistent with the uncertainty we expressed about whether presidential tone could affect stories that are often written in a way that balances two or more perspectives, and do not solely represent the president's point of view. In short, presidents are limited in their ability to dictate the tone of a news story given professional norms that frown on the media solely reporting the president's point of view in a story about a Supreme Court case.

CONCLUSIONS

One of the main arguments in this book is that presidents are interested in discussing Supreme Court decisions because it enables them to show they are responsive to important issues, potentially contributing to their reelection, policy goals, and historical legacies. Yet, we know that the public does not hang on every word the president speaks, and the president has limited opportunities to speak directly to the American people. Because of this, the president's words often reach the public through the news media, and it is through the news media that presidents are most able to demonstrate responsiveness to legal issues of concern to the American people. In this chapter, we examined the extent to which presidents can influence media coverage of their remarks on Supreme Court cases. We argued that presidents are capable of affecting news coverage of their speeches by appealing to the profit incentive of news media and professional norms of journalism.

Consistent with our expectations, we find that presidents can lead news coverage of their remarks in terms of the volume of coverage. In particular, when presidents devote a great deal of attention to discussions of Supreme Court cases in their speeches, this increases coverage of those speeches. When presidents criticize the Court's decisions, this enables the media to convey conflict between the executive and judicial branches, resulting in more coverage of the presidents' speeches. Presidents can also lead coverage by delivering their speeches in national addresses and in press conferences, as well as in Washington, DC. Further, when presidents discuss recently decided cases, this increases coverage of their speeches as such cases are of contemporary relevance to the public. Indeed, if presidents want to generate more news coverage of their commentary on Court cases, our results suggest that presidents can deliver more press conferences in the nation's capital, and do so when Supreme Court decisions are likely to be in the news.

We clearly demonstrate that presidents are effective in increasing news coverage of their remarks on Supreme Court cases. Nevertheless, this finding is not without qualification. Many features of presidential leadership of the news do not translate into heightened coverage. After all, the majority of the president's comments do not make the news, as only about 25 percent of remarks generate news coverage. Moreover, as we have shown, the president's ability to dictate news coverage has declined over time. This is an interesting paradox: just as presidents have had more White House resources to be able to generate news coverage, they have been less successful garnering coverage of their speeches on cases. This fits with research that shows declining coverage of the Court (Johnson and Socker 2012), overall, but it also fits with changes in newspaper reporting patterns (Bennett 2016) and changes in presidential public relations strategies (Hager and Sullivan 1994). Despite the limits of presidential leadership of the news media, our results support one of the president's primary motivations to comment on Supreme Court cases: to generate news coverage of their remarks on issues of national concern.

Though it is evident that presidents are capable of increasing news coverage of their speeches regarding Supreme Court cases, they do not appear to be able to generate positive coverage of those speeches. In fact, very few variables seem to drive the tone of newspaper coverage of their speeches. Thus, it appears that presidents will only have mixed success using the media to translate their comments on issues to the American people. Just as presidents are unable to influence the tone of coverage, certain presidential strategies for leading the media have a clear payoff in terms of influencing the volume of news coverage of speeches. Further, our results indicate that media coverage of the president's speeches is driven primarily by factors the president can control – such as the length, type, and location of the speech, the tone of comments, and whether the speech focuses on recently decided cases – rather than factors specific to the Court's decision. These findings indicate that the media respond primarily to the president, not the Court, in covering presidential speeches about judicial decisions. Consequently, discussing Supreme Court decisions can be a very useful tool for presidents who seek to generate news coverage of their speeches in an effort to reach out to the American public. Besides, publicly discussing the Court's cases – and generating coverage of those discussions – provides a clear mechanism by which presidents can attempt to shape the public's constitutional understandings, thus providing presidents with a readily available and high-profile mechanism to participate in the coordinate construction of the Constitution.

APPENDIX TABLE 6.1. *Influences on the number and tone of newspaper stories covering presidential remarks on Supreme Court cases, 1953–2017*

	Volume	Tone
Presidential Attention	0.20[a]	−0.0001
	(0.03)	(0.001)
Negative Tone	0.31[a]	−0.0002
	(0.18)	(0.007)
Positive Tone	0.21	0.007
	(0.15)	(0.006)
National Address	1.03[a]	−0.001
	(0.27)	(0.007)
Press Conference	1.15[a]	0.008[a]
	(0.14)	(0.005)
Washington, DC	0.97[a]	0.0007
	(0.27)	(0.007)
Pending Case	0.38	0.003
	(0.28)	(0.007)
Minimum Winning Coalition	0.02	0.0002
	(0.18)	(0.006)
US Lost	−0.20	−0.009[a]
	(0.18)	(0.005)
Unconstitutional	−0.11	−0.003
	(0.14)	(0.005)
First Amendment	0.03	
	(0.21)	
Civil Rights	0.09	
	(0.16)	
Liberal Decision	0.67[a]	
	(0.17)	
Amicus Curiae Briefs	0.00	
	(0.00)	
Years from Case	−0.03[a]	
	(0.01)	
Presidential Approval	0.01[a]	
	(0.01)	
Reelection Year	−0.18	
	(0.17)	
Post-Carter Presidencies	−0.67[a]	
	(0.17)	
Constant	−3.11[a]	0.011
	(0.40)	(0.009)
Wald χ^2	403.5[a]	
R^2		0.04
N	924	215

Note: Entries in the Volume column are negative binomial regression coefficients. Entries in the Tone column are ordinary least squares regression coefficients. Robust standard errors are reported in parentheses. [a]$p \leq .05$ (one-tailed tests).

7

Presidents and Public Opinion

On June 26, 2015, the Supreme Court announced its decision in *Obergefell* v. *Hodges*. By a 5–4 vote, the Court determined that the Fourteenth Amendment prohibits states from refusing to grant marriage licenses to same-sex couples. Writing for the Court's majority, Justice Kennedy said, "The ancient origins of marriage confirm its centrality, but it has not stood in isolation from developments in law and society. The history of marriage is one of both continuity and change. That institution – even as confined to opposite-sex relations – has evolved over time" (135 S.Ct. 2584, at 2595).

The notion that Americans' understanding of marriage has evolved over time certainly pertains to public support for same-sex marriage, which shifted dramatically over the past decades. For example, in 1996, the first time Gallup asked about support for same-sex marriages in the United States, only 27 percent of respondents endorsed extending marriage licenses to same-sex couples. By May of 2015, a month before the Court's ruling, 60 percent of Americans supported same-sex marriages (McCarthy 2015). One such American whose view evolved during these decades was Barack Obama. Indeed, it was not until 2012 that President Obama announced his support for same-sex marriages, which corresponded to roughly the point at which a majority of Americans first supported same-sex marriages (McCarthy 2015; Schwarz 2015).

Obama was quick to react to the Court's ruling. On the same day the Court handed down its decision, Obama made extensive prepared remarks about it to the nation. Obama said:

> this ruling is a victory for America. This decision affirms what millions of Americans already believe in their hearts: When all Americans are treated as equal, we are all more free. . . . I know change for many of our LGBT brothers and sisters must have seemed so slow for so long. But compared to so many other issues, America's shift has been so quick. I know that Americans of good will continue to hold a wide range of views on this issue. Opposition in some

> cases has been based on sincere and deeply held beliefs. All of us who welcome today's news should be mindful of that fact, recognize different viewpoints, revere our deep commitment to religious freedom.[1]

Obama would praise the decision another seven times throughout his second term.

The example of President Obama's choice to speak out publicly in favor of *Obergefell* raises some interesting questions. Do presidents praise or criticize cases in an effort to shape public opinion through their bully pulpits? Are presidents capable of influencing public opinion on Supreme Court cases or the Court itself? Do presidents discuss cases in an effort to lead or follow public opinion? Our purpose in this chapter is to tackle these questions. To do this, we bring two types of evidence to bear. First, we present the results of a first-of-its-kind survey experiment that investigates public support for Court decisions, and the Court itself, based on whether the president praised a decision, criticized a decision, or made no comment on the case. Second, we examine the positions presidents have taken on the Court's cases and match them to public support for the issues underlying those cases. We are confident that using both experimental and observational data will shed a great deal of light on these important questions.

This chapter contributes to our understanding of presidential speeches on Supreme Court decisions in two ways. First, it helps clarify the effect of presidential statements on the public. In the previous chapters, we have looked at whether presidential remarks result in favorable actions by the Court (Chapter 2), Congress (Chapter 5), and the media (Chapter 6). Here we extend this to perhaps the president's most important audience – the American people. Second, this chapter helps us to comprehend the extent to which presidents are responsive to public opinion, or try to lead public opinion. In particular, we show that presidents take public positions to demonstrate their responsiveness to issues that are important to the American people, and to display their congruence with American's attitudes on these issues. In turn, this can contribute to presidents' abilities to secure reelection, make good public policy, and enhance their historical legacies by showing they reflect the preferences of the public.

Our results indicate that presidents can shape public support for the Court's decisions in relatively low-salience cases. However, they are incapable of mobilizing public support or opposition to the Court's decisions in high-salience cases, or influencing public support for the Court as an institution. We also find that the positions presidents take on the Court's recently decided cases overwhelmingly correspond to the positions favored by the public on those cases. Thus, this chapter demonstrates that presidents can only lead public opinion under certain conditions, and instead tend to reflect the public's preferences when they take positions on the Court's decisions.

PRESIDENTIAL LEADERSHIP OF THE PUBLIC

Modern presidential leadership is often viewed through the lens of public leadership. Without public support, presidents have difficulty breaking congressional gridlock to pass their legislative agendas, win reelection, or achieve other goals. Presidents' central need for public support means that they often marshal myriad resources to affect it. Whether or not presidents are successful in moving public opinion forms the basis for many conclusions about presidential leadership and the success of a presidency. Yet, the prospects for presidential leadership of public opinion are complicated, with many factors diminishing the chances that presidents will be successful increasing public support for their policy positions. Nevertheless, presidents expend considerable time and energy using their vast resources to lead the public in an effort to contribute to successful public presidencies.

On the one hand, there are several reasons to expect that presidents can lead public opinion. First, the president enjoys the largest audiences of any politician (Baum and Kernell 1999). The public expresses more interest in presidents than other political actors (Hamilton 2004), meaning that presidents are more likely to garner the attention of the American people directly by delivering national addresses or indirectly through news coverage of their public remarks. National addresses are an especially effective means to lead public opinion, at least in the short term, just as continuous public outreach efforts generate more news coverage for the president (Cohen 2010). Second, the president has an extensive communications apparatus (Kumar 2007). The president's team of speechwriters allows for presidents to deliver hundreds of speeches annually throughout the nation and the world. Other communications staff provide research on which points to emphasize, and help to identify which audiences are likely to be most responsive to the president's message. Third, the public's limited knowledge about policy and politics provides the president with an opportunity to shape their opinions on policies, especially when those issues are not otherwise salient to the American people (Rottinghaus 2010). Each of these attributes provides presidents with the opportunity to lead public opinion, even though they may not be sufficient for us to expect that presidents will be able to do so consistently.

On the other hand, there are reasons to believe that presidents will have difficulty leading public opinion. First, the public is generally inattentive to politics and does not always understand the president's message (Edwards 2016, 30). Even though presidents can lead the public through national addresses, few Americans watch (Baum and Kernell 1998) and those who do watch already tend to support the president (Kernell and Rice 2011), resulting in short-lived effects on public opinion (Welch 2003). Second, the president's voice is rarely entirely in unison with other elites. Because of this, the president's attempts at public leadership are often countered by the opposition, which has much to gain among their supporters by opposing a president that they do not like. Often, any temporary increase in public support that the president may enjoy from a national address or rally event does not last when countered by effective messaging from the opposition (Edwards 2003, 170). Third, predispositions drive public support for issues, and partisanship is an especially reliable predictor of the public's support for or opposition to a policy advocated by the president (Berinsky 2009). Thus, partisanship dictates much of the public's reaction to a presidential speech, limiting the number of Americans that may be likely to respond favorably to presidential remarks.

Clearly, it can be challenging for presidents to lead or change public opinion. However, presidents can accomplish other goals through their public commentary. First, presidents take positions to engage their own supporters (Cavari 2017). This can activate their electoral base during reelection campaigns, or at a minimum maintain existing public support (Edwards 2003). Even when public position taking does not increase public support for the president or his policies, it may affect the strength of the public's opinion. For example, although Bill Clinton's public support for allowing gays and lesbians to serve in the United States military did not lead to an overall increase in support for his policy, it did increase the percentage of Americans who strongly supported the policy (Bailey, Sigelman, and Wilcox 2003). Second, presidents may increase the salience of issues to the public or emphasize issues new to the public debate (Edwards 2009, Chapter 3; Eshbaugh-Soha and Peake 2011). Third, the public expects the president to comment on issues of national importance, whether or not they agree with his position (Waterman, Silva, and Jenkins-Smith 2014). Thus, by taking public positions on important matters of public policy, presidents can appear, well, presidential.

In taking public positions, moreover, presidents are able to demonstrate that they are responsive to issues of public concern. This illustrates to the public that they are democratic leaders who consider the public's views in their decision-making. We have presented this idea throughout this book, but it is not one that is unique to presidential leadership of public opinion on the

Court's decisions. Rather, others have identified responsiveness as an essential means for presidents to engage public opinion effectively. Canes-Wrone (2006), for example, shows how presidents respond to public opinion by using public support to decide which issues to emphasize when they go public on their legislative agendas. Eshbaugh-Soha and Peake (2011) maintain that responsiveness is an essential element of the president's public leadership strategy. Even when presidents cannot change public opinion, they may still respond to public concerns about issues such as the economy by prioritizing them and offering policy solutions that benefit the public. Erikson, MacKuen, and Stimson (2002) show how presidents are responsive to the public's policy preferences. Canes-Wrone and Shotts (2004) reveal how presidential responsiveness to the public is conditional on approval ratings and whether it is reelection year. Wood (2009) also concludes that presidents are receptive to public opinion, responding to the policy positions of their partisans in the electorate.

Considering this vein of research as a whole, it is evident that presidential leadership of public opinion is complex. On the one hand, there are reasons to believe the president can affect public attitudes. On the other hand, there are clear limitations to the president's ability to do so. Further, there is evidence to suggest that presidents' main motivation in taking public positions may not be to shape public opinion at all, but rather to illustrate they are sensitive to matters that are important to the American polity. With this in mind, we now turn to exploring the ability of presidents to lead the public in the context of their public speeches on the Court's decisions.

The President, the Court, and the Public

It is evident that existing scholarship provides mixed support for the ability of presidents to lead public opinion. Though this body of research is very informative, it does not look at the ability of presidents to shape public opinion on the Court's decisions. To the best of our knowledge, there is no published research that specifically investigates presidents' ability to influence public opinion on Supreme Court cases. However, there is a small body of work that suggests presidents may be able to shape the views of the public on the Court or its decisions.

Armaly (2018) provides a novel examination into how statements made by extra-judicial actors can influence public support for the Supreme Court. To do this, he studies whether statements made by presidential candidates – Hillary Clinton or Donald Trump – regarding the Supreme Court influence the public's support for the Court as an institution, known as diffuse support.

Using an experimental survey design, Armaly finds that presidential candidates are capable of shaping diffuse support for the Court, particularly among their supporters. Thus, Armaly provides evidence that elite opinion leaders can alter public support for the Court.

Clark and Kastellec (2015) investigate whether public support for the Court can be manipulated based on whether proposals to reduce the independence of the Court (such as term limiting justices or allowing the president and Congress to reverse its decisions) were made by different partisan elites. They found that Democratic respondents were more likely to support Court-curbing measures when they were attributed to Democrats, while Republican respondents were less likely to favor such measures when attributed to Democrats, and vice versa. It therefore appears that partisan elites can influence public support for the independence of the Court, suggesting another way that public attitudes about the Court are manipulable.

What is particularly notable about this research is that it focuses on diffuse support for the Court, rather than specific support. For decades, scholars have argued that diffuse (institutional) support for the Court is relatively stable over time and connected to established beliefs regarding concepts such as democracy and procedural justice (Baird 2001; Caldeira and Gibson 1992; Gibson, Caldeira and Spence 2003; Gibson and Nelson 2015; Mondak and Smithey 1997; Tyler 2006). Conversely, changes in specific support for the Court, which refers to support for the Court's decisions (Easton 1975; Swanson 2007), tend to be more easily changeable. Research indicates that specific support is malleable based on things such as the size of the majority coalition, knowledge of a case, and whether individuals support or oppose the Court's decisions on policy grounds (Hoekstra 2000, 2003; Hoekstra and Segal 1996; Nicholson and Hansford 2014; Tanenhaus and Murphy 1981; Zink, Spriggs, and Scott 2009).

If statements made by presidential candidates or attributed to partisan elites can reduce how the public views the institutional legitimacy of the Supreme Court, this suggests that public support for the Court as an institution may be malleable (Armaly 2018; Bartels and Johnston 2013; Christenson and Glick 2015; Clark and Kastellec 2015). This is important as scholars have noted that the Court relies on a "reservoir of goodwill" that allows the justices to render sometimes unpopular or controversial decisions without facing substantial backlash from the public (Caldeira and Gibson 1992). Given this, if diffuse support for the Court can be changed relatively easily based on attacks on the Court, the Court may face a legitimacy problem if it frequently draws the ire of other public actors.

This research also suggests that presidents may be able to manipulate public support for the Court and its decisions based on their public rhetoric toward the Court's decisions. It is well established that the public does not pay close attention to the Court or its decisions (Franklin and Kosaki 1989; Gibson and Caldeira 2009; Hoekstra 2000; Morin 1989; Tanenhaus and Murphy 1981). As a result, the public may look to opinion leaders to form their attitudes toward the Court and its decisions (Armaly 2018; Zaller 1992). As noted above, the president is perhaps the most visible opinion leader in the country, garnering substantial media attention (Baum and Kernell 1998). Thus, when presidents take public positions on Supreme Court decisions, there is good reason to believe those positions might affect how Americans view the decisions, and perhaps even the Court itself. Simply put, the public can use presidential positions on the Court's opinions as a heuristic to help them form their own opinions about the Court's cases (specific support) and the Court as an institution (diffuse support).

In taking public positions supporting the Court's decisions, presidents can lend legitimacy to those decisions. As we have shown throughout this book, presidential praise for the Court's decisions is hardly associated with every case that presidents approve of. Rather, presidents appear to choose strategically when to offer public admiration for the Court's decisions. Because this is a rare event, it may stand out to the public. Average citizens can look to the president to help form their own attitudes on the Court's decisions given their general lack of knowledge about the Court and its policy outputs. Moreover, when presidents publicly praise the Court's decisions, they can add an additional layer of legitimacy to the decisions by signaling that two branches of government are in harmony with respect to the case's outcome. This can potentially contribute to public acceptance of the decision and more favorable views of the Court as an institution. Accordingly, we expect that, when the president praises a Court decision in his public rhetoric, public support for the decision and the Court as an institution will increase.

Conversely, when presidents publicly criticize the Court's decisions, they can serve to undermine those decisions. By choosing to publicly criticize the Court's decisions, presidents open themselves up to criticism for violating the norm of judicial independence (Barnes 2010; Dennison 2018; Lane 2018). Because of this, presidents generally reserve public admonishment of the Court's decisions for those decisions that are particularly salient and disagreeable to them, as we demonstrated in Chapter 4. When the public observes presidential criticism of a Court decision, this can send a strong signal that the decision is flawed from a legal or policy standpoint. Because the average American citizen is hardly a legal expert, this may serve to convince the public that the Court ruled incorrectly. In turn, this may decrease public support for the decision and possibly the Court itself. Thus, we expect that, when the president criticizes a Court decision in his public rhetoric, public support for the decision and the Court as an institution will decrease.

These empirical expectations are based on the idea that presidents may be able to shape public attitudes toward the Court and its decisions via their public speeches. However, we have reason to believe that they may have an easier time influencing public opinion about specific support than diffuse support. Notwithstanding recent research suggesting outside actors may be able to influence diffuse support for the Court (Armaly 2018; Clark and Kastellec 2015), the literature on diffuse support suggests that it is relatively stable over time (Baird 2001; Caldeira and Gibson 1992; Gibson, Caldeira and Spence 2003; Gibson and Nelson 2015; Mondak and Smithey 1997; Tyler 2006). For this reason, it should not be especially malleable as a result of short-term praise or criticism by an actor like the president, since diffuse support is largely based on engrained beliefs in concepts such as democracy and procedural justice. On the contrary, research indicates that specific support is more open to change in the short term based on factors such as exposure to stories about the Court's decision and partisan cues (Boddery and Yates 2014; Hoekstra 2000, 2003; Hoekstra and Segal 1996; Nicholson and Hansford 2014; Zink, Spriggs, and Scott 2009). Given this, it seems more plausible that presidents will be able to shape specific support for the Court's decisions than diffuse support for the Court as an institution.

Further, the ability of presidents to shape public opinion on the Court or its decisions is likely dependent on the salience of the issue area of the case discussed by the president (Hoekstra 2003; Hoekstra and Segal 1996). When issues are salient, attitudes toward them tend to be stronger and less vulnerable to change (Collins 2008b; Edwards and Wood 1999; Hoekstra and Segal 1996; Krosnick 1988; Peake 2001; Petty and Cacioppo 1986). Conversely, attitudes involving less salient issue areas may be more malleable, and susceptible to change based on the opinions of political elites. For example, Rottinghaus (2010) demonstrates that presidents are capable of leading public opinion when the public is persuadable, including when presidents take positions on issues that are relatively low in salience. Similarly, Villalobos and Sirin (2012) show that presidents can influence public opinion on low-salience issues, but struggle to do so on more important issues. Thus, we believe that presidents will be less successful at shaping the public's opinion of the Court and its decisions in salient cases.

Experimental Research Design

To examine whether presidential speeches on the Court's cases influence public perspectives of the Court and its decisions, we use an experimental research design. This allows us to manipulate systematically the key factors we are interested in learning about, maximizing our ability to draw causal inferences. Such is the case because respondents in our survey experiment are randomly assigned to various treatment groups, allowing us to attribute any change in public support for the Court or its decisions to exposure to presidential speeches, rather than other factors (e.g., Druckman et al. 2006).

We conducted our survey experiment on Amazon's Mechanical Turk (MTurk) platform. MTurk is a relatively low-cost way of recruiting respondents, who are paid for their participation in the survey. Although respondents do not constitute a random national sample, MTurk has become a very common tool in the social sciences to conduct survey experiments, and research indicates that the sample populations in MTurk are generally valid (Berinsky, Huber, and Lenz 2012; Clifford, Jewell, and Waggoner 2015; Mullinix et al. 2015). For these reasons, MTurk has become one of the primary tools used by researchers to evaluate public attitudes toward the Supreme Court (Armaly 2018; Boddery and Yates 2014; Clark and Kastellec 2015; Christenson and Glick 2015).

We conducted our survey in February of 2019. Recall that we sought to investigate the influence of presidential speeches on public opinion in both high- and low-salience cases. Given this, we set up the experiment such that respondents were randomly assigned to one of six groups based on: 1) whether the case discussed by the president was of high or low salience; and 2) whether the president praised, criticized, or made no mention of the Court's decision (the control group). Power analysis suggested that we needed a minimum of 100 respondents in each group based on an expected 0.7 increase on the measure of specific support with a mean of 4.0 (on a 1 to 7 scale) and a standard deviation of 1.5 at a power of 0.9. (The actual mean is 4.8 with a standard deviation of 1.8.) Because this research is the first-of-its kind, we wanted to be safe and sought to include 150 respondents in each condition. As a whole, 902 respondents took the survey, and there are 146 to 153 respondents in each condition.[2] Respondents are all United States citizens at least 18 years of age.

After completing a series of demographic and political questions, respondents were asked to read a newspaper story about a fictional Supreme Court case. (Respondents were not informed it was a fictional case until they were debriefed at the conclusion of the survey.) For the low-salience issue area, we choose wetlands protection and modeled the case after *Rapanos* v. *United States* (2006). For the high-salience issue area, we chose immigration and modeled the case after *Arizona* v. *United States* (2012).

We choose Barack Obama as the president who commented on the case and crafted his remarks after actual comments he made about Supreme Court decisions. We selected President Obama for two reasons. First, because President Trump is particularly polarizing (Bump 2019; Weiss 2018), we worried that attributing statements to Trump might decrease the generalizability of our results, since respondents may take particularly strong cues off Trump. Second, as we explain in Chapter 9, President Trump speaks quite differently than other presidents about Supreme Court decisions and the Court itself, often relying on brief statements (or Tweets) criticizing or praising decisions with little depth or substance. This, coupled with the polarization associated with Trump, made it very difficult for us to draft language that we believe respondents would credibly attribute to President Trump involving the president praising or criticizing an identical decision. Conversely, President Obama tended to speak about the Court's decisions in a more thoughtful manner, and we believed we could craft both positive and negative language on the same case that respondents would credibly attribute to President Obama on both of the issues areas investigated here. Further, because President Obama spoke more similarly to past presidents on the Court's cases than President Trump, we believe the choice of Obama would enhance the generalizability of our results. With that said, we recognize that our results pertain to statements attributed to President Obama.

Respondents in the low-salience wetlands protection group read the following story:

> WASHINGTON (AP) – Today, the Supreme Court ruled that the federal government has broad authority to regulate wetlands under the Clean Water Act. The decision involved individuals in Arizona who filled a wetland with sand in order to construct a new office space, without filing a permit. The Arizona business owners argued that they did not need to file the permit since the area was not connected to navigable waters and therefore not a wetland. The Environmental Protection Agency fined the business owners since the wetland that was filled was connected to local waterways through two small tributaries and therefore constituted a wetland. The Supreme Court agreed, holding that navigable waterways have been broadly interpreted by previous Court decisions to include areas connected to larger waterways via tributaries and streams.

Respondents in the control group simply read this story. Respondents in the *Praise* group read the following at the end of the story:

> In response to the decision, President Obama said, "Today, the Supreme Court made a decision that will allow us to enforce our environmental laws. No one should be able to pollute or alter waterways that provide vital drinking water and recreational opportunities to the people of the United States. I agree with the Court's decision and I look forward to ensuring it is implemented swiftly and fully."

Respondents in the *Criticize* group read the following at the end of the story:

> In response to the decision, President Obama said, "Today, the Supreme Court made a decision that allows the federal government to fine property owners for making improvements to their property. This decision will harm business owners seeking to contribute to the growth of the US economy. I disagree with the Court's decision and I look forward to working with Congress to pass legislation to limit the ability of the Environmental Protection Agency to administer these fines."

Respondents in the high-salience immigration group read the following story:

> WASHINGTON (AP) – Today, the Supreme Court ruled that local police have the authority to force individuals to present papers demonstrating that they are in the country legally. This decision involved an Arizona law that allowed local police officers to require individuals suspected of being in the country illegally to show that they are authorized to be in the United States. Arizona passed the law in response to growing concerns about the number of individuals entering the country illegally through the Southern border. Opponents of the law argued that it was a form of racial profiling and gave local police too much power. The Supreme Court held that allowing local police to check the immigration status of individuals suspected of being in the country illegally was permissible since it did not conflict with or obstruct federal immigration enforcement.

As before, respondents in the control group simply read this story. Respondents in the *Praise* group read the following at the end of the story:

> In response to the decision, President Obama said, "Today, the Supreme Court made a decision that will allow us to enforce our immigration laws and protect our borders. Arizona has passed a tough, but fair law that will allow us to address the growing immigration problem facing the country, while respecting the rights of law-abiding citizens. I agree with the Court's decision and I look forward to ensuring it is implemented swiftly and fully."

Respondents in the *Criticize* group read the following at the end of the story:

> In response to the decision, President Obama said, "Today, the Supreme Court made a decision that allows local police to check the immigration status of anyone they even suspect to be here illegally. No one should ever live under a cloud of suspicion just because of what they look like. I disagree with the Court's decision and I look forward to working with Congress to pass comprehensive immigration reform that addresses our security needs, and upholds our tradition as a nation of laws and a nation of immigrants."

After reading the vignettes, respondents were asked a series of questions about the case and the Supreme Court. To capture specific support for the Court's decision, respondents were asked, "Do you agree or disagree with the Supreme Court's decision in this case?" This was measured on a 7-point scale from "strongly disagree" to "strongly agree" (e.g., Clawson and Waltenburg 2003; Gibson, Caldeira, and Spence 2003; Mondak 1994). To measure diffuse support for the Court, we used the 7-item battery of questions described in Gibson and Nelson (2015). Respondents were asked to answer the following questions on a 7-point scale, from "strongly disagree" to "strongly agree:"

> It is inevitable that the US Supreme Court gets mixed up in politics; therefore, we ought to have stronger means of controlling the actions of the US Supreme Court.
>
> The US Supreme Court ought to be made less independent so that it listens a lot more to what the people want.
>
> Judges on the US Supreme Court who consistently make decisions at odds with what a majority of the people want should be removed from their position as judge.
>
> Supreme Court justices are just like any other politicians; we cannot trust them to decide court cases in a way that is in the best interests of our country.
>
> If the US Supreme Court started making a lot of decisions that most people disagree with, it might be better to do away with the Supreme Court altogether.
>
> The US Supreme Court gets too mixed up in politics.
>
> The right of the Supreme Court to decide certain types of controversial issues should be reduced (Gibson and Nelson 2015, 167–168)

To capture diffuse support for the Court, we summed respondents' answers to these questions and divided by seven to put them on the same 7-point scale as our measure of specific support.[3] Because our dependent variables, specific support for the Court's decision, and diffuse support for the Court range from 1 to 7 (with higher values reflecting more specific or diffuse support), we utilize ordinary least squares regression with robust standard errors to examine the influence of presidential speeches. As in previous chapters, we present our results graphically to facilitate easy interpretation. We obtain substantively identical results when we perform difference of means tests, as would be expected given that there is a good deal of balance among respondents across the treatment conditions, as reported in Appendix Table 7.1.

In addition, we control for respondents' political and demographic attributes, including political party affiliation, race, gender, age, and education (Clark and Kastellec 2015). *Democrat* is coded 1 if respondents think of themselves as Democrats, and 0 otherwise. *Republican* is coded 1 if respondents think of themselves as Republicans, and 0 otherwise. The comparison group are those identifying themselves as independents, identifying with a third party, or stating no preference. *White* is coded 1 if respondents identified their race as white, and 0 otherwise. *Black* is coded 1 if respondents identified their race as black or African American, and 0 otherwise. *Hispanic* is coded 1 if respondents identified their race as Hispanic or Latin American, and 0 otherwise. *Asian* is coded 1 if respondents identified their race as Asian, and 0 otherwise. The comparison group are those identifying as mixed race, American Indian or Alaska Native, Native Hawaiian or Pacific Islander, and other. *Male* is coded 1 if respondents identified their gender as male, and 0 if otherwise. *Age* is the respondent's age in years at the time of the survey. *Some College* is coded 1 for respondents who attended, but did not graduate, from college, and 0 otherwise. *College Graduate* is coded 1 for respondents who graduated from college, and 0 otherwise. The comparison group consists of respondents with a high school education or less.

Survey Experiment Results

Figure 7.1 reports the results of our survey experiment regarding specific support for Supreme Court decisions. These graphs represent the predicted change in support for the Court's decision given a one-unit change in the independent variable of interest, holding all other variables at their mean or modal values. The circles represent the point estimate of the marginal effects, and the horizontal lines coming off the circles are 90 percent confidence intervals. Variables are statistically significant if the 90 percent confidence intervals do not cross the solid line at zero.[4]

The top figure is the results of the wetlands protection case, and the bottom figure pertains to the immigration case. These results are consistent with our expectations.[5] They show that presidents are able to shape public support for the Court's decisions in low-salient cases (wetlands protection), but cannot do

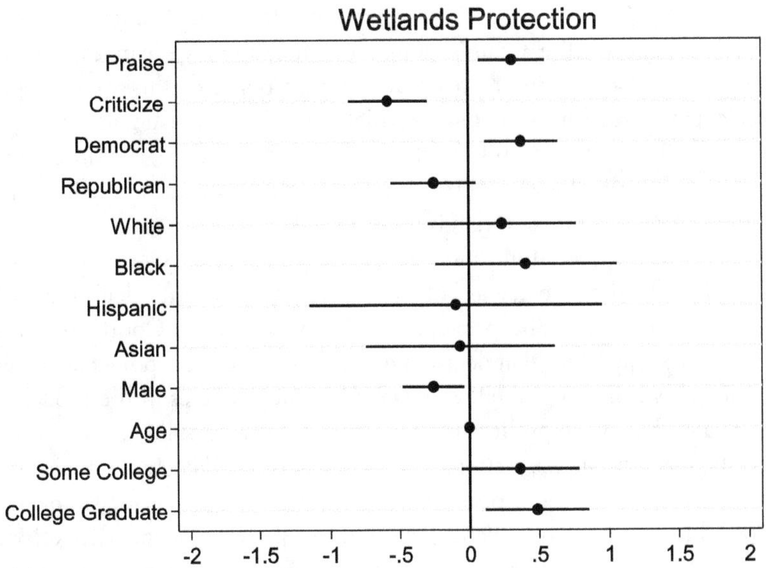

N=447
R-squared = 0.11
Mean of Dependent Variable = 5.3

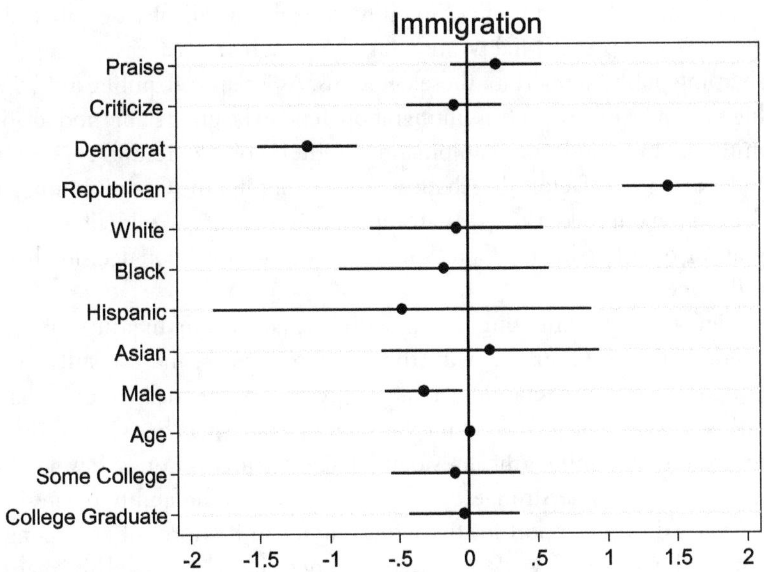

N=455
R-squared = 0.28
Mean of Dependent Variable = 4.3

FIGURE 7.1. Influences on specific support for a Supreme Court decision

so in high-salience issue areas (immigration). In substantive terms, when the president praises the Court's non-salient decisions, we can expect to see support for that decision increase by about 0.3 points on the 7-point approval scale, compared with situations in which the president made no statement on the case. To put the magnitude of this effect in perspective, it is similar in size to the difference between Democrats and independents when it comes to support for the Court's wetlands protection decision.

Notably, the magnitude of the effect of criticism of the Court's decisions by presidents is almost twice as large as praise for the Court's decisions in low-salient cases. When the president criticizes one of the Court's non-salient decisions, support for that decision decreases by about 0.6 points on a 7-point scale. This is the largest effect out of all of the variables in the model. This indicates that, when presidents rebuke the Court's low-salience decisions, the public reacts particularly strongly to that criticism and decreases their support for the Court's decision. Because this type of presidential criticism opens the door for allegations of violating the norm of judicial independence (Barnes 2010; Dennison 2018; Lane 2018), there is some risk involved in pursuing this rhetorical strategy. It appears that this risk may be mitigated in part by the potential for a relatively large influence on public support for the Court's decision.

In contrast to the president's ability to lead low-salient cases, there is no evidence that presidential position taking on high-salience cases is capable of sharping public support for those decisions. As we argued, public attitudes on high-salience issues, such as immigration, tend to be quite stable and relatively immune to short-term manipulation. Our empirical results support this. Indeed, the only factors that shape public support for the Court's immigration decision in our model are partisanship, age, and gender. Presidential speeches praising or criticizing the Court's high-salience immigration decision have no influence.

Figure 7.2 presents our results with respect to our measure of diffuse support for the Court. As with the previous figures, these results support our theoretical expectations. That is, presidents are incapable of shaping diffuse support for the Court through their public speeches. This is the case regardless of whether the presidential speech focuses on a low- or high-salience issue. The strongest evidence supporting the ability of presidents to shape diffuse support for the Court comes in the form of criticizing the Court's low-salience wetlands protection decision. Although this treatment approaches conventional levels of statistical significance ($p = 0.07$, one-tailed), its effect is fairly small in magnitude, and it is signed in the opposite direction of what one would expect based on existing scholarship

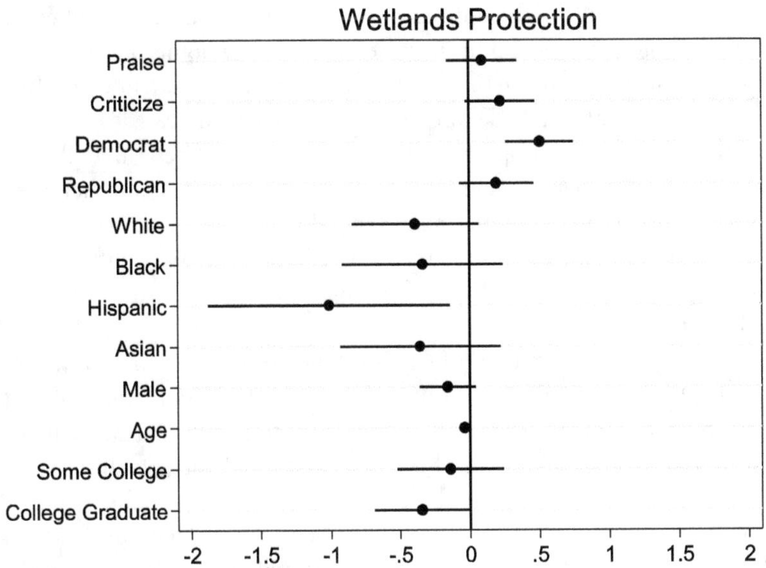

N=447
R-squared = 0.15
Mean of Dependent Variable = 3.7

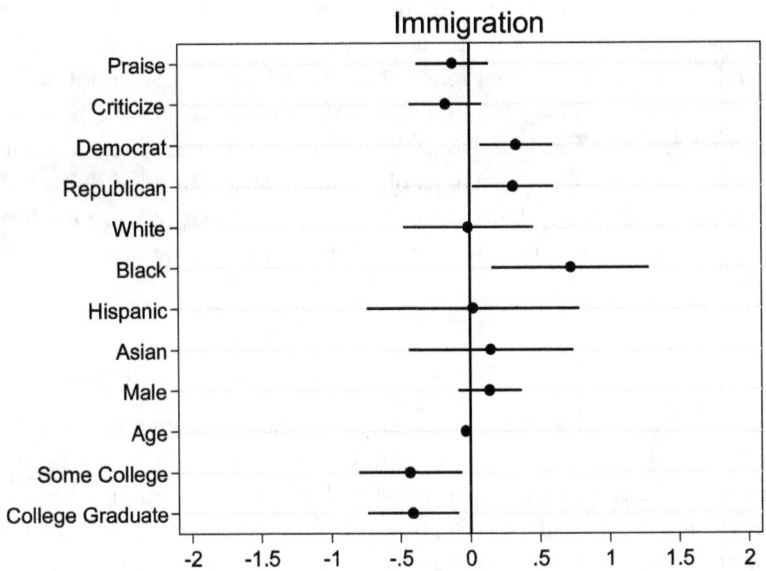

N=455
R-squared = 0.13
Mean of Dependent Variable = 3.8

FIGURE 7.2. Influences on diffuse support for the Supreme Court (e.g., Armaly 2018; Clark and Kastellec 2015). Substantively, it indicates that diffuse support for the Court increases by about 0.2 points on a 7-point scale when presidents criticize the Court's decisions in low-salient cases. In other words, presidential attacks on the Court's decisions can lead to a slight increase in diffuse support for the Court. This suggests that the public might cue off negative statements made by the president and increase their support for an institution that they generally hold in higher regard than the president (Gibson, Caldeira, and Spence 2003). To put it differently, presidents should be warned that, "if you plant ice you're gonna harvest wind" (Hunter 1975).

Although this work is the first-of-its-kind to examine the ability of presidents to shape specific and diffuse support for the Court and its decisions, one may interpret our results as contradicting adjacent scholarship by Armaly (2018) and Clark and Kastellec (2015) that suggests diffuse support for the Court is malleable under certain conditions. We believe our results are inconsistent with this work for two reasons. First, both of these studies focused on examining general criticism aimed at the Court as an institution, not individual decisions. For example, Armaly (2018, 604) attributed statements such as "The Court gets too mixed up in politics" to presidential candidates; and Clark and Kastellec (2015, 514) associated statements about ideas such as limiting the tenure of federal judges to partisan elites. Conversely, our study examines specific statements about the Court's policy outputs – its decisions. Second, Armaly (2018) and Clark and Kastellec (2015) look at different actors. Armaly focuses on presidential candidates, and Clark and Kastellec examine partisan elites. In contrast, we focus on the specific actions of a United States president. Given these differences, it should not be entirely surprising that our results diverge. Simply put, although related, each of these studies is aimed at answering a different question.[6]

PRESIDENTIAL RESPONSIVENESS TO PUBLIC OPINION

Having examined whether presidents can influence public opinion on the Court and its cases, we now turn to the related question of whether presidents discuss cases in an effort to lead or follow public opinion. As noted above, the difficulties presidents face when trying to lead public opinion implies presidents may have additional motivations for engaging the public. One such motivation is to show that they are responsive to public opinion. Under many circumstances, presidents will use their public speeches to take positions that illustrate their commitment to democratic leadership or their responsiveness to public opinion. In this sense, presidents are rational to speak publicly and take positions on issues that are already popular with the public, especially given the difficulty presidents have engaging and motivating a relatively disinterested American public. As Geer (1996) argues, responsiveness is an essential component of presidential leadership and is necessary in a democracy. Although scholars have examined this question from many angles, we are not aware of systematic research that looks at this in the context of presidential position taking on Supreme Court decisions.

Presidential Responsiveness to Public Opinion on Court Cases

One of the primary reasons why presidents speak about Supreme Court cases is to demonstrate their attentiveness to issues of public concern. Doing so ensures that the president is acting democratically even amid the many difficulties that presidents face leading public opinion. Like other scholars, we conceive of responsiveness as analogous to congruence (Canes-Wrone and Shotts 2004).[7] When presidents support issues favored by a majority of the public, their views are congruent with public opinion, irrespective of whether the president is responsible for shaping the public's opinion. We discuss the advantages and disadvantages of taking positions congruent with public opinion. Given our results in Chapter 2, demonstrating that presidents seldom take positions in an effort to influence the outcome of the Court's pending decisions, we do not contend that presidents take positions congruent with the public in an attempt to influence the Court's decisions. Instead, our focus here is on the Court's decided cases.

The president can benefit in three primary ways by taking a position congruent with public support for an issue adjudicated by the Court. First, and as we showed in Chapter 3, presidents can take positions for electoral reasons. Position taking on popular decisions give presidents an opportunity to demonstrate to the public that they share the positions of the majority of the public, which helps build the constituency of electoral support that they need to win reelection. This may be particularly beneficial to presidents as Supreme Court opinions have generally remained salient to the American people over the course of the modern presidency (Collins and Cooper 2012; Epstein and Segal 2000). Simply put, presidents can do much to motivate their electoral bases by speaking about important issues before the Court.

Second, taking positions congruent with the public on popular issues may benefit the president in Congress. As we showed in Chapter 5, presidents occasionally use their public remarks to call on Congress to respond to Supreme Court rulings. Presidents may be able to generate more congressional support for action if their positions mesh with public opinion on the issue, particularly if that issue is salient to the public and Congress.[8] Simply put, an issue that is popular and salient to the American people is more likely to generate a positive legislative response to the president given legislators' obvious electoral incentive to demonstrate that they are responsive to issues on the public's agenda (Canes-Wrone 2006).

Third, presidents can take positions on popular issues to affect news coverage. One of the most enduring factors that affects presidential commentary on Court cases concerns media coverage of those cases. Not only are presidents more likely to comment on cases covered in the news (as we show in Chapters 3 and 4), they are also able to affect the amount of news coverage when they comment on a case (as we show in Chapter 6). By taking positions congruent with the public, presidents may be able to take advantage of favorable news coverage, thus enhancing their standing with the public.

In spite of the potential benefits that come from taking positions that are congruent with public opinion, we do not believe that presidential remarks on the Court's cases will always align with popular opinion. Presidents are strategic actors who consider many factors when they decide to comment on issues, especially on issues over which they have discretion. Because they can choose which issues to address, presidents may find it worthwhile to take positions incongruent with public opinion when doing so can benefit their presidencies. There may be circumstances where taking a position in contrast to the public allows presidents to appear as strong leaders and further their own policy goals, including being consistent with their previously-stated positions on those policies. When applied specifically to policy goals, Canes-Wrone (2006, 105) calls this "policy leadership."[9] That is, presidents take positions not because the public supports them, but because presidents think that they will result in good public policy. Moreover, because there are potential costs to presidents who change their long-held positions on issues after the public expresses a different opinion on those issues, there are many situations where the president may have previously taken a position and advocated in favor of that position in both public and private arenas. Once presidents have taken a position on an issue, it is more difficult for presidents to change that position and so they are unlikely to do so without sufficient justification. Thus, there are likely to be at least some situations in which the president will disagree with the public on Supreme Court decisions.

Research Design

Our goal in this section is to determine the extent to which the positions presidents take on the Court's cases mesh with public opinion. Because we have collected data on every Supreme Court case on which presidents took a position, this seems like a straightforward research design. That is, we can compare all of the positions that presidents took on the Court's decisions to public opinion polls on the same issue area. However, this is complicated by the fact that public opinion polls rarely correspond to the issue areas featured in the Court's decisions, and it is an extremely time consuming task to locate public opinion surveys on the same questions addressed by the Court given the volume of both.

Fortunately for us, Thomas Marshall, the author of several books on public opinion and the Supreme Court (Marshall 1989, 2008), was kind enough to share his data with us. His data contain the universe of public opinion surveys matched to the Court's cases from 1953 to 2017, a total of approximately 600 cases associated with a public opinion poll (Marshall 2018). To match Marshall's data with the data used in this book, we took the following steps. First, we identified those cases found in his lists of Court cases on which there is public opinion data and matched them to cases in our dataset on which presidents took positions. Second, we modified this list to exclude cases that were not decided concurrently with the president's remarks. Since Marshall's polls are contemporaneous to the date of the decision, we only included remarks made by the incumbent president at the time of the decision.[10] This left us with 53 unique cases in which there was both a presidential statement on the case and a public opinion poll on the case.

To capture presidential congruence with the public's opinion about the issue featured in the case, we first determined the public's position on the issue. In nearly all instances, we concluded that the public supported (or opposed) a decision when 50 percent or more of respondents agreed (or disagreed) with the Court's ruling in the case. The two exceptions involved instances in which there was not a majority in support of, or in opposition to, the Court's decision. *Bowsher* v *Synar* (1986), a separation of powers case, registered 66 percent "don't knows," but 16 percent more opposition to, than support for, the outcome. *Reynolds* v. *Sims* (1984), a highly salient legislative districting case, registered 23 percent "don't knows," but 17 percent more support for, than opposition to, the decision. Thus, we included both cases in the data.

Having identified the public's position on each case's outcome, we then matched the positions presidents took on the cases with the public's position on the cases using the data discussed in Chapter 4, with regard to whether the president took a positive or negative position on the Court's decisions. If the president's position matched the public's position, we code this as congruent. If the president's position differed from that of the public, we code this as incongruent. This left us with 40 cases in which we were able to match the president's position on the case at the time the case was decided to public opinion on the case in the same period.[11]

Presidential Responsiveness Results

Figure 7.3 reports presidential congruence with public support for Supreme Court decisions. The black portions of the bars indicate cases in which presidents took positions supported by the public, and the white portions reveal cases in which presidents took positions that differed from the public. Overall, presidents made statements congruent with public opinion 82.5 percent of the time and disagreed with the public only 17.5 percent of the time. On average, presidents agreed with public opinion in their statements on the Court's decisions 2.1 times per term, compared with disagreeing with public opinion 0.44 times per term, a statistically significant difference ($p = 0.01$, one-tailed). Further, only a single president was out of step with public opinion in the majority of his comments. This was Richard Nixon, who spoke out against the Court's decision in *US* v. *Nixon* (1974), against the will of both the Court and the public. This decision was devastating to Nixon, requiring him to turn over tape recordings of sensitive conversations associated with the Watergate investigation, leading to his eventual resignation. For this reason, we provide strong evidence of presidential responsiveness to public attitudes on the Court's cases, indicating that presidents at least in part take public positions on the Court's decisions to show they are responsive to the public's positions.

President Clinton took the most congruent positions on the Court's cases, totaling 12 statements across his two terms. Interestingly, he also made the most incongruent statements, making two remarks that defied public opinion during his second term. These statements pertained to *Pegram* v. *Herdrich* (2000), which involved the Employee Retirement Income Security Act of 1974, and *Washington* v. *Glucksberg* (1997). In *Glucksberg*, the Court considered the constitutionality of Washington State's ban on physician-assisted suicide. The Court ruled in favor of Washington, even though this was at odds with the American people, 65 percent of whom opposed the Court's position. President Clinton supported the Court's decision,[12] which placed him in conflict with

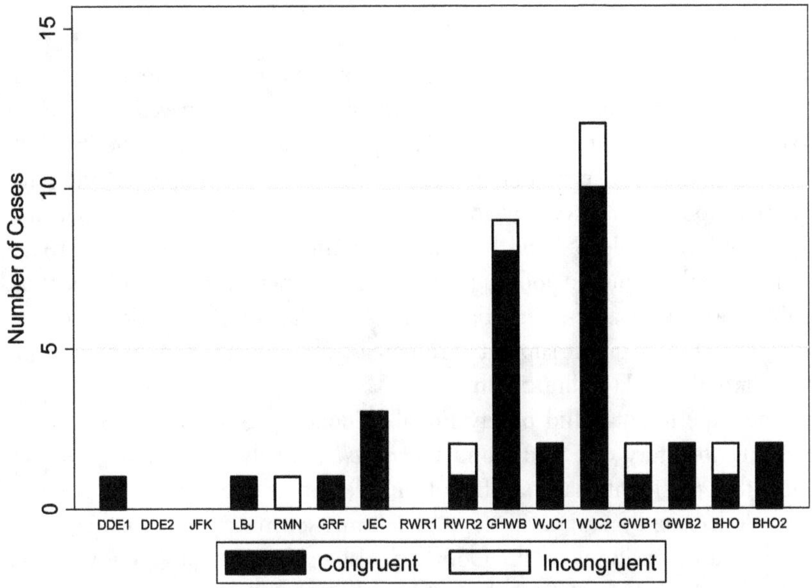

FIGURE 7.3. Presidential congruence with public support for Supreme Court decisions, 1953–2017

the will of the American people, a potentially risky move considering that only 3 percent of the public did not have an opinion on the issue of physician-assisted suicide.

President Obama's repeated discussions of *National Federation of Independent Businesses* v. *Sibelius* (2012) further illustrate a president willing to take a public position that was at odds with public opinion. Obama spent considerable time speaking about the case in the months after it was decided. This, of course, should not be surprising given that the Affordable Care Act was his signature domestic policy achievement. Nevertheless, in so doing, Obama was speaking largely to a skeptical audience as 74 percent of Americans opposed the individual mandate upheld in *Sebelius*. In this way, the president's position aligned with the Court's, but it was out of step with public opinion. Even so, the president was in no position to pander to public opinion on the issue – even though he was in the middle range of job approval and campaigning for reelection – given it was a top priority of his administration. Thus, although presidents generally take positions that are congruent with public opinion, they may defy public opinion in an effort to build support behind their policy priorities.

CONCLUSIONS

As demonstrated in the opening to this chapter, President Obama spent considerable time and energy publicly praising the Court's *Obergefell* decision. In so doing, he was able to attach himself to a position shared by the majority of the American public, 60 percent of whom believed same-sex couples should have the right to marry (McCarthy 2015), thus showing his democratic responsiveness. But was he able to shape the opinions of Americans that opposed marriage equality? Public opinion polls suggest not. Indeed, there was little movement on public support for same-sex marriage in the year following the decision: one year after the decision, public support only increased by 1 percent, within the margin of error of the poll (Gallup 2018b).

The experimental and observational evidence presented in this chapter indicate the story of Obama and *Obergefell* is likely a common one. We show that presidents have a difficult time leading the public to support the Court's decisions on salient issues such as same-sex marriage. Nonetheless, by taking public positions on the Court's decisions that are congruent with the public, presidents can illustrate to the public that they are democratically responsive. This can benefit them electorally and reputationally, as the public expects presidents to comment on issues of national importance and to reflect the public's positions on those issues.

More broadly, this chapter clarifies the effect of presidential statements on public attitudes toward the Court and its decisions. It shows that, consistent with existing work on presidential leadership, presidents have a hard time motivating opinion change on high-salience issues. This suggests that presidents' primary goal in taking public positions on the Court's decisions may not be to affect attitude change in the public. Rather, presidents may take public positions to demonstrate to the public that they are responsive to important issues (as we showed in Chapters 3 and 4), and the public's preferences on those issues. This implies that, at least on high-profile issues, presidents may be following, rather than leading, public opinion on the Court's decisions. Although we also show that presidents can shape public opinion on low-salience issues before the Court, taking positions on low-salience cases is not a common strategy for presidents, as shown in Chapters 3 and 4. It is therefore unlikely that presidents would take positions on relatively obscure cases in an effort to shape public opinion on low-salience issues.

This chapter also speaks to the president's role in the coordinate construction of the Constitution. As we have shown throughout this book, presidents do not shy away from taking public positions on important issues implicated in the Court's decisions. In so doing, they contribute to the constitutional dialogue that takes place among the three branches of government. However, this chapter reveals that their ability to effectuate public attitude change is limited to low-salience cases. Although our experimental survey does not directly address whether presidents are capable of shaping public dialogue on the Court's cases, the results nonetheless provide evidence that this may be a difficult task on issues highly salient to the American public. Moreover, our findings in this chapter indicate that presidents overwhelmingly take positions consistent with the public's preferences on the Court's decisions. This suggests that, to the extent presidents can influence public debate on constitutional issues, it may be to primarily reinforce already existing beliefs, particularly on high-salient issues. Considered in light of evidence that the Court can influence public attitudes toward salient issues (e.g., Franklin and Kosaki 1989; Hoekstra 2000, 2003; Hoekstra and Segal 1996; Johnson and Martin 1998; Linos and Twist 2016), this chapter suggests presidents may play a more limited role than the Court in influencing the public's constitutional understandings.

APPENDIX TABLE 7.1. *Randomization analysis from survey experiment*

	Wetlands			Immigration		
	Praise	Control	Criticize	Praise	Control	Criticize
Democrat	0.36	0.38	0.49	0.46	0.45	0.46
Republican	0.27	0.28	0.25	0.24	0.29	0.24
Independent	0.29	0.31	0.23	0.26	0.23	0.27
White	0.79	0.75	0.85	0.72	0.83	0.78
Black	0.08	0.10	0.05	0.15	0.05	0.06
Hispanic	0.02	0.02	0.01	0.02	0.02	0.01
Asian	0.05	0.11	0.06	0.07	0.03	0.08
Male	0.53	0.53	0.52	0.59	0.46	0.56
Age	38.9	37.6	38.6	38.5	40.8	39.1
High School	0.17	0.09	0.11	0.11	0.12	0.10
Some College	0.15	0.23	0.22	0.19	0.25	0.23
College Graduate	0.68	0.69	0.67	0.70	0.63	0.67
N	146	151	150	149	153	153

Entries are the means for each variable. The following differences are statistically significant at $p \leq 0.05$ (two-tailed): blacks receiving the immigration praise and immigration control treatments; blacks receiving the immigration praise and immigration criticize treatments; Democrats in the wetlands praise and wetlands criticize treatments; high school in the wetlands praise and wetlands control treatments; Asians in the wetlands praise and wetlands control treatments. As a whole, 5 of the 72 pairwise comparisons were significantly different, corresponding to 6.9 percent of observations, slightly higher than the randomness expected from chance at 0.05 level (Clark and Kastellec 2015, 529).

APPENDIX TABLE 7.2. *Influences on specific and diffuse support for the Supreme Court*

	Specific Support		Diffuse Support	
	Wetlands Protection	Immigration	Wetlands Protection	Immigration
Praise	0.31[a]	0.21	0.10	−0.12
	(0.14)	(0.20)	(0.15)	(0.16)
Criticize	−0.58[a]	−0.10	0.23	−0.17
	(0.17)	(0.21)	(0.15)	(0.16)
Democrat	0.38[a]	−1.15[a]	0.51[a]	0.34[a]
	(0.16)	(0.21)	(0.15)	(0.16)
Republican	−0.25	1.44[a]	0.20	0.31[a]
	(0.19)	(0.20)	(0.16)	(0.18)
White	0.24	−0.08	−0.39	−0.01
	(0.32)	(0.38)	(0.28)	(0.28)
Black	0.41	−0.17	−0.34	0.72[a]
	(0.39)	(0.46)	(0.35)	(0.34)
Hispanic	−0.10	−0.47	−1.00[a]	0.02
	(0.64)	(0.82)	(0.53)	(0.46)
Asian	−0.07	0.16	−0.36	0.15
	(0.41)	(0.47)	(0.35)	(0.36)
Male	−0.26[a]	−0.32[a]	−0.16	0.14
	(0.13)	(0.17)	(0.12)	(0.14)
Age	0.00	0.01	−0.04[a]	−0.03[a]
	(0.00)	(0.01)	(0.01)	(0.01)
Some College	0.36	−0.10	−0.14	−0.43[a]
	(0.26)	(0.28)	(0.23)	(0.23)
College Graduate	0.48[a]	−0.04	−0.34[a]	−0.41[a]
	(0.22)	(0.24)	(0.21)	(0.20)
Constant	4.84[a]	4.25[a]	5.51[a]	5.07[a]
	(0.44)	(0.50)	(0.38)	(0.39)
R^2	0.11	0.28	0.15	0.13
N	447	455	447	455

Note: Entries are ordinary least squares regression coefficients. The dependent variable is support for the Court's decision (specific support) or the Court as an institution (diffuse support), both on a 1–7 scale. Robust standard errors are reported in parentheses. [a]$p \leq .05$ (one-tailed tests).

8

Going Public on Supreme Court Cases before the Modern Presidency

President Franklin Delano Roosevelt had a combative relationship with the Supreme Court. Perhaps most famously, Roosevelt so disagreed with the Court's rulings related to the constitutionality of his New Deal policies that he proposed to create additional seats on the Court and "pack" them with justices sympathetic to his economic policy goals (Leuchtenburg 1966). Although this plan never came to fruition, it illustrates Roosevelt's contempt for the Court and his willingness to take actions that violate the norm of judicial independence and undermine the judicial branch. This included aiming some particularly harsh language at the Court, such as this gem from a Fireside Chat in March of 1937: "We have . . . reached the point as a Nation where we must take action to save the Constitution from the Court and the Court from itself. We must find a way to take an appeal from the Supreme Court to the Constitution itself. We want a Supreme Court which will do justice under the Constitution – not over it. In our Courts we want a government of laws and not of men."[1]

Interestingly though, when afforded an opportunity to attempt to direct the outcome of a pending case by making his position clear to the justices and the public, Roosevelt was much more timid. For example, after a reporter asked whether his plans for labor relations reform were dependent on the Court's pending decision in *NLRB* v. *Jones & Laughlin Steel Corp* (1937), Roosevelt replied with a succinct "no," rather than using the question as an opportunity to stake a clear position on the case.[2] Considering the extent to which Roosevelt criticized the Court on matters related to cases involving his other economic policies (Blackstone and Goelzhauser 2014), it might be a surprise that the president restrained himself in this instance.[3]

As we show in this chapter, Roosevelt's refusal to discuss a pending Court case was consistent with the actions of other historical presidents. Indeed, of the very small number of instances in which historical presidents remarked on pending Court decisions, none of them ever took a position on a pending case. Although modern presidents have also not discussed pending cases with any great frequency, they have much more often taken positions when afforded an opportunity to talk about a pending case. In fact, modern presidents have taken positions 74 percent of the time in which they discussed yet undecided cases on the Court's agenda. This comparison shows one way that historical and modern presidents differ in their approaches to addressing Supreme Court cases.

The purpose of this chapter is to further our understanding of presidential rhetoric on the Court's cases by exploring this phenomenon from Washington to Truman. To be clear, we do not expect historical presidential references to Court cases to be extensive for two primary reasons. First, because going public was an infrequently employed strategy prior to the modern era (Laracey 2002; Tulis 1987), it follows that presidents would rarely take public positions on the Court's cases. Second, the relationship between the presidency and the judiciary was rudimentary for much of the nineteenth century, in part because the Court rarely made decisions that either contradicted executive branch preferences or overturned acts of Congress (Scigliano 1971; Whittington 2001). Thus, presidents would have had few reasons to target Court cases with their written or spoken statements.

Nevertheless, exploring the historical side of presidential rhetoric on Supreme Court cases is important to paint a comprehensive picture of this subject. It will also allow us to speak to two significant points related to both going public and executive-judicial relations. First, we know that historical presidents went public in ways that differed from modern presidents (Laracey 2002). This chapter thus helps us to understand whether and to what extent historical characterizations of going public extend to presidential references to Supreme Court cases. Second, one of the goals of this book is to contribute to our understanding of the extent to which presidents engage in the coordinate construction of the Constitution. Looking at historical presidencies will help us to ascertain how the presidents' role in fostering constitutional understandings may have changed over time, and how this relates to presidential perspectives regarding the norm of judicial independence.

Extending our work from previous chapters, we examine presidential speeches from the country's founding through the Truman administration (1789–1953). We study all instances in which presidents made both spoken and written remarks on Supreme Court cases. Given that his administration devoted substantial attention to the Supreme Court (e.g., Blackstone and Goelzhauser 2014; Holland 2004), our analysis pays particular attention to remarks made by Franklin Roosevelt. We find that, as expected, going public on the Court's cases was not a common rhetorical strategy during this time. When presidents did reference the Court's cases, they overwhelmingly discussed the Court's decided cases, but rarely criticized those decisions prior to the Franklin Roosevelt administration. Thus, this chapter demonstrates how historical presidencies are both similar to, and different from, modern presidencies when it comes to rhetoric toward the Supreme Court.

PRESIDENTIAL RHETORIC AND THE SUPREME COURT IN THE HISTORICAL ERA

As we discussed in the introduction of this book, our understanding of presidential rhetoric on the Supreme Court is limited and tends to focus primarily on the president's role in the nomination of federal judges. This is particularly true with regard to examining how historical presidents have discussed the Court. Similarly, like most scholarship on the presidency, there is much more research regarding the ways modern presidents go public relative to historical presidents. This does not mean, however, that researchers have shied away from exploring the early public presidency. Rather, scholars have demonstrated that going public was a feature of early presidential administrations (Laracey 2002) and that presidential rhetoric has changed over time (Tulis 1987). Moreover, Scigliano's (1971) account of the presidency and the Court describes in detail the interrelationship between the executive and judicial branches from Jefferson to Franklin Roosevelt. We briefly review existing research on historical presidential rhetoric on the Supreme Court, which centers primarily on judicial nominations, Roosevelt's Court-packing plan, and presidential conflicts with the Court.

Judicial Nominations

Much historical research on presidential interactions with the Court centers on the judicial nomination process. For example, Abraham (2008) and Gerhardt (2000) provide comprehensive overviews of the strategies used by presidents, including using public rhetoric, to help to ensure the confirmation of their federal court nominees. Yet, these works devote the majority of their attention to the confirmation process since the Franklin Roosevelt Administration. Other work that explores the selection of federal judges also tends to stop short of a full treatment of all presidents throughout history. Goldman's (1997) classic book on federal court appointments, for example, begins with Franklin Roosevelt, noting that this president's policy agenda was a top reason for selecting circuit court judges.

Cameron and Park (2011) examine presidents on the earlier side of the modern presidency, including Hoover, Franklin Roosevelt, and Truman, but similarly do not offer a comprehensive look into what we consider the historical presidency. They also speak to the differences in how these presidents went public (or did not) to affect the confirmation of their Supreme Court nominees. For instance, despite their overall conclusion that presidents go public when their nominees are in danger of losing confirmation, Hoover did not follow this strategy when his nomination of John J. Parker was in danger of defeat due to strong interest group opposition. Although Cameron and Park refrain from answering why Hoover remained silent on this nominee, it is likely that he did so because going public on judicial nominees was not yet considered to be a fruitful or appropriate strategy for presidential leadership, much as going public on legislation was uncommon until the later twentieth century (Tulis 1987). This is not to say that presidents were unconcerned about the success of their nominations. Rather, this work reveals that early presidents did not go public to affect Senate votes, likely because this was not yet an established strategy of presidential leadership. Prior to Reagan – and as illustrated in the case of Judge Parker – interest groups and private lobbying were the primary vehicles to pressure senators over nominations (Maltese 1995a). For example, Nixon did not go public frequently to affect the nomination of Clement Haynesworth. Rather, the White House lobbied senators behind the scenes in a manner very similar to using a legislative liaison to increase support for a policy priority in Congress. Reagan marked the beginning of an entrenched strategy of heightened public attention to judicial nominees, with an increase in speeches when the nominees were in danger of losing (Maltese 1995a, 113).

Roosevelt's Court-Packing Plan

Among studies of historical presidents' interactions with the judiciary, a great deal of research has focused on Franklin Roosevelt's Court-packing plan (e.g., Caldeira 1987; Holland 2004; Leuchtenburg 1966; McKenna 2002; McMahon 2004; Nelson 1988). Although Roosevelt's Court-packing rhetoric was generated in response to what he perceived to be unfavorable decisions by the Supreme Court in cases such as *United States* v. *Butler* (1936), in which the Court struck down the Agricultural Adjustment Act, Roosevelt did not often speak directly about the Court's decisions (Leuchtenburg 1966). Rather, his rhetoric tended to be more general, focusing on what he saw as a judicial branch that was reaching beyond its constitutional authority (Blackstone and Goelzhauser 2014). Thus, much of Roosevelt's public remarks in this era represent an institutional struggle between the Court and the president, whereby the Court-packing plan would rebalance the relative power of the three federal branches, enhancing the presidency while simultaneously diminishing that of Congress and the Supreme Court (McMahon 2004: 69; Whittington 2001). Moreover, Roosevelt did not tie the issues most important to his presidency to the Court until his 1936 reelection campaign (Nelson 1988), something that modern presidents regularly do when they reference Supreme Court cases, as we have demonstrated. Ultimately, Roosevelt was unsuccessful at convincing Congress and the American people of the merits of his Court-packing plan, despite his public rhetoric, his relative popularity, and Democratic control of Congress (Scigliano 1971, 55).

Presidential Conflicts with the Court

In addition to Franklin Roosevelt's battles with the Court, other presidents have conflicted with the judicial branch, often over the scope of presidential power vis-à-vis the Court (Whitttington 2001, 2007). For example, Scigliano (1971, chapter 2) recounts how Thomas Jefferson disagreed with Federalist Chief Justice John Marshall concerning the Court's power of judicial review; Andrew Jackson resisted enforcing the Supreme Court's ruling involving tribal sovereignty in *Worcester* v. *Georgia* (1932); and Abraham Lincoln preferred a much broader interpretation of his authority to suspend the writ of habeas corpus than the Court granted him. Yet, among these presidents, none publicly admonished the Court regarding their decisions related to these issues. Scigliano (1971, 35) explains, for example, "that Jefferson never openly acted or spoke against the judicial branch, or any decision rendered by it ... His criticisms and other comments were confined to his private correspondence." Similarly, even if Jackson made his oft-quoted statement that "John Marshall has made his decision. Now let him enforce it" in response to *Worcester* v. *Georgia* (which does not seem to be the case), it is attributed to being part of a private correspondence, rather than a public remark (Boller and George 1989, 53; Greeley 1864, 106). Further, Lincoln, who repeatedly criticized the Court's *Dred Scott* v. *Sandford* (1857) decision, which held that slaves were not citizens within the meaning of the Constitution, on the campaign trail, chose not to call out the decision directly as president. Instead, Lincoln framed his battles with the Court in general terms relating to the authority of the Court to interpret the Constitution vis-à-vis the other branches of government (Paulsen 2008). Thus, although presidents have been in conflict with the Court throughout American history, that conflict does not appear to have been revealed to the public via the president's remarks on the Court's cases until Franklin Roosevelt. Instead, historical presidents' public references to the

Court have primarily involved other issues, most notably their appointments of Supreme Court justices (Blackstone and Goelzhauser 2014, 184).

GOING PUBLIC BY HISTORICAL PRESIDENTS

Extending the theoretical framework used throughout this book, we maintain that presidents, including historical presidents, pursue three primary goals while in office: good public policy, reelection, and historical achievement (Canes-Wrone 2001; Light 1999; Moe 1985). In turn, presidents use their legitimate power and authority to realize these goals. Even though historical presidents did not go public to the same extent as modern presidents, they have nonetheless used their public speeches to achieve their goals (Laracey 2002). Indeed, there is evidence that modern and historical presidencies are more similar than most research has led us to believe (Teten 2008). This suggests that it is plausible that eighteenth-, nineteenth-, and early twentieth-century presidents not only shared comparable goals, but also used similar means to achieve them. If so, then even historical presidents would have had reason to address Supreme Court cases to the extent that those cases related to their goals as chief executive. Since the Court is often the final arbiter of the law in the American system of separated powers, it can bolster or counteract presidential policy making. Consequently, the Court's decisions present presidents with ample occasions to comment on the Court's docket as they pursue their own goals.

Our chief goals in this chapter are to investigate how often historical presidents discuss Supreme Court decisions in their public statements, whether they primarily comment on pending or decided cases, the issue areas of the cases they discuss, and the tone of their remarks on those decisions. To explore this, we first develop our understanding of how presidents went public prior to the rise of the modern presidency. Although most work on going public involves the modern presidency, historical presidents also issued public remarks or wrote public statements as they governed. Some of these, such as Lincoln's Gettysburg Address, are seen as particularly important representations of historical presidencies. Second, we provide an overview of the president's relationship to the Supreme Court in the historical era, including a treatment of how presidential views of the norm of judicial independence may have changed over time.

Public Rhetoric by Historical Presidents

The theory of going public is based on the idea that presidents use public speeches and other activities to achieve their goals as chief executive. This involves speaking in an effort to motivate the public to influence Congress (Kernell 1997), inspiring bureaucrats to implement policy (Eshbaugh-Soha 2006), or influencing news coverage of their administration, among other activities (Cohen 2010). Yet, much of our understanding of public leadership is grounded in the modern presidency, during a time in which changing institutional conditions and improving technology drove presidents to build public support for their presidencies, and centralize public leadership in the White House.

There is evidence that nineteenth- and early twentieth-century presidents viewed public leadership differently. Central to this line of thinking is the work of Tulis (1987, 2000), who conceives of presidential rhetoric in two phases or "constitutions." In the first phase, presidents were constrained by the US Constitution. The framers actively discouraged public leadership, fearing that a charismatic leader might engage in demagoguery and undermine the new Federalist republic that shunned public appeals by its leaders. Thus, not only did earlier presidents deliver written, and not spoken, messages to Congress, the framers also devised the Electoral College so that the masses would not directly elect the president. Barring any need to directly appeal to the public in an election, presidents had few incentives to deliver public speeches. Moreover, the lack of an efficient vehicle to speak nationally (such as radio or television) and the absence of the necessary institutional resources to write and deliver daily speeches (such as the Office of Communications) were also impediments to a more expansive public presidency in the nineteenth century.

This does not mean that historical presidents failed to go public. The methods and the incentives presidents had to communicate publicly differ from the current era, to be sure. But prominent research is clear that historical presidents went public to achieve their goals and spoke specifically about important policy issues facing their presidencies. Even without modern communications technologies, Laracey (2002) demonstrates how nineteenth-century presidents, such as Jefferson and Jackson, regularly communicated their policies to the American people through partisan newspapers. Presidents used other means to go public, as well. President Lincoln, for example, liked to express his views through either policy speeches or written letters (Laracey 2009). President Cleveland's published letter about the Sherman Silver Purchase Act was designed to cultivate public support for his position (Hoffman 2002). President Taylor made a series of public speeches during his 1849 tour of the northeastern United States. He covered both domestic policy topics, like slavery, and foreign policy concerns, such as the acquisition of Cuba (Ellis and Walker 2007).

The idea that historical presidents would publicize their administrations, regardless of the means of communication, is not as unusual as Tulis (1987) appears to have suggested. Even though he portrayed the "first constitution" as being devoid of public outreach, others show that presidents did go public. Reaching out to the American people may have been inconsistent with some of the framers' views of the role of the presidency, but it is consistent with anti-federalist ideals of government by the common person, and is reflected in popular support for the election of Andrew Jackson as president (Laracey 2002). Surely, the ways in which presidents go public have evolved over time. Indeed, the early days of Tulis's (1987) "second constitution" reveal the evolution of the presidency into an institution that relies on popular appeals and more spoken and shorter remarks. Even though they were not the first presidents to do so (e.g. Ellis and Walker 2007; Hoffman 2002), Theodore Roosevelt and Woodrow Wilson both engaged in public activities to promote their presidencies and policy priorities, and did so more frequently than their predecessors. In fact, one can see several parallels between historical and modern efforts at going public given that both historical and modern presidents relied primarily on reaching the public through newspapers (Laracey 2002) or on varied media given the difficulty presidents have speaking to the public directly (Edwards 2003). So, despite the obvious differences in how presidents might appeal to the public, their efforts to reach the public may have been similarly constrained.[4] Therefore, although evidence suggests that historical presidents did not go public as often as modern presidents – and did so through different means – they still communicated publicly as a means to achieve their goals.[5]

Going Public on Supreme Court Decisions

Applying our understanding of going public among historical presidents to presidential discussions of Supreme Court cases presents a different dilemma. Even though historical presidents went public occasionally to speak about or influence policy, they did not do so as frequently as modern presidents have. Moreover, by focusing on a single type of presidential rhetoric – that involving remarks regarding Supreme Court decisions – we further reduce the number of presidential statements that we might evaluate. This is particularly true since the time period we examine (1789–1953) was an era in which the Court and its decisions were not considered to be as important as they would become in the mid- to late twentieth century (Epstein and Segal 2000, 74).

The lack of public attention to Supreme Court vacancies helps to illustrate this point. The Senate Judiciary Committee did not even begin the practice of holding open public hearings on all Supreme Court nominations before the 1955 nomination of John Harlan (Collins and Ringhand 2013). Furthermore, only rarely were Supreme Court nominations discussed publicly before 1929, as a two-thirds vote was required to move nomination hearings out of the closed-door executive session (Maltese 1995a). Along with the politicization of the Supreme Court came more public attention to the hearings and efforts by presidents to affect those nominations by going public (Maltese 1995a). Indeed, the growing public importance of the Court in American democracy resulted in an increase in presidential speeches regarding both nominations (Cameron and Park 2011) and Supreme Court decisions (Eshbaugh-Soha and Collins 2015).

Again, the bulk of research on going public and the rhetorical presidency in the nineteenth century centers on public speeches that do not reference the Supreme Court specifically.[6] This line of research – like the going public literature of the modern era – focuses on presidential speeches targeted at other political institutions or the American people. To repeat a point made previously: we simply do not know whether historical presidents have spoken about Supreme Court cases, even though it is clear that historical presidents did go public in their own ways to target other institutions and the public. It is plausible that since presidents used their public papers and speeches to affect other aspects of governance, they also used them to discuss Supreme Court cases. Of course, because historical presidents went public less frequently than their modern counterparts, we expect to see that historic presidents devoted less attention to the Court's cases than modern presidents.

In addition to the reality that historical presidents made fewer public appeals than modern presidents, there is one feature that might further limit historical presidents from mentioning the Court in their public rhetoric: the norm of judicial independence. This norm holds that the justices should be free to render their decisions absent from interference from the president or Congress (Reddish 1995). Given limited presidential attention to the Court and the absence of a public spotlight on judicial nominations, there is reason to believe that the norm of judicial independence was stronger during earlier eras of American history than it is today. In earlier eras, presidents chose to air their grievances regarding the Court's decisions in private, rather than in public speeches (Scigliano 1971). This suggests that historical presidents took strides to avoid violating the norm of judicial independence in their public rhetoric, in the fear that doing so could hurt their reelections, ability to make public policy, and historical legacies. Even so, it is likely that in those few instances where presidents saw the Court's decisions as relevant to their goals as president, that they would discuss those decisions in their public statements.

Although Scigliano (1971) provides evidence that historic presidents preferred discussing the Court's decisions in private, Franklin Roosevelt broke this trend by publicly criticizing the Court and its decisions in a series of speeches intended to garner congressional and public support for his Court-packing plan (Caldeira 1987). Prior to his presidency, presidents appeared to have had little interest in discussing the Court's decisions in their public rhetoric, choosing instead to use private correspondence to do so. But, the Franklin Roosevelt Administration may have ushered in a new era in which the Court's decisions were fair game for discussion in presidents' public speeches (McMahon 2004). We now turn to bringing empirical evidence to bear on this possibility.

DATA

Our database of historical presidential comments on Supreme Court cases follows the same coding scheme we used to collect data on presidential remarks since 1953, as discussed in Chapter 1. After identifying all Supreme Court cases historical presidents mentioned in their public speeches, we evaluated whether the president spoke about the case before or after the Court issued its ruling based on the date of the speech and the date the decision was handed down according to Spaeth et al. (2017). In addition, merging our data with the Spaeth et al. (2017) database of historical cases also allows us to examine the issue areas of the cases that historical presidents discussed, and to compare those to the issue areas in the cases featured in the statements of modern presidents.

We also coded the tone of presidential remarks on decided cases, following the coding rubric discussed in Chapter 4. Positive comments expresses praise, confidence in, or agreement with the Court's decisions. Negative remarks are critical of or offer disagreement with the Court's decisions. Neutral comments include discussions of cases in which presidents do not take a clear negative or positive position on the case or offer a mix of positive and negative comments.

Consistent with the approach taken throughout this book, we restrict our analysis to the presidents' public remarks. This means that we do not include presidential discussions of Supreme Court cases that appear in private, such as correspondences. As noted above, we have reason to believe that discussing the Court's cases in private may be a characteristic of historical presidents. Scigliano (1971, 48–49) contends, for example, that Franklin Roosevelt privately considered attacking the Supreme Court if its rulings in the *Gold*

Clause Cases (1935), which involved the constitutionality of congressional legislation abrogating clauses in public and private contracts requiring the payment of gold, went against the government's position. And even though the president had crafted a radio address to defy the Court's rulings, he never delivered it because the Court did not rule against the president's position. Having said this, even if private remarks were particularly revealing about a president's opinions about the Court's decisions, examining these private papers is beyond the scope of our analysis. After all, we are primarily interested in public remarks that can potentially help the president achieve several goals as president, including affecting the implementation of decisions, engendering public support or opposition to cases, influencing the public's view of the Constitution, and helping to build a historical legacy. Presidential efforts to criticize or praise the Court's decisions in private suggest a different set of goals than the ones we have identified as being central to the president's motivation for issuing public remarks on Supreme Court cases. The president's private remarks are also likely targeted to a different audience, although we remain agnostic as to the specific target or motivation for writing private memos related to the Supreme Court.

Although we look at the presidents' public statements, most of these were not in the form of spoken remarks, as is the case with modern presidents. Written comments were much more common among historical public statements, which reflects the norm of communication during the nineteenth century. They also underscore different motivations for presidential comments on Supreme Court cases when compared with modern presidents. As we have shown throughout the book, modern presidents speak more frequently than they write about cases. Not only does this illustrate greater responsiveness to matters of public concern, it also shows that modern presidents have intended to act more democratically than their predecessors, whether as a vehicle to respond to the public's policy preferences or as a means to generate support for their much more public reelection campaigns.

EMPIRICAL RESULTS

We begin by examining the amount of attention presidents devoted to the Court's cases throughout the entire historical era, which we conceive of as 1789 through 1953. We then discuss the issues involved in these cases and make comparisons with modern presidents. Next, we present the tone of presidential remarks on the Court's cases. Given the volume of attention Franklin Roosevelt devoted to the Court in his public rhetoric (Blackstone and

Goelzhauser 2014), we pay special attention to the tone of Roosevelt's comments in his combative relationship with the Court.

Presidential Attention to Supreme Court Cases

Figure 8.1 reports the number of remarks historical presidents made on decided and pending cases. The black portion of the bars indicates the number of times presidents discussed decided cases, and the white portion of the bars provide this information for pending decisions. There are several notable features of this graph that paint a broad picture of the nature of public commentary concerning Supreme Court cases from the Washington to Truman Administrations. First, only about half of presidents mentioned a Supreme Court case in their public rhetoric, with Andrew Jackson being the first president to do so. Of these, nine presidents mentioned only a single case in a single speech. In all, these presidents mentioned cases a total of 124 times, ranging from a low of one to a high of 53 for Franklin Roosevelt. These findings are vastly different from those related to modern presidents. The 937 Supreme Court cases mentioned by modern presidents represents almost a 650 percent increase over presidents who governed prior to 1953.

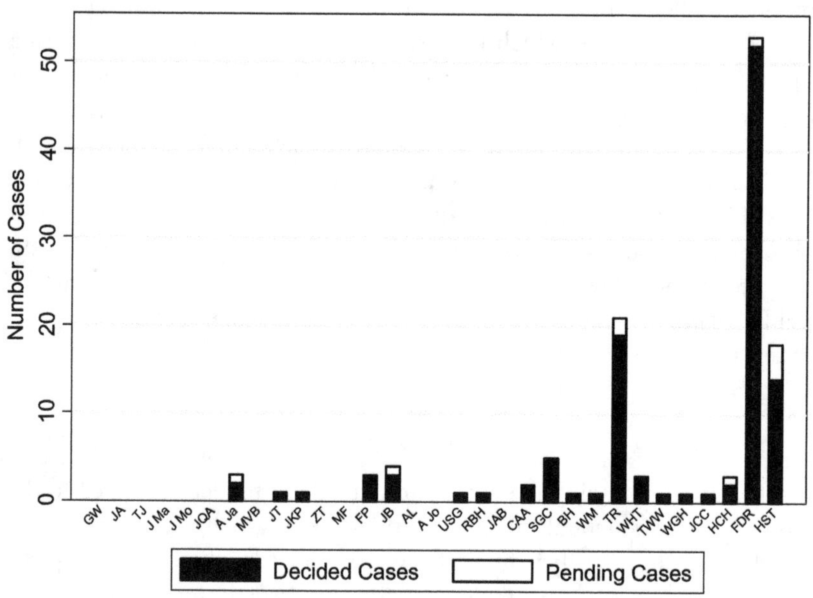

FIGURE 8.1. Number of presidential comments on US Supreme Court cases, 1789–1953

Excluding Franklin Roosevelt's 53 mentions reveals 71 presidential comments on Supreme Court cases made by the remaining 18 presidents who issued a public remark on a Court case. Thus, no matter how one views the data, attention devoted to Supreme Court decisions in public speeches by modern presidents positively dwarfs that of their predecessors. This is a function of the realities that presidents were not as publicly active during this period and that the Court had not yet begun weighing as much into substantive matters of public policy in the field of civil rights and liberties, compared with the modern era.

Second, the vast majority of speeches devoted to cases involve discussions of already decided cases. Indeed, only 10 speeches (8 percent) involved presidents discussing a pending case; in the remaining 114 speeches presidents referred to decisions the Court had already handed down.[7] This finding is in line with our results presented in Chapter 1 concerning modern presidents, which also revealed that modern presidents overwhelmingly discussed decided, and not pending, cases. In fact, the discussion of pending cases is quite similar for historic and modern presidents, at 8 percent and 6 percent of all comments on the Court's cases, respectively. This indicates a longstanding concern for the norm of judicial independence, which suggests that it is unfitting for presidents to attempt to influence the pending decisions of the Court through their public rhetoric. However, one notable difference is that no historical president actually took a position on a pending case. Rather, they discussed them generally. Conversely, modern presidents took positions on pending cases 74 percent of the time in their discussions of yet undecided cases, clearly revealing a break in tradition from their historical counterparts.

Third, along with Franklin Roosevelt, the presidencies of Theodore Roosevelt and Harry Truman are clear exceptions to the minimalist approach adopted by other historical presidents. Theodore Roosevelt spoke 21 times about cases decided by the Supreme Court, including references to two pending cases. Truman also dedicated the bulk of his attention to decided cases, discussing them on 14 occasions, but also referencing three pending cases in four speeches. This is not to say that Truman was particularly aggressive in mentioning these pending cases. On the contrary, each of Truman's comments about pending Court cases were responses to reporters' questions in press conferences. Truman's remarks in each instance were brief and involved little more than a statement of "no comment." In other words, although Truman did respond to reporters' questions about pending cases, in no instance did he take a public position on those cases. Finally, Franklin Roosevelt spoke much more frequently than other historical presidents, discussing Supreme Court cases 53 times, with only a single speech mentioning a pending case. Since Franklin Roosevelt is such an outlier, we devote special attention to his speeches. Here we turn to a more detailed discussion of Theodore Roosevelt and Harry Truman.

It makes sense that the Theodore Roosevelt and Truman presidencies would stand out in comparison with their historical counterparts. First, Theodore Roosevelt is considered the first pre-modern president, coining the "bully pulpit" phrase, and speaking as a surrogate of the American people (Edwards 2003). In short, he was truly the first president to engage in what we might consider the modern act of going public. Second, Truman governed after Franklin Roosevelt and during a time of increasing judicial activity, particularly in the field of civil rights and liberties (Epstein et al. 1994, 74–75). Although not all of Truman's remarks referenced cases related to issues such as segregation, he was asked to comment on several cases pending in the Court, though he refused to do so. Truman also referenced Supreme Court decisions concerning offshore oil drilling to criticize Republican presidential candidate Dwight Eisenhower (although not by name). Perhaps surprisingly, Truman commented on *Youngstown Sheet & Tube Company* v. *Sawyer* (1952), in which the Court rejected his attempts to seize American steel mills as part of the ongoing Korean War, only once. However, this discussion came in an unusual message to Congress that focused solely on explaining his decision-making concerning the steel strike, which led to the Court's ruling.[8]

Finally, the distribution of written and spoken remarks follows our expectations (results not shown). Overall, over 63 percent (78 out of 124 total references) of presidents' comments on the Court's decisions were written, as opposed to spoken. This is consistent with our belief that historical presidents would issue more written than spoken comments on Court cases given the style of nineteenth-century presidential communication, which involved fewer, but longer, written remarks. Indeed, the vast majority of presidential comments on cases made during the nineteenth century were written, and all but two of 23 comments made by presidents before Theodore Roosevelt were written. Although twentieth-century presidents also issued a fair share of written comments on the Court's cases, both Franklin Roosevelt and Harry Truman spoke frequently about cases, too. Of the 46 spoken remarks by all historical presidents, these two presidents issued 41 of them.

The Issue Areas of Cases Mentioned by Presidents

Table 8.1 reports the issue areas of the cases historical and modern presidents have discussed in their public rhetoric, based on the typology of cases found in

TABLE 8.1. *The most frequently addressed Supreme Court case issue areas by historical and modern presidents, 1789–2017*

Historical Presidents (1789–1953)	Modern Presidents (1953–2017)
Economic Activity (30.1)	Civil Rights (29.7)
Federal Taxation (22.6)	First Amendment (19.1)
Civil Rights (16.9)	Privacy (11.7)
Judicial Power (11.3)	Miscellaneous (9.6)
Federalism (4.8)	Criminal Procedure (8.8)
Unions (4.0)	Federalism (8.5)
Miscellaneous (4.0)	Due Process (3.4)
Criminal Procedure (2.4)	Economic Activity (3.1)
First Amendment (1.6)	Judicial Power (2.9)
Due Process (1.6)	Unions (1.7)
	Federal Taxation (1.2)
	Interstate Relations (0.2)

The numbers in parentheses indicate the overall percentage for each issue area. Numbers may not sum to 100 due to rounding.

Spaeth et al. (2017, 2018). As this table reveals, there are some stark differences between historical and modern presidents. Perhaps most notably, historical presidents commented on economic and tax issues much more frequently than modern presidents. Indeed, more than 50 percent of historical presidents' remarks relate to cases involving economic activity and federal taxation, compared with only 4 percent for modern presidents. Conversely, modern presidents devoted substantial attention to matters of civil rights and liberties compared to historical presidents. More than 70 percent of modern presidents' remarks were on cases involving civil rights, the First Amendment, privacy, criminal procedure, and due process, compared with only 23 percent for historical presidents.

We believe that these findings reflect the role the Supreme Court was playing in society at the time of the presidents' speeches, the importance of various issues to the American public, and presidents' responsiveness to those issues. For instance, in the modern era, the Court is a key player in civil rights and liberties disputes, which are highly salient to the public. Thus, it is not surprising that modern presidents frequently discuss civil rights and liberties cases. In contrast, prior to the Warren Court, the justices played a much more active role in economic matters, which were particularly salient to the public, especially during the beginning of the twentieth century (Pacelle 1991). For example, Theodore Roosevelt frequently referenced economic disputes such as the *Employers' Liability Cases* (1908), which determined that the Employers' Liability Act was unconstitutional. Interestingly, Roosevelt was decidedly neutral in his comments regarding these cases, despite the fact that economic regulation was central to his policy agenda (Goldman 1997). Similarly, historical presidencies often referenced cases involving federal taxation during periods in which the nation's tax policies were expanding. Most of these remarks took place during the tenure of Franklin Roosevelt, including references to *United States* v. *Butler* (1936), which declared the Agricultural Adjustment Act unconstitutional and was referenced by Roosevelt more than a dozen times. Of the civil rights and liberties cases referenced by historical presidents, many involved issues relating to slavery, which was dividing the nation, including James Buchanan's four remarks on the Court's *Dred Scott* decision.

In all, it is evident that topics of the cases referenced by historical and modern presidents follow the salient issues facing the nation. Theodore Roosevelt referenced anti-trust cases in conjunction with his efforts, and the nation's move, toward greater regulation of big business. Franklin Roosevelt challenged the Court's rulings regarding economic and taxation issues, both of which were central to the nation's struggles during the Great Depression. James Buchanan wrote about *Dred Scott* given its obvious importance to slavery, the most important issue facing the nation during his presidency. This is consistent with our analysis of modern presidents in Chapters 3 and 4, which showed that they too are attentive to the salient issues facing American society. This suggests that that both historical and modern presidents discuss Supreme Court decisions in part to show their democratic responsiveness to issues of national concern.

The Tone of Presidential Commentary

Figure 8.2 reports the tone used by historical presidents in their discussions of the Court's cases. The white portions of the bars indicate positive tone; the black portions reveal negative tone; and the gray portions report neutral tone. Overall, most comments made by historical presidents were neutral in nature, at 41 percent of remarks. Presidents delivered a roughly equal amount of negative and positive comments, making up about 30 percent and 29 percent of their statements, respectively.

Neutral comments were particularly common in the nineteenth century, constituting 60 percent of presidential statements on the Court's decisions. For example, although John Tyler issued a statement that concerned an appeal to the governor of Rhode Island about violent domestic uprisings, his reference to *Rhode Island* v. *Massachusetts* (1838) was matter-of-fact. Tyler

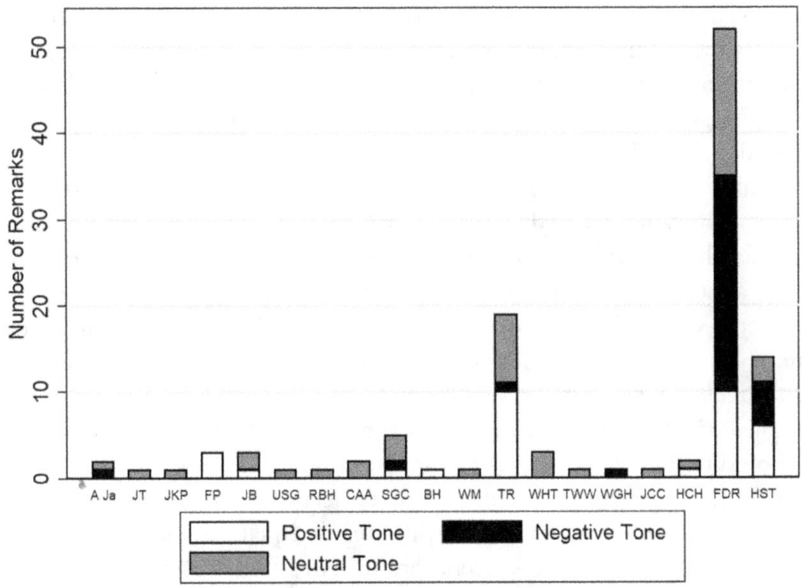

FIGURE 8.2. Tone of presidential comments on US Supreme Court cases, 1789–1953

simply noted that, "legislative usage . . . had been decided by the Supreme Court of the United States"[9] In another speech, Tyler conveyed a Spanish minister's dissatisfaction with the Court's ruling in *United States* v. *The Amistad* (1841),[10] although his own comments were neutral and legally dismissive of the minister's claims. Theodore Roosevelt referenced *Chin Bak Kan* v. *US* (1902) in a neutral fashion, mentioning that the Supreme Court called citizenship an "inestimable heritage."[11] President James Buchanan discussed *Dred Scott* four times, including in his Inaugural Address, two days before the decision was rendered. Although he seemed pleased with the Court's decision – at least in the context of helping to quell instances of "unhappy agitation"[12] between free and slave states – all but one remark was neutral in tone. Given that slavery was a key issue of the era, and one of Buchanan's goals as president was to maintain the status quo (Stampp 1990), these examples illustrate how, even for historical presidents, referencing Supreme Court cases was more common for high profile cases relevant to the president's own policy goals, even if they did not take firm positions on the outcomes of those cases.

Negative rhetoric was rarer among historical presidents. In fact, the only nineteenth-century presidents to openly criticize the Court were Andrew

Jackson and Ulysses S. Grant. Moreover, although Theodore Roosevelt began to raise the public profile of Supreme Court cases in his comments, he, too, only openly criticized one Court decision, *United States* v. *Trans-Missouri Freight Association* (1897), which applied the Sherman Act to railways.[13] Of Theodore Roosevelt's immediate successors, only President Harding was critical of a Court decision, expressing regret about *Hammer* v. *Dagenhart* (1918), which he claimed undermined Congress's ability to regulate adequately child labor.[14] And although Franklin Roosevelt was critical of Court cases amid his public defense of increasing the number of justices on the Supreme Court (Blackstone and Goelzhauser 2014), President Truman did not resume Roosevelt's more extensive criticism of Court decisions, as only 36 percent of his comments were negative. Nevertheless, Truman's five negative remarks easily places him second to Franklin Roosevelt in terms of the most negative references to Court cases among historical presidents.

Historical presidents praised the Court's decisions about as much as they criticized its decisions, and did so with roughly equal frequency throughout the nineteenth and twentieth centuries in terms of the percentage of their remarks. For example, Franklin Pierce spoke favorably of the Court's decision in *Cooley* v. *Board of Wardens* (1852), in which the Court upheld a Pennsylvania law that required ships navigating the Port of Philadelphia to hire local pilots, despite a challenge that the policy ran afoul of the Commerce Clause. In recounting the constitutional debate regarding the power of the federal government vis-à-vis the states, Pierce stated:

> Congress does not possess constitutional power to impose restrictions of this character upon any present or future State of the Union. In a long series of decisions, on the fullest argument and after the most deliberate consideration, the Supreme Court of the United States had finally determined this point in every form under which the question could arise, whether as affecting public or private rights – in questions of the public domain, of religion, of navigation, and of servitude."[15]

Pierce, a supporter of states' rights, thus saw the advantage of justifying his ideals publicly by referencing the Court's support for those positions, ranging from slavery to maritime navigation.

Examples from the twentieth century also illustrate how presidents can praise the Court's decisions as a means to build support for their positions. Theodore Roosevelt, who cared deeply about environmental conservation, spoke favorably about a series of Court decisions regarding the authority of states vis-à-vis Congress to make improvements to navigable waters.[16] Similarly, Truman spoke favorably about a long-standing dispute between

Kansas and Colorado over water rights in three speeches for the purposes of building support for the United Nations and the World Court. In these remarks, Truman tried to leverage public views of the Supreme Court as a respected adjudicative body to build similar support for a World Court that could referee international disputes. For example, he argued:

> We must make the United Nations continue to work, and to be a going concern, to see that difficulties between nations may be settled just as we settle difficulties between States here in the United States. When Kansas and Colorado fall out over the waters in the Arkansas River, they don't go to war over it, they go to the Supreme Court of the United States, and the matter is settled in a just and honorable way. There is not a difficulty in the whole world that cannot be settled in exactly the same way in a world court.[17]

The Franklin Roosevelt Administration

Because Franklin Roosevelt offered the most comments on Supreme Court cases among historical presidents, we provide a closer look into his presidency. Figure 8.3 presents the number of comments by year and according to the tone of Roosevelt's remarks. As before, the white portions of the bars indicate positive tone, the black portions negative tone, and the gray portions neutral tone. During his nearly 13 years as president, Franklin Roosevelt referenced Supreme Court cases 53 times, averaging about 4 cases in each of these years in office. Roosevelt did not mention a case before May 1935, however, and the bulk of his comments took place during the heat of his battles with the Court over its New Deal decisions in 1935, 1936, and 1937, with 39 mentions in these 3 years alone. Amid discussions of his failed Court-packing plan, Roosevelt mentioned the Court's cases 20 times in 1937. Interestingly, in no way did President Roosevelt use his speeches to lobby the Court over its pending decisions. Rather, all but one mention occurred after the case had been decided. The lone exception came in the form of a question regarding the pending case of *NLRB* v. *Jones & Laughlin Steel Corporation*. President Roosevelt simply responded that the case was not relevant to his positions on legislation related to minimum wage, child labor, or maximum hours regulations.

Among Franklin Roosevelt's 52 mentions of decided Court cases, the data reveal that he took a fairly balanced approach in terms of the type of his remarks (results not shown). The distribution of spoken to written comments is 28 to 25, with the president addressing most cases in response to questions at his press conferences. In addition to talking about 3 cases in fireside chats,

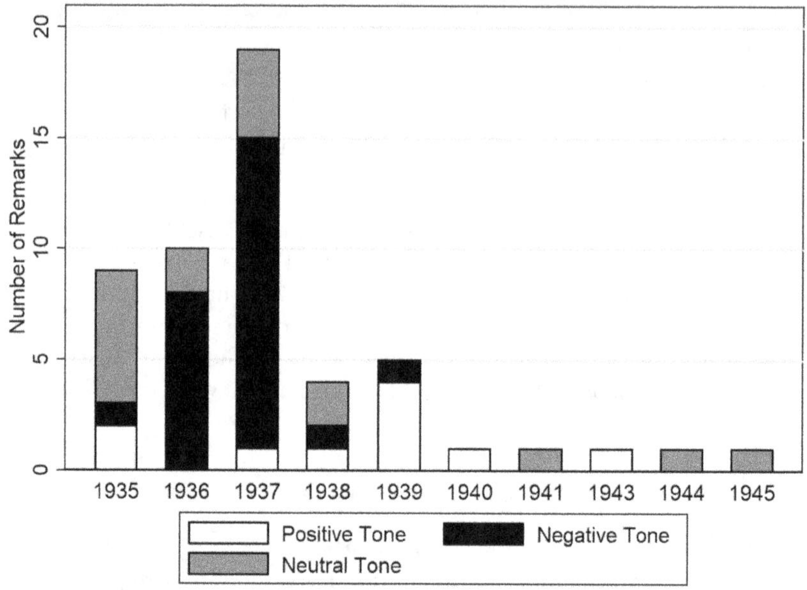

FIGURE 8.3. Tone of speeches made by Franklin Delano Roosevelt on decided US Supreme Court cases

Roosevelt also referenced 7 cases in spoken addresses he delivered throughout the nation and in Washington, DC. Roosevelt referenced 8 cases in written statements, 5 cases in written letters (typically to a member of Congress in support of, or opposition to, legislation), and 11 cases in written messages to Congress.

In terms of tone, Roosevelt's remarks tended to be primarily negative, clearly reflecting his battles with the Court over its unwillingness to support New Deal legislation. Overall, 48 percent of Roosevelt's comments were negative, compared with 33 percent neutral, and 19 percent positive. Almost all of the positive comments came after the "switch in time that saved nine" in spring of 1937, after which Roosevelt began praising the Court's decisions upholding the New Deal. For example, in response to a reporter's question on *NLRB* v. *Jones & Laughlin Steel Corp.* the day after the decision was handed down, Roosevelt positively beamed in his playful exchange with reporters. In this case, the Court upheld the Wagner Act, thus expanding Congress's Commerce Clause authority and signaling its deference to Congress on economic matters. Roosevelt said:

> Off the record, and really off the record and just in the family, I have been chortling all morning, ever since I picked up the papers. I have been having

a perfectly grand time. When I picked up one of the papers, the dear old *Herald-Tribune*, and saw the editorial entitled, "A Great Decision," I harked back . . . It is a joy.[18]

His most frequently cited case was *United States* v. *Butler* (mentioned 16 times), followed by *Schechter Poultry Corp.* v. *United States* (1935) and *Morehead* v. *New York ex rel. Tipaldo* (1936), in which the Court struck down a New York minimum wage law, at four remarks each. Notably, Roosevelt mentioned *Schechter* four times during a one-week period in 1935. In *Schechter*, the Court ruled Congress's delegation of legislative authority to the president under the National Industrial Recovery Act of 1933 was unconstitutional. This major part of the president's New Deal program allowed Roosevelt to regulate wages and prices. Roosevelt was highly critical of the Court in each of his four mentions of *Schechter*. These cases, seen by Roosevelt as impediments to his New Deal, were especially important to Roosevelt and were vital factors that led him to propose and attempt to garner support for his Court-packing plan (Leuchtenburg 1966). Consequently, like modern presidents, Roosevelt discussed Supreme Court cases in his public rhetoric in an effort to advance his policy goals.

And there is anecdotal evidence that Roosevelt's Court-packing plan – and presumably the rhetoric that went with it – helped to shape his success on later issues essential to his New Deal programs. As Holland (2004, 85) notes, Chief Justice Hughes appears to have changed his position on minimum wage legislation from dicta in *Schechter* to his support for upholding the Fair Labor Standards Act in *United States* v. *Darby Lumber* (1941). One might infer that the Court-packing efforts had the intended effect, but one cannot reasonably attribute the results of a 1941 case to the actions of a president four years earlier by tying the outcome in *Darby Lumber* to Roosevelt's rhetoric on *Schechter*. However, it is not unfair to conclude that Roosevelt's efforts concerning the Court – and his public comments on more than two dozen cases – laid the foundation for future presidents to also incorporate the public discussion of judicial politics into their governing strategies.

CONCLUSIONS

The purpose of this chapter was to extend our understanding of how presidents speak about Supreme Court cases to the historical era prior to the modern presidency. Our empirical analyses allow us to draw several conclusions. First, as expected, historical presidential discussions of Supreme Court cases were rare. Indeed, not all historical presidents referenced cases. In fact, the first reference to a case came in 1833 and almost half of the presidents from 1789 to 1953 refrained from discussing Supreme Court decisions in their public speeches. Second, most presidential comments involved already decided Supreme Court cases, and most were neutral in tone. In this sense, historical presidents did not use the bully pulpit in an attempt to influence the justicess' pending decisions nor did they overwhelmingly criticize the Court's decided cases. Third, Theodore Roosevelt, Franklin Roosevelt, and Harry Truman deviated from the dominate pattern of other historical presidents. Theodore Roosevelt was an activist president who commonly used public rhetoric to achieve his goals (Stampp 1990). He advocated that presidents should act as stewards of the people, relying on a broad interpretation of executive prerogative to govern publicly and with the best interests of the American people in mind. Franklin Roosevelt was particularly active in discussing the Court's decisions, in large part due to his conflicts with the Court over the constitutionality of New Deal legislation. Truman offers a bridge from Franklin Roosevelt to the modern presidency. Although he referenced cases neither as much as Roosevelt nor Eisenhower, he seems to have considered issuing statements on the Court's decisions to be an appropriate part of his public rhetoric. Finally, when historical presidents did discuss the Court's cases in their public remarks, they tended to address those cases that involved salient matters of public concern, thus demonstrating their democratic responsiveness in a manner similar to modern presidents.

The era of the historical presidency also offers additional insight into the debate between the coordinate construction and judicial supremacy approaches to understanding the interrelationship between the presidency and the Supreme Court on matters of constitutional interpretation. Based on our analysis, it appears that historical presidents generally refrained from using their public rhetoric to challenge the authority of the Court as the primary interpreter of the Constitution or to pressure the justices to rule in a particular way by taking positions on pending cases. However, Theodore Roosevelt violated this tendency on occasion, and Franklin Roosevelt essentially terminated it. This opened the door for modern presidents to speak about, and often be critical of, the Court's decisions when they see some benefit to doing so. Thus, as a whole, historical presidents were reluctant to use public rhetoric to assert themselves as coequals to the Court on matters of constitutional interpretation, suggesting they were more comfortable with judicial supremacy views of the relationship between the Court and the executive. However, that this was their general approach to public remarks does not mean that historical presidents were not often in conflict with the Court. Rather, it suggests that historical presidents tended to have more reverence for the norm of judicial independence when it came to their public remarks, choosing to air their criticisms of the Court and preferred positions on the Court's pending decisions in private (Scigliano 1971).

9

Conclusions

Donald Trump has a storied history of criticizing courts, judges, and their decisions, including the Supreme Court. As we have illustrated throughout this book, the Court is not immune from condemnation by the president. But, President Trump's attacks on the judiciary are different (e.g., Brennan Center for Justice 2018; Chemerinsky 2018). When previous presidents criticized the Court, they tended to do so in a respectful manner, typically expressing their disagreement with the Court's interpretation of the Constitution, as opposed to attacking individual justices. Indeed, even Andrew Jackson's apocryphal comment that "John Marshall has made his decision. Now let him enforce it," is ultimately a dispute about the constitutional powers of the Court compared with the president, not a personal attack on Chief Justice Marshall (Rosen 2017).

President Trump often takes a different tack. Instead of providing pointed criticism of disagreements about constitutional interpretation, he often attacks individual judges and courts as institutions, and focuses on the winners and losers in case outcomes. This approach started before his inauguration and often takes place on Twitter, one of his preferred modes of communication. For example, before he announced his candidacy for president, Trump boldly criticized not just the Court's decision in *National Federation of Independent Business* v. *Sebelius* (2012), but also the Chief Justice personally: "If Justice Roberts had done the right thing and voted against ObamaCare, our country would be in a lot better shape right now! TOTAL TURMOIL" (November 10, 2013). As a candidate, Trump continued these lines of attack. For instance, in a Tweet, Trump said of United States District Judge Gonzalo P. Curiel, who presided over a lawsuit against "Trump University," "I have a judge in the Trump University civil case, Gonzalo Curiel (San Diego), who is very unfair. An Obama pick. Totally biased-hates Trump" (May 30, 2016). Trump continued to disparage Judge Curiel repeatedly as a candidate, including in an infamous June 2016 interview on CNN, where he said, "Let me just tell you, I've had horrible rulings, I've been treated very unfairly by this judge. Now, this judge is of Mexican heritage. I'm building a wall, OK?" (Wolf 2018).

These types of attacks did not dissipate once Trump was sworn in as president. In response to a lower court loss in what would become *Trump v. International Refugee Assistance Project* (2017), the President tweeted, "In any event we are EXTREME VETTING people coming into the US in order to help keep our country safe. The courts are slow and political!" (June 5, 2017). He referred to Judge James Robart, who granted a temporary restraining against President Trump's travel ban, a "so-called judge" (February 4, 2017). Judge Robart would receive more than 100 death threats following this tweet (Mauro 2018).

Trump's repeated attacks on federal judges led to a rare and public rebuke by Chief Justice John Roberts in late 2018. Upset that a favorite target of conservatives – the Ninth Circuit Court of Appeals – issued a temporary restraining order to block the Trump Administration from barring migrants from seeking asylum, Trump lashed out against the Ninth Circuit and the judge who ruled against the President's position. He called Judge Jon Tigar, "an Obama judge," and said that "it's not going to happen like this anymore." He further stated, "Every case that gets filed in the 9th Circuit, we get beaten. And then we end up having to go to the Supreme Court, like the travel ban, and we won" (Chemerinsky 2018).

In a highly unusual public reaction to Trump's criticism of the judiciary, Chief Justice John Roberts responded to a question by an Associated Press reporter by condemning the president's criticism. Citing the intuitional integrity of the courts and the independence of judges and the judiciary, Chief Justice Roberts stated, "We do not have Obama judges or Trump judges, Bush judges or Clinton judges. What we have is an extraordinary group of dedicated judges doing their level best to do equal right to those appearing before them" (Sherman 2018). Trump shot back in a tweet: "Sorry Chief Justice John Roberts, but you do indeed have 'Obama judges,' and they have a much different point of view than the people who are charged with the safety of our country" (November 21, 2018). In response, federal and state judges speaking at the National Judicial College expressed their profound frustration by the president's lack of respect for the independence of the judiciary and the role of judges in American society (Mauro 2018).

Again, it is not uncommon for presidents to criticize judicial decisions they disagree with. They do this for a variety of reasons related to their desires to secure reelection, make good public policy, and enhance their historical legacies. Yet, Trump's direct and repeated attacks on the judiciary and its judges suggest an approach that deviates considerably from accepted norms of executive-judicial branch relations. Simply put, President Trump appears to be different from other presidents when it comes to publicly discussing judicial decisions. While the above examples make this clear with regard to the tone of President Trump's criticism of judges and their decisions, we believe it is important to provide a more systematic investigation into President Trump's discussion of Supreme Court cases.

In addition to examining the first 21.5 months of the Trump presidency, this concluding chapter also allows us to accomplish three additional goals. First, in presenting data on the Trump Administration, we also review the book's findings and place Trump's approach to Supreme Court cases in that context. Second, we provide a big picture assessment of presidential rhetoric on Supreme Court decisions and discuss how this book has contributed to our understanding of a variety of topics. Finally, we examine some of the limitations of our book and offer several avenues for future research on this important topic.

WHAT ABOUT TRUMP?

The opening vignettes in this chapter suggest that President Trump approaches the norm of judicial independence differently than his predecessors. Indeed, the popular consensus appears to be that Trump is more combative and more willing to violate norms of presidential-judicial relations in his public rhetoric (Brennan Center for Justice 2018; Chemerinsky 2018; Liptak 2018; Rosen 2017), and the examples we provide support this perception. But we still lack answers to some pressing questions about President Trump's rhetorical strategies toward the Court. For example, how does Trump's public discussion of Court decisions compare with other presidents in their first two years? Does Trump's approach reveal differences in how he relates to Congress, the media, and the public? Given Trump's reliance on Twitter to communicate, do the president's tweets exhibit different patterns of presidential-judicial relations than his more traditional public remarks?

Trump's Public Comments on Supreme Court Cases

Recall that the initial distinction we made in this book was between those comments presidents made before and after the Supreme Court issued a ruling. We investigated the popular impression that presidential remarks on pending cases are evidence of presidents attempting to use their public rhetoric to bully the Court into deciding cases in the president's favor. This

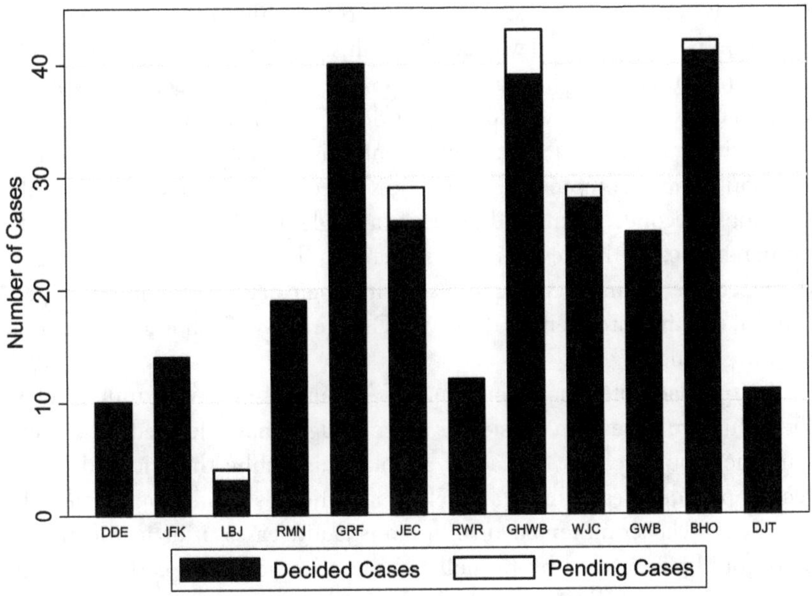

FIGURE 9.1. Presidential remarks on the Supreme Court's pending and decided cases during their first 21.5 months, 1953–2018

would be akin to presidents using speeches to attempt to pressure Congress to support their policy agendas, very much in the tradition of going public outlined by Kernell (1997). Conversely, we considered presidential remarks on decided cases to be driven by a set of other goals, with a primary motivation being to address issues of national concern presented in cases. This allows presidents to demonstrate their responsiveness to the public and to take positions to help them satisfy policy, reelection, and historical achievement goals.

To examine President Trump's public rhetoric on the Court's decisions, we used the same search strategy explained throughout this book, using the *Public Papers of the President* (American Presidency Project 2019) as our data source. In addition to determining whether the president commented on a pending or decided case, what those cases were, and the tone of the president's remarks, we also coded whether Trump's commentary was written or spoken. Our data on President Trump span from January 20, 2017, to November 5, 2018 – 21.5 months. In order to draw appropriate comparisons with other presidents, we compare Trump with the first 21.5 months of the first terms of President Eisenhower through Obama.

Figure 9.1 provides counts of both pending and decided cases mentioned during each president's first 21.5 months in office. The black portion of the bars represents comments on decided cases, and the white portion reflects comments on pending cases. Two features of this graph stand out with regard to President Trump. First, he made a relatively low number of comments on the Court's cases compared with other presidents, at only 11 remarks. Indeed, in this entire era (1953–2018), only presidents Eisenhower (10 comments) and Johnson (four comments) spoke less frequently about the Court's decisions. Second, Trump did not utter a single word in his public remarks on pending cases. However, it is important to note that very few presidents discussed the Court's pending cases during their first 21.5 months in office. Indeed, only five presidents did so, with George H. W. Bush leading the pack at four comments.

Trump's lack of remarks on Supreme Court cases is very much below the volume of attention presidents since Reagan have devoted to referencing the Court's cases. Instead of aligning his public rhetoric with more recent presidencies, Trump's level of attention is more consistent with presidents who commented on Supreme Court cases prior to the rise of going public identified by Kernell (1997) and others. It is certainly possible that President Trump will issue more comments on Supreme Court cases during the latter half of his first term in office – particularly if he references *Trump* v. *Hawaii* (2018), a major victory for his travel ban, frequently on the campaign trail as President Obama did in 2012 with respect to the Court upholding the Affordable Care Act in *Sebelius*. In addition, it is likely that we will see Trump reference more cases in the second half of his first term as many cases that implicate his administration's priorities are working their way to the Supreme Court. Whether this happens or not, the data in Figure 9.1 show that Trump has chosen to issue substantially fewer public remarks about Supreme Court cases than his predecessors, which is at odds with presidential behavior over the past 30 years.

In terms of the focus of his remarks, President Trump most frequently discussed *Trump* v. *Hawaii*. Trump praised the decision four out of the five times he mentioned it. (The other mention was a neutral reference to the case in a written proclamation.[1]) Related to his campaign promise to repeal and replace the Affordable Care Act, Trump also referenced *Sebelius* twice. Similar to other presidents, Trump cited *INS* v. *Chadha* (1983). However, this was in a single statement at the signing of the Countering America's Adversaries through Sanctions Act.[2] Aside from the five references to *Trump* v. *Hawaii*, the remaining cases were decided before Trump took office, although *INS* v. *Chadha* was the only case that the President mentioned that predated the Obama Administration.

Among these 11 remarks, four were spoken comments, with the other seven of the President's comments communicated in prepared, written statements. Perhaps surprisingly given Trump's reputation, only two of these remarks were negative in tone. Both of these negative comments referenced *Sebelius* and the President's objection to the individual mandate. Even though the Court upheld the individual mandate as constitutional under Congress' power to tax, the Trump Administration eliminated it as part of his first-year tax cut legislation. Trump's comments reflect this development:

> And before Christmas, we passed the largest tax cut and reform in American history, including ANWR and including the fact that the individual mandate was terminated, which is a tremendously important thing and a very popular thing, I must tell you. People are supposed to pay for the privilege of not having health care; that was not good. Unfortunately, the courts didn't cut it, but we cut it.[3]

Both of his negative comments on *Sebelius*[4] were in spoken and unscripted remarks. This fits with the perception that, although Trump may be more disrespectful of the courts than other presidents, this is most likely to occur when Trump speaks and goes off script. When the White House is able to curtail the president's impulsiveness by gaining control over the content of the president's message, such as in written statements, the language is consistent with norms of presidential deference to the Court. Indeed, the president's other remarks were either positive or, in the case of a September 24, 2017, comment on *Trump* v. *Hawaii*, neutral, and all but one of these were delivered in prepared, written statements. For example, President Trump's statement of disapproval of the "arbitration agreements rule," cites support for Supreme Court precedent in a manner similar to other presidents. Specifically, Trump wrote, "The CFPB's rule is also in tension with the policy expressed by Congress in the Federal Arbitration Act, as recognized repeatedly by the Supreme Court, favoring resolution of disputes through arbitration."[5]

In all, President Trump's comments on Supreme Court cases – as found in the *Public Papers of the Presidents* – are different from previous administrations in two ways. First, Trump has spoken less frequently about Supreme Court cases than recent presidents, fully ignoring cases pending before the Court. Second, the president has issued more written than spoken remarks on the Court's cases, and, perhaps surprisingly, he tended to be more positive than other presidents were, although this may be due in large part to focusing much of his attention on a single case (*Trump* v. *Hawaii*) that reflected a top administration priority. In both of these ways, President Trump's public comments on Court decisions align more with patterns we observed for presidents who governed before the Reagan Administration, rather than more recent presidents.

The Effects of Trump's Public Remarks

In addition to describing and explaining the type, amount, and tone of all presidential commentary on Supreme Court cases throughout this book, we also investigated the impact that these comments had on the Court, Congress, the media, and public opinion. Although we have only 21.5 months of data, a peek into the effect of Trump's comments on Supreme Court cases may reveal the extent to which his presidency is similar to, and different from, previous administrations. We examine this proposition in the context of presidential calls for congressional action and the impact that Trump's comments on Supreme Court cases have had on news coverage and public opinion.

Recall from Chapter 5 that presidents since Eisenhower made a number of calls to Congress for legislative action in response to Supreme Court decisions, averaging about 20 percent of their commentary on the Court's decided cases. Indeed, all presidents in the modern era asked Congress for legislation on at least four occasions, with some presidents being particularly insistent on a legislative response. For example, Gerald Ford called on Congress 10 times to pass legislation in response to *Buckley* v. *Valeo* (1976). Further, presidents were successful at various stages of the legislative process. Overall, 54 percent of presidents' unique calls led to some form of congressional action, with 31 percent of those actions resulting in passed legislation.

Unlike these examples of presidential leadership of Congress, however, President Trump issued no explicit calls for congressional action in either his spoken or written comments. He has criticized Congress in signing statements where he referenced Supreme Court cases, but he made no direct calls for congressional action related to a Supreme Court decision. As we discuss below, President Trump did issue one call on Congress, but this was through Twitter, an element of presidential communication not previously examined in this context.

The failure to call for congressional action on the Court's decisions may be indicative of Trump's legislative strategy more generally, rather than his specific responses to Court cases. A typical going public strategy of recent presidents is to announce a policy priority and then follow up with a series of focused speeches to build public and legislative support for it. The idea behind going public in this way is to raise the salience of an issue by increasing news coverage and encouraging Congress to respond to the president's leadership. One recent prominent example is George W. Bush's efforts to reform social security. After announcing his intention in his 2005 State of the Union Address to privatize Social Security, Bush traveled the nation in a "60 stops in 60 days" tour. He touted his reforms in key states and congressional districts and generated a significant amount of news coverage. Despite these efforts, public opinion did not move on the issue, and the Senate never voted his proposal out of committee (Eshbaugh-Soha and Peake 2006).

President Trump has not gone public in this manner. Without question, Trump has used the State of the Union Address to underscore his policy priorities, but his public relations strategy has not been to sustain attention to those policy priorities. He has not followed up any of his national addresses with campaigns to build policy support and he has tended to defer to Congress on his domestic policy priorities, including health care reform, tax cuts, and budget appropriations. In short, President Trump has not gone public in a manner similar to past presidents, whether to call on Congress to act more generally or specifically by asking the legislature to respond to a Supreme Court decision.

In addition to calling for congressional action on the Court's decisions, we have also demonstrated that presidents can use their speeches to share their perspectives on the Court's cases with the public through news coverage. Even as presidents seek out additional ways to reach the public directly – such as through Twitter and other social media – most Americans still prefer to watch news on television or read it through newspapers (Mitchell 2018). Thus, when the president speaks, it is up to the news media to ensure that it makes a sound. However, presidents face considerable difficulty leading the media. For example, news coverage of the president tends to be more negative than positive (Farnsworth and Lichter 2006) and more superficial than substantive (Hallin 1992). Besides, despite exhaustive efforts to generate coverage by the White House, there is no guarantee these public relations efforts will result in coverage of the president (Cohen 2008; Kumar 2007).

These issues also persist for news coverage of the Supreme Court (Magnuson and Walcker 2017), generally, and, as we showed in Chapter 6, for presidential comments on Supreme Court cases, specifically. Coupling the overall decline in presidential news coverage with a similar decline in coverage of the Supreme Court means that presidential news management is likely to be strategic and generate some, but not significant, news coverage of the president's remarks on Supreme Court cases.

Chapter 6 revealed several patterns of news coverage since the Eisenhower Administration. First, coverage of presidential commentary was highest prior to the Ford Administration. Aside from Lyndon Johnson's coverage, Eisenhower, Kennedy, and Nixon all received more news reporting of their Supreme Court commentary than any other president did. Relative to the amount of attention presidents have devoted to commenting on Supreme Court cases – attention that has increased over time – recent presidents have struggled to generate news coverage of their remarks. This is in part due to the changing nature of presidential news coverage, generally (Cohen 2008), but also because the means by which the media covers presidential remarks has changed. For example, the *New York Times*'s practice of reprinting the transcripts of presidential remarks ended in the 1970s, requiring presidents to do more than just speak to generate news coverage.

Second, when and how presidents speak about Court cases matters significantly for news coverage of presidential commentary. As we showed in Chapter 6, presidents are unlikely to generate news coverage by speaking about cases prior to their decision. Rather, the media tends to cover presidential remarks on the Court's decided cases that address issues of national concern. This is particularly true when those remarks are made in a national address or at a press conference, thus showing that presidents can lead news coverage of Supreme Court cases if they take advantage of the strategic tools available to them.

Returning to President Trump's commentary on Supreme Court cases, we followed our research strategy in Chapter 6 and searched the *New York Times* for stories related to Trump's remarks on the Court's cases. This search revealed that 18 percent of the president's comments generated coverage: four stories covering two written statements. First, President Trump garnered one news story the day after he issued a statement in support of the Supreme Court's decision in *Trump* v. *Hawaii*.[6] In the case, the Court allowed the president's travel ban to take effect after agreeing to hear arguments on the ban in October. Quoting both the president's statement and a Tweet, the *Times* balanced the president's point of view with the Court's decision, and provided background on the legal difficulties facing the president's travel ban.

Second, President Trump's Proclamation on September 24, 2017, which revised provisions in his travel ban established in an executive order, generated three different stories. The focus of these stories was in some mixture based on the president's written proclamation, the Supreme Court's decision to cancel oral arguments in response to the president's revisions, and an analysis of the international response to the Administration's revisions. The proclamation banned travel from additional, non-Muslim countries (such as Chad) signaling to the Court, perhaps, that the travel ban did not target countries based on their religious majorities.

That Trump's written statement and proclamation generated news coverage differs from our findings in Chapter 6. There we showed that written statements tend not to make the news, which instead favors spoken comments. Nevertheless, both of President Trump's written statements that made the news reflected the president's formal attempt to shape the policy discussion related to his travel ban, a ban that was already highly salient to the national news media. Although our sample is limited to his first 21.5 months in office, it nevertheless illustrates that President Trump has not followed the precedent set by previous presidents of trying to lead coverage through spoken remarks on the Court's cases.[7]

In addition to trying to shape the agendas of Congress and the media, presidents also seek to influence public attitudes toward constitutional issues and the Court's decisions. Indeed, this is one of the main reasons why presidents wish to generate news coverage of their public comments: to communicate their positions to the American people. This helps presidents demonstrate that they have considered issues of national importance and it may assist them in achieving a number of goals, including reelection, good public policy, and historical recognition. In Chapter 7, we showed that presidents can shape public attitudes toward the Court's decisions in low-salience issue areas, but have difficulty doing so in high-salience cases. We further demonstrated that presidents overwhelmingly take positions congruent with public attitudes on the issues featured in the Court's cases, thus showing their democratic responsiveness.

Turning again to President Trump, our limited data reveal that the Trump does not appear to have altered public opinion on his two major and repeated references to Court cases, *Sebelius* and *Hawaii*. Trump's criticism of *Sebelius* came in December of 2017 and January of 2018. Public support for the Affordable Care Act decreased from 50 percent in November of 2017 to 48 percent in November of 2018, but this change was within the margin of error (Gallup 2018c). Trump's praise for *Hawaii* came in December of 2017 (twice) and October of 2018. Public support for keeping immigration at its current level was not moved by the president's remarks. In June of 2017, 38 percent of Americans supported keeping immigration at current levels, compared with 37 percent in January of 2019, with the change falling within the margin of error (Gallup 2019).

In addition, President Trump appears to hold a different strategic motivation in taking positions on Supreme Court cases than his predecessors. Recall that he praised *Trump* v. *Hawaii*, including a clear statement (and Tweet) in support of the Court's decision. Although his position places him in agreement with the Court's views, he did not take this position in response to public support for this policy. According to a June 2018 poll, only 49 percent of Americans approved of the Court's decision to uphold the Trump Administration's travel ban (Quinnipiac University Poll 2018a).[8] President Trump also criticized the Supreme Court's support for the individual mandate in the *Sebelius* case. He did so despite the reality that favorable views of the Affordable Care Act in January 2018 had reached 50 percent (Kaiser Family Foundation 2018).[9]

Neither of these examples places President Trump completely at odds with our argument for why presidents may choose to speak about Court cases. Recall that one of presidents' primary motivations for speaking about a case is to position them for reelection. Comments in support of both the travel ban and eliminating the individual mandate fall squarely in line with Republican support, Trump's primary constituency. Thus, instead of taking positions that align with national public opinion to benefit his reelection goals, President Trump's strategy appears to be to respond to a subset of public opinion – that of his Republican base – in an effort to shore up partisan support (Quinnipiac University Poll 2017, 2018b).[10]

President Trump, Twitter, and Supreme Court Cases

In comparison with other presidents, Donald Trump has issued fewer comments on Supreme Court cases with a correspondingly limited impact on Congress, the media, and public opinion. Moreover, President Trump's remarks in the *Public Papers of the Presidents* do not reveal the same level of disrespect for the judicial branch and its judges found in the examples that opened this chapter. In fact, more often than not, the President has used his public commentary to praise the Court's decisions.

One likely reason for these differences involves the medium by which the president communicates. In his written statements, Trump has almost universally praised the Court's decisions. But these statements are those of White House counsel and policy experts, not necessarily the president. Simply put, through written statements, the White House has more control over President Trump's message. When Trump has more discretion, such as in his spoken comments, he is more willing to criticize the Court. Given that President Trump relies heavily on Twitter to communicate his messages (Kreis 2017), by focusing on presidential statements in the *Public Papers of the Presidents*, we have offered an incomplete picture of Trump's rhetoric on the Court's decisions. This is particularly important since White House counsel and speechwriters may have even less control over Trump's Twitter feed than they have over even his speeches. Consequently, if we were to find evidence of disparaging behavior toward the Supreme Court's decisions, it is likely we would find this in his tweets (e.g., Gross and Johnson 2016).

To determine the extent to which Trump used Twitter to reference Supreme Court cases – if at all – we examined a publicly available list of all presidential tweets.[11] We downloaded all of President Trump's tweets from January 20, 2017, through November 5, 2018, which corresponds to the end of our data collection using the *Public Papers of the Presidents* (and allows us to make comparisons with other presidents during their first 21.5 years on office). We then searched each tweet for the term "court."[12] Once we determined that the reference to the word "court" was a reference to a Supreme Court case, we read each of the president's tweets to determine which Supreme Court case or cases he referenced.

This information is reported in Figure 9.2. This graph contains the same data in Figure 9.1 on the extent to which presidents discuss pending and decided cases during their first 21.5 months in office, with the addition of data on Trump's tweets. This figure corroborates our belief that focusing only on the *Public Papers of the Presidents* for President Trump paints an incomplete picture of his rhetoric toward the Court's cases. First, when tweets are

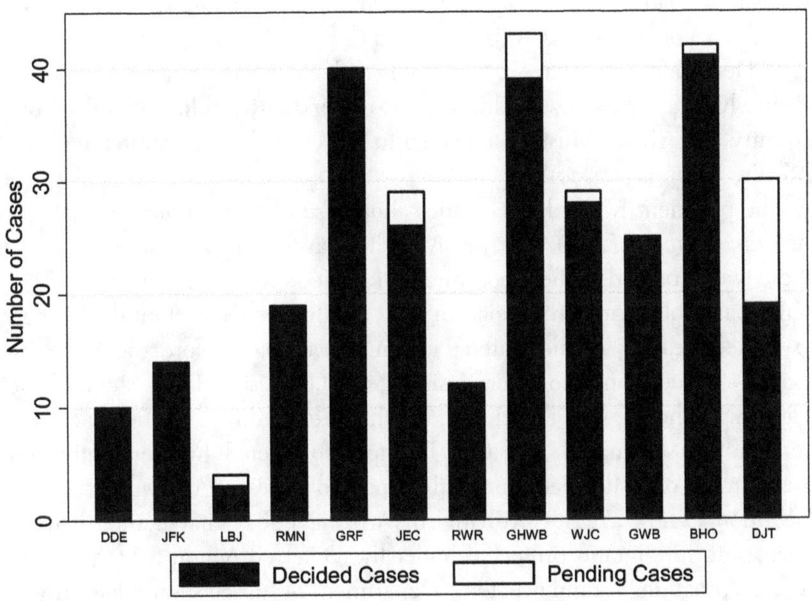

FIGURE 9.2. Presidential remarks on the Supreme Court's pending and decided cases during their first 21.5 months, including President Trump's tweets, 1953–2018

added into Trump's data, he is no longer among the presidents who least frequently discussed the Court's cases in their public rhetoric during their first 21.5 months in office. Rather, he discussed the median volume of the Court's cases since the Reagan Administration. Second, Trump is no longer somewhat of an outlier for having never discussed a pending Supreme Court case. Quite the opposite: he discussed more pending Court cases in his first 21.5 months than any president in American history. All of these statements took place on Twitter, where the White House has minimal control over the president's message. This suggests that researchers may have to approach the study of Trump's public remarks differently than previous presidents by including his Twitter feed in data collection efforts.

As a whole, Trump discussed the Court's cases in 19 tweets, covering 21 total cases and 10 unique cases. The majority of Trump's tweets involved pending (11), not decided (10) cases. Of the 11 pending cases Trump discussed, he took positions in eight tweets (73 percent). Three tweets involved *Trump* v. *Hawaii*, including one tweet calling for its appeal and two urging the Court to uphold the travel ban, including one arguing, "We need to be smart, vigilant and tough. We need the courts to give us back our rights. We need the Travel Ban as an extra level of safety!" (June 3, 2017). Trump also tweeted twice in support of the appeal of what would become *Turzai* v. *League of Women Voters of Pennsylvania* (2018), a case involving legislative redistricting: "Democrat judges have totally redrawn election lines in the great State of Pennsylvania. @FoxNews. This is very unfair to Republicans and to our country as a whole. Must be appealed to the United States Supreme Court ASAP!" (February 24, 2018).

The president tweeted three times about *Trump* v. *International Refugee Assistance Project* (2017), also involving his travel ban. Interestingly, two of these tweets related to the Department of Justice's role in the creation of the travel ban, both made on June 5, 2017: 1) "The Justice Dept. should ask for an expedited hearing of the watered down Travel Ban before the Supreme Court – & seek much tougher version!"; 2) "The Justice Dept. should have stayed with the original Travel Ban, not the watered down, politically correct version they submitted to S.C." Trump also offered his perspective on Department of Justice decisions with respect to *Brewer* v. *Arizona Dream Act Coalition* (2018), a case involving an Arizona policy that denied drivers' licenses to immigrants protected under the Deferred Action for Childhood Arrivals program. Trump tweeted, "Department of Justice should have urged the Supreme Court to at least hear the Drivers *[sic]* License case on illegal immigrants in Arizona. I agree with @LouDobbs. Should have sought review" (March 21, 2018). It is interesting that the president uses Twitter, a forum that focuses on brevity and thus offers little opportunity for the depth one might expect in discussions of policy or litigation strategies, to comment on the decisions of the Department of Justice.

Turning to the tone of his Twitter remarks, 80 percent of the references to the Court's decided cases were positive in nature in terms of the Court's decision. Therefore, it appears that Trump is not particularly negative on Twitter when he discusses the Court's decisions. This includes mentioning *South Dakota* v. *Wayfair Inc.* (2018) three times, once to poke at Jeff Bezos, the founder of Amazon.com and the owner of the *Washington Post.* Trump used Twitter to comment on the decision, which allowed states to collect sales taxes from internet sales associated with companies who did not have a physical location in that state. Trump opined on how the case may undermine Amazon's profit margins (July 23, 2018). In two separate tweets, he praised the Court's decisions in *Janus* v. *AFSCME* (2018), in which the Court handed a devastating blow to the ability of unions to collect fees from non-members, and *Jennings* v. *Rodriguez* (2018), which held that immigrants subject to mandatory detention are not entitled to periodic bond hearings.

Of particular note is the president's tweet on April 17, 2018. Although he is mistaken that the Court just ruled on this case, the president referenced the case of *Sessions* v. *Dimaya* (2018), in which the Court ruled that the Immigration and Nationality Act's provision related to crimes of violence is unconstitutionally vague. The decision squarely countered President Trump's strong stance on immigration and deportation. Instead of bashing the decision, as one might expect, however, President Trump called on Congress to act: "Today's Court decision means that Congress must close loopholes that block the removal of dangerous criminal aliens, including aggravated felons. This is a public safety crisis that can only be fixed by . . . Congress – House and Senate must quickly pass a legislative fix to ensure violent criminal aliens can be removed from our society. Keep America Safe!" This represents the only instance in which President Trump called for congressional action on a Supreme Court case. It is fascinating that he used Twitter, a non-traditional form of communication, to make a traditional plea to Congress to remedy the Court's decision.

Overall, including the president's tweets substantially increases Trump's total public attention to Supreme Court cases. Adding these remarks to President Trump's body of commentary places him more in line with presidents since Reagan. Further, while it is not directly comparable with the other types of remarks found in the *Public Papers of the Presidents*, Trump's use of Twitter is not solely superficial. Rather, Twitter provides him with the opportunity to comment on issues of national concern, even if those messages have little legal depth or detail owing to their brevity. Instead of fashioning a written statement, holding a press conference, or delivering a speech, the president can simply tweet his views on a Supreme Court decision immediately and briefly. Interestingly, at least as it concerns references to Supreme Court cases, President Trump has not been particularly critical. The reputation that he has for using Twitter to disparage others is not especially applicable to his discussions of Supreme Court cases. This, of course, is not to say that he treats members of the judicial branch with the respect accorded to them by previous presidents. Rather, he tends to focus this negative rhetoric on lower court judges and the judicial branch as an institution, instead of the Court's specific decisions (Brennan Center for Justice 2018). It will be telling to observe how President Trump handles situations in which the current conservative Supreme Court rules against his administration's policy priorities, should they arise.

THE BIG PICTURE

The purpose of this book was to thoroughly examine presidential rhetoric on the Supreme Court's decisions. To accomplish this, we developed a theory of presidential interactions with the Court based on insights from research on a wide array of topics involving the president, the Court, the Constitution, Congress, the media, and the public, among others. To examine the validity of our theoretical propositions, we compiled an original database of presidential commentary on the Court's decisions from Washington to Trump, and conducted a novel survey experiment. In providing a first-of-its-kind treatment of this subject, we have supplied a wealth of insight into a variety of important matters involving the president and the Court, and constitutional interpretation more generally.

First, this work speaks directly to presidential deference to the norm of judicial independence. According to this norm, judges should be permitted to make their decisions free from interference from other actors, including the president. Thus, when presidents take positions on the Court's decisions, they can be criticized for violating this norm. This is particularly true when presidents take positions on the Court's pending decisions, which some have interpreted as efforts to bully the justices to decide in the president's favor. Indeed, our survey results in Chapter 1 demonstrate that the majority of the public does not support presidents taking positions on pending decisions in an effort to influence the outcome of the Court's cases, but nor are they especially keen on presidents taking a position once cases have been decided.

This perspective is closely associated with the judicial supremacy standpoint of constitutional interpretation, which holds that the Court is the final arbiter of constitutional disputes. In contrast to this view, the coordinate construction of the Constitution viewpoint holds that all three branches of government, and the public, play a role in constitutional interpretation. Consequently, when presidents take positions on the Courts decisions – pending or decided – they are exercising their independent and coordinate authority to interpret the Constitution, not violating the norm of judicial independence.

Our empirical results should provide some solace to those concerned that presidents regularly try to bully the justices through their public rhetoric or violate the norm of judicial independence. Presidents rarely take positions on the Court's pending decisions. They have done so in only about 4 percent of their statements on the Court's decisions. Moreover, when they do take public positions, they are not primarily motivated to do so to influence the Court's decisions. Rather, the weight of the evidence in Chapter 2 indicates that they take positions on issues that are important to the public and their partisan bases in an effort to enhance goals related to their reelections, preferred policies, and historical legacies. These same motivations apply to presidential comments on the Court's decided cases, as we showed in Chapters 3 and 4. Thus, by taking public positions on the Court's decisions, presidents interject themselves into the national policy debate about what the Constitution means at a given moment in time. This is not inconsistent with deference to the norm of judicial independence. Further, from a normative standpoint, this can be good thing. It allows an elected actor – the president –to provide his perspective on the Constitution, instead of leaving that task solely to nine unelected judges.[13]

Second, this book sheds light on the strategy of going public and the effectiveness of this means of communication. Although there is a voluminous body of scholarship examining why presidents go public and the impact of this rhetorical strategy, this is the first work to explore going public on the Court's decisions. We find that all presidents in the modern era have gone public on the Court's decisions and they do so to pursue their goals of reelection, making good public policy, and achieving historical recognition. For example, during reelection years, presidents speak more about the Court's cases, both recent and historical, in an effort to attach themselves to the specific policies that the Court has adjudicated, such as abortion, health care reform, and affirmative action. Presidents write more about the Court's decisions during periods of divided government to influence the implementation of policy by the federal bureaucracy, thus helping to achieve their policy making goals. Further, presidents can enhance their historical legacies by tying their presidencies to landmark Supreme Court decisions, such as *Brown* v. *Board of Education* (1954), *Roe* v. *Wade* (1973), and *Engel* v. *Vitale* (1962).

This book also provides evidence as to the effectiveness of going public on the Court's decisions with respect to the Court, Congress, the media, and the public. We showed that presidential attempts to influence the outcome of the Court's cases by taking public positions on its pending cases are largely ineffectual. We demonstrated that presidents call for Congress to take action on the Court's decisions in about one-fifth of their statements on the Court's cases, and Congress appears to take these calls seriously. We illustrated that presidents are capable of generating news coverage of their speeches on the Court's cases, although they are unable to influence the tone of that coverage. Our innovative survey experiment provided evidence that presidents can affect public support for the Court's decisions in low-salience issues areas, but they have a hard time affecting public opinion in high-salience cases, or public support for the Court as an institution. We also showed that presidents tend to follow, rather than lead, public opinion when they take positions on the Court's cases, thus demonstrating their responsiveness to the public.

Third, this work also tracks the development of this rhetorical strategy over time. We found that going public on the Court's decisions was not a common strategy among historical presidents. Indeed, almost half of presidents from 1789 to 1953 refrained from discussing the Court's cases in their public statements. Andrew Jackson, who had a conflictual relationship with the Court, was the first president to discuss the Court's decisions in his public remarks, but he did not devote much attention to the Court's cases. Other presidents generally held back on discussing the Court's cases in their public remarks. Theodore Roosevelts' tenure marked the end of the norm of generally not discussing the Court's cases in public, and this norm was eviscerated by Franklin Delano Roosevelt, another president often in conflict with the Court. Of course, this is not to say that historical presidents always agreed with the Court's decisions. Rather, they generally aired these disagreements in private, rather than in their public speeches, suggesting a greater deference for the separation of powers and the norm of judicial independence than their more modern counterparts.

In the end, and based on the evidence in this book, we believe that presidential comments on the Court's decisions are appropriate and even welcome in a constitutional democracy such as ours. Contrary to some popular allegations, presidents are generally not trying to bully the justices in their public remarks. Instead, they are injecting their own perspectives on matters of constitutional interpretation into the national debate. Given that presidents can generate media coverage of their remarks, this can serve to increase public awareness and interest in constitutional matters. We think this is a good thing, even if we doubt that presidents can substantially increase the average citizen's engagement with the Constitution.[14] Despite this limitation, we contend that the potential benefits of this form of presidential rhetoric outweigh any costs associated with largely unfounded claims that this form of speech violates the norm of judicial independence.[15]

DIRECTIONS FOR FUTURE RESEARCH

Although we aimed to provide a comprehensive examination of presidential rhetoric on Supreme Court decisions, like any work, there are limitations to this research. Our purpose here is to identify some of these confines in the hopes other scholars will use this book as a starting point for further investigations into this significant topic. First, because one of our goals was to provide a generalizable account of the ways that presidents discuss the Court's decisions in their public remarks, we choose to focus primarily on the presentation of quantitative data to explain this phenomenon. In so doing, we sacrificed some depth for breadth. We encourage future researchers to investigate this topic using other approaches, such as interviews with key actors, participant observation, and archival research. For example, we imagine that speaking with or observing White House speech writers can shed a great deal of light on the content of these speeches. In addition, archival research, particularly into presidents' private papers, can help illustrate the personalities and conflicts underlying some of the public remarks featured in this volume. This may be especially revealing concerning presidents' high-profile remarks on Supreme Court cases, such as President Obama's 2010 State of the Union Address reference to *Citizen's United*. Researching presidents' private correspondences will also enable researchers to compare presidential motivations for going public on the Court's cases with their motivations for discussing the Court's cases with other actors in private.

Second, there are other ways to explore the effects of presidential speeches than those featured here. For example, researchers might examine whether presidential speeches on the Court's decided cases in a particular issue area influence legal change in that area, the consistency of the individual justices' votes in those cases, or their decisions to write separate opinions. Scholars might also determine how quickly and efficaciously the bureaucracy responds to presidential remarks, including those targeted at Department of Justice decision-making in President Trump's tweets. Another line of inquiry could be to examine whether Congress sends signals to the president that it is receptive to altering the Court's decisions. Researchers might employ a similar research design as our survey experiment to answer questions related to the public's attitudes on different styles of presidential rhetoric, such as tweets versus more in-depth discussion of the Court's decisions. In addition, examining whether presidential speeches on Court decisions have contributed to fluctuations in the Court's legitimacy in the eyes of the public over time is a worthy endeavor.

Third, because our focus here was on the presidents' interactions with the Supreme Court, we did not address presidential statements on lower-court decisions. Although we are confident these are not as common as remarks on Supreme Court decisions, we nonetheless observed many of them in our data collection efforts. For example, as noted in the beginning of this chapter, President Trump targeted lower-court decisions and judges with respect to unfavorable decisions involving "Trump University" and his travel ban. We believe future research should examine the tendency for presidents to comment on cases that have been heard in lower courts, which can offer insights into how presidents think about the decisions of lower-profile institutions and how they relate to their governing strategies.

Finally, though our focus here is on the relationship between the President of the United States of America and the Supreme Court of the United States of America, we recognize that this form of executive-judicial relations occurs in other settings. For example, Kentucky Governor Matt Bevin had harsh words for a Kentucky Supreme Court decision that overturned a pension law, calling it "an unprecedented power grab by activist judges" (Cassens Weiss 2018). In Australia, Prime Minister Julia Gillard created quite a row when she referred to the High Court of Australia's decision in an asylum case as turning the law "on its head," and accused the Chief Justice of making inconsistent decisions (Packham 2011). In Israel, some called for the firing of Justice Minister Ayelet Shaked after she repeatedly criticized decisions of the Supreme Court of Israel, with one member of the Knesset referring to her remarks as "a dangerous act of violence" (Baruch 2016). As these examples makes clear, there are plentiful opportunities to investigate how executives discuss judicial decisions in their public rhetoric and what that means for our understanding of the norm of judicial independence.

Notes

1 GOING PUBLIC AND THE SUPREME COURT

1. "The President's News Conference with President Felipe de Jesus Calderon Hinojosa of Mexico and Prime Minister Stephen J. Harper of Canada," April 2, 2012. The statement involved *National Federation of Independent Business* v. *Sebelius* (2012). The individual mandate required that people purchase health care insurance or pay a tax penalty for failing to do so.
2. "Remarks at the Associated Press Luncheon and a Question-and-Answer Session," April 3, 2012.
3. "Remarks by President Obama in a Press Conference after the G7 Summit," June 8, 2015. The statement referred to *King* v. *Burwell* (2015).
4. Blackman (2016) provides a comprehensive summary of the response to President Obama's remarks, offering observations that reinforce those concerned with the president's comments, while referencing others who reject these concerns.
5. "Question-and-Answer Session with Reporters Following a Meeting With Former President Reagan in Los Angeles, California," April 26, 1989.
6. "Remarks at the Women's Legal Defense Fund Luncheon," June 20, 1996.
7. "Remarks on the Michigan Affirmative Action Case," January 15, 2003.
8. "Statement on the United States Supreme Court Decision on Abortion," June 16, 1983.
9. "Remarks at a Rally on Inner-City Compassion in Cleveland, Ohio," July 1, 2002.
10. Based on a search in the *Public Papers of the Presidents* for "Bork" in 1987 (American Presidency Project 2017).
11. "Address to the Nation on the Supreme Court Nomination of Robert H. Bork."

12. We surveyed 902 American citizens over the age of 18 via the Amazon Mechanical Turk platform. A full description of the survey protocols appears in Chapter 7.

2 GOING PUBLIC ON PENDING DECISIONS

1. "Remarks on the Michigan Affirmative Action Case," January 15, 2003.
2. Although media coverage of Bush's speech was overwhelmingly negative, not all reactions to President Bush's speech were critical. For example, Bush was praised for his stance by African Americans affiliated with Project 21, a conservative leadership network (US Newswire 2003).
3. For example, Clinton's remarks on *Printz* v. *United States* (1997), which involved the implementation of background checks for potential handgun purchases found in the Brady Bill, were delivered during the midst of his reelection campaign, but generated virtually no newspaper coverage at all. See for example, Clinton's speech on June 20, 1996, "Remarks at the Women's Legal Defense Fund Luncheon."
4. This appears to be the case, at least for the State of the Union Address (Bradshaw, Coe, and Neumann 2014), although no study of which we are aware compares the impact of prepared versus responsive remarks on presidential leadership of the news agenda. Even so, this reasoning is consistent with studies that restrict analysis of going public to influence Congress to prepared remarks (Barrett 2004).
5. "The President's News Conference," June 29, 2011.
6. "The President's News Conference," June 27, 1989.
7. "Remarks to College Reporters and a Question-and-Answer Session," April 28, 2016.
8. Measuring timing relative to the date the first US government brief was filed reveals a nearly identical distribution of comments. This measure is correlated with the measure reported in Figure 2.2 at $r = 0.98$.
9. There are only 39 speeches in the data in Figure 2.2, as President Obama took a position on *al-Marri* v. *Spagone* (2009), which was not orally argued as it was dismissed as moot.
10. All but one of these responses was to a reporter's question. President Obama responded to an audience member's question about *National Federation of Independent Business* v. *Sebelius* in August 2011.
11. "Remarks at the Women's Legal Defense Fund Luncheon," June 20, 1996.
12. "Interview with the President Remarks and a Question-and-Answer Session with Representatives of Black Media Associations," February 16, 1978.
13. To calculate this for question-and-answer sessions, we ignored reporters' questions and only included the president's remarks.

14. "Question-and-Answer Session with Reporters Following a Meeting with Former President Reagan in Los Angeles, California," April 26, 1989.
15. "Remarks on the Michigan Affirmative Action Case," January 15, 2003.
16. On very rare occasions, presidents make public statements discussing the appeal of lower court decisions to the Supreme Court. For example, President Carter addressed the appeal of *INS* v. *Chadha* (1983) from the Ninth Circuit in a relatively lengthy statement ("*Chadha* v. *Immigration and Naturalization Service* Statement on the Ninth Circuit Court of Appeals Decision," December 24, 1980). Though such remarks are interesting, they are so infrequent that it would be difficult to draw any conclusions as to their influence on the Court's agenda-setting process.
17. This finding suggests that presidential position taking on the Court's cases may damage the Solicitor General's credibility in the eyes of the justices (e.g., Wohlfarth 2009). However, we are hesitant to draw this conclusion given the small number of cases in which presidents take positions on the Court's pending cases.
18. When we exclude the number of questions asked of the attorney supported by the Solicitor General as an amicus, we obtain substantively similar results. The correlation between the two measures is 0.98.

3 GOING PUBLIC ON DECIDED CASES

1. "Remarks to Participants in the March for Life Rally," January 22, 1987.
2. "Remarks on Affirmative Action at the National Archives and Records Administration," July 19, 1995.
3. One example among many includes Bush's interview with Scott Pelley of CBS News's "60 Minutes" at Camp David, Maryland (January 12, 2007).
4. This seems to be the conventional wisdom, although the 2012 presidential election did not follow this tendency, as neither Obama nor Romney made much issue of the Supreme Court, whether cases or potential nominees (Barnes 2012). Moreover, we know of no scholarly research that shows presidents cater to their base by referencing Supreme Court cases when campaigning.
5. We recognize that presidents occasionally discuss salient cases when reporters ask them about those cases. Although such activities are driven primarily by the media, they nonetheless provide an opportunity for presidents to take positions on the Court's most significant cases, which can further their reelection goals and promote their historical legacies.

6. The month is one of several possible units of analysis to explain presidential attention to cases with one potential alternative being the case level. Our approach in this chapter is to explain the frequency of public commentary, much like previous research that has attempted to explain the frequency of all speeches (Eshbaugh-Soha 2010; Hager and Sullivan 1994; Powell 1999; Ragsdale 1984). In Chapter 4, we use the case as the unit of analysis.
7. It matters little to our results whether to analyze the number of unique cases or all cases mentioned in a month as these counts are correlated at 0.98.
8. Although the Supreme Court's job approval rating ticked up in July 2018, it has hovered below 50 percent since late 2011. Overall, its average approval rating since August 2000 is 51.5 percent with a high of 62 percent in that August 2000 poll. During this period, Gallup asked, "Do you approve or disapprove of the way the Supreme Court is handling its job?" only 32 times or just over twice each calendar year, on average (Gallup 2018a). Including the Court's approval in our model is not feasible given how infrequently polling organizations ask this question.
9. Although the state of the economy could also affect presidential attention to Supreme Court cases, including both the misery index (Bureau of Labor Statistics 2017) and job approval affects the significance of both variables due to multicollinearity ($r = -0.41$). We model approval ratings since they are more directly tied to the president's public activities than the state of the economy.
10. Although October through June is the Court's traditional session, the Court hands down decisions during other months, most notably in July. When we include July in the operationalization of this variable, the results do not differ. We also considered including a variable capturing the month of June, since the Court tends to hand down its most salient cases at the end of its term (Epstein, Landes, and Posner 2014). We ultimately excluded that variable from the model because it is correlated with *Court Decisions* at the 0.71 level.
11. We ran an alternative model specification that included fixed effects for presidents. Including these dummy variables adds to the explanatory power of the model, but the only significant differences are that the post-Reagan presidency and divided government variables fail to reach statistical significance. Thus, we faced a trade-off whether to include fixed effects, even though we have no rationale for individual presidents being more or less likely to address Court decisions, or to include *Post-Carter Presidencies*, which the literature proposes should be influential. We opted to exclude fixed effects in an effort to model our data most consistently with our theoretical expectations based on previous work on presidential speechmaking.

12. Although correlograms are suggestive of first-order autocorrelation for each of our dependent variables in the absence of a lagged dependent variable, modeling a lagged dependent variable is probably overly cautious, since excluding one has no significant impact on the results. There is no risk of cointegration because neither the dependent nor independent variables are integrated. In addition, there is minimal evidence of multicollinearity as none of the variables are correlated higher than 0.49, and the variance inflation factor does not exceed 1.51 for any variables in the model. Moreover, the results are not overly sensitive to the inclusion or exclusion of particular variables.
13. For a general discussion of the negative binomial regression model, see Long (1997). Another modeling strategy is to normalize the monthly counts to mean daily averages to account for different lengths of months, which we do not report because the results are substantively similar to those presented.
14. We use 90 percent confidence intervals since our hypotheses are directional. This is the equivalent to one-tailed significance tests at the 95 percent level.
15. For those interested in a more traditional presentation of our empirical results, this information appears in Appendix Table 3.1.
16. Although there may be some concern that the president's remarks drive media coverage of Supreme Court cases, regressing our measure of media coverage on presidential speeches (lagged one month) reveals a statistically insignificant impact of speeches on media coverage.
17. We maintain that this result is suggestive because the inclusion of presidential fixed effects renders the *Divided Government* variable statistically insignificant.
18. "Special Message to the Congress Proposing Legislation To Reconstitute the Federal Election Commission," February 16, 1976.
19. Even our view of this finding has evolved. In the initial publication of these findings (Eshbaugh-Soha and Collins 2015), we claimed that these findings were inexplicable. Yet, they actually reinforce the overall theme of the book that presidents preserve the norm of judicial independence by commenting on cases after they have been decided and, among recent cases, this is more likely to occur when the Court is out of session. Despite this revised interpretation, the findings in our *Presidential Studies Quarterly* piece and those presented in this chapter are quite consistent, even after adding data on the remainder of President Obama's time in office.

4 THE TONE OF PRESIDENTIAL RHETORIC ON SUPREME COURT DECISIONS

1. "Address Before a Joint Session of the Congress on the State of the Union," January 27, 2010.
2. "The President's News Conference," March 1, 2013.
3. "Remarks on Energy and Climate Change," April 16, 2008.
4. "Special Message to the Congress on the Need for Additional Passport Control Legislation," July 7, 1958.
5. "Statement on the United States Supreme Court Ruling on the Defense of Marriage Act," June 26, 2013.
6. "Remarks at a Fundraising Dinner for Senator Jesse Helms in Charlotte, North Carolina," June 20, 1990.
7. Justices also seem aware of this possibility. For example, Chief Justice Earl Warren and Justice Felix Frankfurter negotiated a unanimous decision in *Brown* v. *Board of Education*, believing that a unanimous decision would be more easily accepted by the public (Tushnet and Lezin 1991). Empirical support for this proposition, however, is mixed (compare, for example, Zink, Spriggs, and Scott 2009 to Salamone 2014).
8. "The President's Weekly Address," January 23, 2010.
9. The data include all orally argued cases formally decided on the merits by the Court. We used the case citation as the unit of analysis.
10. See, for example, Bush's "Remarks at the Opening of the *Brown* v. *Board of Education* National Historic Site in Topeka, Kansas," May 17, 2004.
11. For example, cumulatively presidents Bush, Clinton, and Bush made more than 40 references to *INS* v. *Chadha* (1983) in signing statements.
12. See, for example, Clinton's "Exchange with Reporters Aboard Air Force One," December 14, 2000.
13. The notable exception here involves the discussion of *Roe* v. *Wade* (1973) by Republican presidents advocating for the reversal of the decision. There are few other examples of presidents who were not in office at the time a case was decided discussing the decision for the purpose of generating support for or opposition to the decision itself. That *Roe* is unique in this regard corresponds to Collins and Ringhand's (2013) evidence that senators use *Roe* as a vehicle for discussing abortion more generally in Supreme Court confirmation hearings. In this way, references to overturning *Roe* may be primarily symbolic as the case has become synonymous with abortion rights broadly defined.
14. In addition to the substantive reasons for excluding cases decided before the incumbent president took office, there are also methodological concerns associated with including such cases. First, it is not evident how far back in time one should go in including cases prior to a president taking office. Further, the inclusion of such cases will increase the size of the dataset monumentally (since each president

would be tagged to each case decided a given number of years before they took office), but the value of the dependent variable will be zero for virtually all of these additional observations (because presidents take positions on historical cases so rarely). Thus, while we recognize the limitation that the empirical results of our research design pertain only to position taking by incumbent presidents, we believe it is the soundest research design from both theoretical and methodological standpoints.

15. "The President's News Conference with Prime Minister Silvio Berlusconi of Italy in Rome," June 12, 2008.
16. "The President's News Conference," July 9, 1976.
17. "The President's News Conference," June 22, 1972.
18. We also examined whether the president's ideological proximity to Congress influenced the tone of remarks, but failed to find a significant relationship.
19. Appendix Table 4.1 presents a more traditional presentation of our empirical results in tabular format.

5 PRESIDENTIAL CALLS TO CONGRESS

1. George H. W. Bush, "Remarks at a Luncheon Hosted by the New York Partnership and the Association for a Better New York in New York, New York," June 22, 1989.
2. George H. W. Bush, "The President's News Conference," June 27, 1989.
3. Not only did President Bush's public response to the Court's decision in *Texas v. Johnson* generate action by Congress, it also made its way into American popular culture. In the Simpson's episode, "The Day the Violence Died," Krusty the Clown aired a parody of the School House Rock cartoon short, "A Bill on Capitol Hill." This "Amendment to be" jingle directly addresses the attempt to amend the Constitution to prevent flag burning. The little boy concluded that if we could amend the Constitution, we could make "all sorts of crazy laws." On the musical front, country legend Merle Haggard penned "Me and Crippled Soldiers," which included the lyrics, "Might as well burn the Bill of Rights as well. And let our country go straight to hell. Only me and crippled soldiers give a damn."
4. George H. W. Bush, "Remarks Upon Receiving a Replica of the Iwo Jima Memorial and an Exchange With Reporters," June 12, 1990.
5. Indeed, even though most concede that Reagan was able to mobilize public opinion in the manner described by Kernell (1997) (by calling on the public to contact legislators, which increases the president's support in Congress), West (1988) shows that it was not the mass public that was motivated to respond to the president, but rather already engaged economic elites who had a clear incentive to see Reagan's tax cuts pass Congress.

6. George W. Bush, "Message to the Congress Transmitting a Legislative Proposal To Give the President a Line-Item Veto," March 6, 2006
7. William J. Clinton, "Statement on the Supreme Court Decision on Campaign Financing," January 24, 2000.
8. Richard Nixon, "Address to the Nation on Equal Educational Opportunities and School Busing," March 16, 1972.
9. Richard Nixon, "Special Message to the Congress on Obscene and Pornographic Materials," May 2, 1969.
10. John F. Kennedy, "248 – Special Message to the Congress on Civil Rights and Job Opportunities," June 19, 1963.
11. Jimmy Carter, "25th Anniversary of *Brown* v. *Board of Education* Remarks at a White House Observance of the Supreme Court Decision," May 17, 1979.
12. An alternative way to approach this is by looking at whether Congress passed legislation using the call for action as the unit of analysis. In all, 27 of 77 repeat calls for legislation (35 percent) led to the president signing a bill into law, compared with 21 of the 90 unique calls for congressional action (23 percent), a statistically significant difference ($p < 0.05$).
13. We also examined whether the tone of the president's remarks influenced bill passage using the call for action as the unit of analysis. Congress passed legislation 26.4 percent of the time in response to positive calls, compared with 26.3 percent of the time in response to negative calls for action, a statistically insignificant difference. However, Congress passed legislation 53 percent of the time in response to mixed calls, a statistically significant difference compared with positive and negative calls.
14. Because we limited this chapter to the presentation of descriptive information, we are cautious to draw any causal conclusions as to whether presidential statements make an independent impact on the probability that Congress will react to Supreme Court decisions.

6 PRESIDENTIAL LEADERSHIP OF NEWS COVERAGE

1. Recall our survey results reported in Chapter 1 showed that about 25 percent of respondents disapproved of presidents taking *any* position on the Court's decided cases. We can imagine that, if we asked about presidents *criticizing* the Court's decisions, that percentage would be even higher.
2. There is a much larger body of literature that examines news coverage of the Supreme Court than we discuss here. Among these studies are descriptive accounts of newspaper coverage of cases. Ericson (1977), for

example, documents the number of decisions that various newspapers covered in the 1974 Supreme Court term. Not surprisingly, the *New York Times* (112/145) covered written decisions more frequently than either the *Ann Arbor News* (87/145) or the *Detroit News* (44/145). Other research finds regional variation in Court coverage. For example, cases originating in a particular location are most likely to see coverage from that region's newspaper, and cases that originate in Washington, DC, receive more coverage in national newspapers (Hoekstra 2003; Sill, Metzgar, and Rouse 2013).

3. We also investigated whether the ideological distance between the president and the Court might increase coverage of the president's speeches about Court decisions as a form of conflict. We did not find any evidence this was the case and thus chose to focus on whether the president's position prevailed in the case.
4. We excluded 13 cases mentioned by presidents in their speeches from our statistical analyses that involved cases that were not formally decided by the Court as a result of denials of certiorari, settlement, and mootness because these cases did not garner full treatment by the Court and thus do not appear in the Spaeth et al. (2018) database.
5. To evaluate whether there is a regional bias with respect to coverage of presidential statements about cases that originated in New York, we included a variable in the model indicating that the case emanated from New York, which failed to contribute to the predictive power of the model.
6. Some may question our decision to focus on the *New York Times* on the grounds that it has a liberal bias (e.g., Groseclose and Milyo 2005). However, at least as it concerns presidential news coverage, Cohen (2008) shows that variation in job approval ratings – not the political party of the president – explains fluctuations in the tone of *New York Times* coverage from 1949 through 1992. In addition, our own data demonstrate that Republican presidents have enjoyed more positive coverage than Democratic presidents when their comments on Supreme Court cases are covered in the *New York Times*. Thus, the *Times* does not appear to have a liberal bias when it comes to coverage of the president, generally, or presidential speeches on the Court's decisions, specifically.
7. There is a variety of ways to code tone based on the number of positive and negative words in a story. An alternative to this coding is to divide the difference between positive and negative words by the total number of words in a story that exhibit tone. The correlation between the two measures is very high ($r > 0.85$), and the alternative measure results in no difference in the findings we report. We prefer our measure since it also includes neutral words, which may dominate a story.
8. "Remarks to Participants in the March for Life Rally," January 22, 1988.
9. "The President's News Conference," August 8, 1956.

10. "State of the Union Message to the Congress on Law Enforcement and Drug Abuse Prevention," March 14, 1973.
11. When we include these control variables, we obtain substantively similar results.
12. "The President's News Conference," March 14, 1956.
13. Appendix Table 6.1 presents a more traditional presentation of our empirical results in a table format.
14. The *Times* did not cover President Carter's written statement on the Ninth Circuit Court of Appeals ruling concerning *INS* v. *Chadha*, despite the fact that Carter took a position on the case with regard to its appeal to the Supreme Court. "*Chadha* v. *Immigration and Naturalization Service* Statement on the Ninth Circuit Court of Appeals Decision," December 24, 1980.
15. We also used a Heckman selection model in which the selection equation was whether there was newspaper coverage of the president's speech, and the outcome equation was the tone of that coverage. Model diagnostics indicated that the selection model was not necessary and the results of that model corroborate those reported in Figure 6.5. Appendix Table 6.1 presents a tabular presentation of our empirical results.

7 PRESIDENTS AND PUBLIC OPINION

1. "Remarks on the United States Supreme Court Ruling on Same-Sex Marriage," June 26, 2015.
2. Randomization checks indicate the respondents are quite balanced across the treatment conditions. Appendix Table 7.1 reports the means of the respondents in each condition based on demographic variables.
3. An alternative approach is to rescale these variables from 0 to 1 (Bartels and Johnston 2013; Gibson and Nelson 2015). Rescaling our measure of diffuse support in this manner does not change the substance of our results.
4. Appendix Table 7.2 provides a tabular presentation of the results.
5. To ensure survey respondents devoted an appropriate amount of attention to taking the survey, we asked a factual question after respondents read the story regarding the state in which the dispute took place. Overall, 89.3 percent of respondents correctly identified Arizona (87 percent in the wetlands group and 91 percent in the immigration group). Excluding respondents who answered this question incorrectly does not substantively change our results.
6. We also examined whether specific support for the Court's decisions is conditional on respondents' affect toward President Obama (e.g., Armaly 2018). We failed to find evidence this was the case.

7. Monroe (1998, 8) posits that determining congruence, properly defined, requires "surveys using the same question wording to be conducted more than one time." It also involves measuring the direction of both opinion and policy change. If both move in the same direction, then there is "congruence" between public preferences and public policy. Since public opinion data often do not allow for such an examination, Monroe tests whether the relationships between public opinion and policy are consistent, or simply in agreement. Because we are not looking at changes in public opinion vis-à-vis presidential positions on Court cases over time, but simply whether the public and president are in agreement on the outcome of Court cases, we think that our approach to studying the relationship between presidential positions and public opinion on Supreme Court cases is more aligned with Monroe's concept of consistency. Nevertheless, we use the word congruence to avoid confusion and so that we might build on the most proximate area of scholarship to own our contribution.
8. Unfortunately, we cannot easily match our congressional response data in Chapter 5 with public opinion data on Supreme Court decisions to determine whether presidents are indeed more likely to generate a congressional response if they reference cases that are popular and salient with the American people. Polls are simply not numerous enough for us to make this determination (Marshall 2008). If Canes-Wrone's (2006) findings are generalizable to this subset of presidential speeches, nevertheless, then we would expect to find that one of the factors motivating presidents to call for legislation in response to a Court decision is the public's support for (or opposition to) a ruling.
9. Alternatively, presidents may pander to public opinion, choosing to take positions on issues that the public may support, but with which the president disagrees would be in citizens' best interests. Canes-Wrone (2006) calls this "policy pandering." Since we are agnostic as to whether presidents would support a case's outcome simply to align their preferences with public support for an issue, we do not explicitly investigate this type of public leadership in this chapter. It is certainly possible for presidents to take positions simply to align their views with public opinion, especially at times when public awareness of the policy is high.
10. For example, Nixon referenced *Gideon* v. *Wainwright* (1963) in 1971. Marshall's polling data are from 1963, the year the case was decided. Since this poll was taken nine years before Nixon took a position on the case, we cannot be sure that this poll reflects public opinion at the time of Nixon's remark. Accordingly, we exclude this presidential mention from our analysis.

11. From the original 53 cases in which there was a presidential statement on the case and a public opinion survey on the case, we excluded 13 (24.5 percent) instances in which the president spoke about the case, but did not take a position as to the case's outcome, or the president took both positive and negative positions on the case in differing speeches contemporaneous to the decision.
12. "Statement on the Supreme Court Decision on Physician-Assisted Suicide," June 26, 1997.

8 GOING PUBLIC ON SUPREME COURT CASES BEFORE THE MODERN PRESIDENCY

1. "Fireside Chat," March 9, 1937.
2. "Excerpts from the Press Conference," January 26, 1937.
3. Of course, it was probably not difficult for the justices to ascertain Roosevelt's position on the case given other public statements he made, as well as private discussions in Washington (Leuchtenburg 1966). Even without public pressure from the president, the Court ruled in his favor, determining that the National Labor Relations Act of 1935 was consistent with the Commerce Clause of the Constitution.
4. There is a much larger debate concerning the extent of going public among nineteenth-century presidents found in the first few chapters of Medhurst's (2008) edited volume. We do not engage this debate at length, but simply conclude that there is enough evidence to show that nineteenth-century presidents did, at least occasionally, engage in activities that could be considered going public.
5. Even though Tulis (1987) notes that presidents appear able to parlay public appeals into increased success in Congress, this is not without cost as heightened rhetoric also increases the public's expectations for presidential leadership. This can potentially undermine the implementation of the president's policies (Zarefsky 1986), and the presidency itself (Lowi 1985), through popular demagoguery. Furthermore, presidential rhetoric has become more simplistic over time (Lim 2008) and has mirrored the larger political context in which presidents govern (Shogan 2006).
6. We say this given that Medhurst (2008) makes virtually no mention of the judicial branch of government, and certainly not in relation to presidential rhetoric. Neither Laracey (2002) nor Tulis (1987) reference going public or presidential rhetoric vis-à-vis the Court, either.
7. Although we do not include them in our analysis, presidents remarked more frequently about the Supreme Court in general, as compared with its cases (Blackstone and Goelzhauser 2014). For example, both Washington and Adams commented on the early structure of the Supreme Court,

particularly as it concerned the circuit courts created by the Judiciary Act of 1789. Many presidents discussed the workload of the Supreme Court and requested additional resources for justices in annual messages to Congress. President Hoover referenced the Supreme Court generally in connection with the budgeting of the modern Supreme Court building that occurred during his administration. He also criticized candidate Franklin Roosevelt several times for comments that Roosevelt made about justices belonging to the Republican Party during a campaign speech.

8. "Special Message to Congress on the Steel Strike," June 10, 1952.
9. "Special Message," April 9, 1844.
10. "Special Message," February 27, 1843.
11. "Third Annual Message," December 7, 1903.
12. "Second Annual Message to Congress on the State of the Union," December 6, 1858.
13. "Seventh Annual Message," December 3, 1907.
14. "Second Annual Message," December 8, 1922.
15. "Fourth Annual Message," December 2, 1856
16. "Special Message," January 15, 1909.
17. "Informal Remarks in Nebraska," June 5, 1948.
18. "Excerpts from the Press Conference," April 13, 1937.

9 CONCLUSIONS

1. "Proclamation 9645—Enhancing Vetting Capabilities and Processes for Detecting Attempted Entry Into the United States by Terrorists or Other Public-Safety Threats," September 24, 2017.
2. "Statement on Signing the Countering America's Adversaries Through Sanctions Act," August 2, 2018.
3. "Remarks During a Cabinet Meeting," January 10, 2018.
4. See also "Remarks on Signing Legislation on Tax Reform and on Funding for the Departments of Homeland Security, Defense, and Health and Human Services and an Exchange With Reporters," December 22, 2017.
5. "Statement of Administration Policy: H. J. Res. 111 – Disapproving the Rule, Submitted by the Consumer Financial Protection Bureau, Known as the Arbitration Agreements Rule," July 24, 2017.
6. "Statement on the Supreme Court's Decision Regarding the Executive Order on Protecting the Nation From Foreign Terrorist Entry Into the United States," June 26, 2017.
7. It is helpful to understand the types of stories President Trump competed with for coverage on the day after his remarks on the Court's decisions. Two examples help to illustrate this. First, even though Trump issued a written statement on the terrorist attack in New York City on December 11, 2017, in

which he referenced the *Hawaii* case and other efforts he thought would combat terrorism, his remarks did not make the *Times*. The focus of that day's coverage was on the Alabama Senate race between Roy Moore and Doug Jones, with Jones (the Democratic candidate) winning a surprise victory in the Deep South. Second, Trump criticized the individual mandate (and *Sebelius*) during remarks at a Cabinet Meeting, but the news focused on what he said behind closed doors, where he criticized the nation of Haiti and the continent of Africa, while praising Norway.

8. "As you may know, the Supreme Court upheld President Trump's travel ban against citizens of five Muslim majority countries. Do you approve or disapprove of this decision?" Quinnipiac University Poll, June 27–July 1, 2018 (49 percent approve, 46 percent disapprove, 5 percent unsure).
9. "As you may know a health reform bill was signed into law in 2010, known commonly as the Affordable Care Act or Obamacare. Given what you know about the health reform law, do you have a generally favorable or generally unfavorable opinion of it?" Kaiser Family Foundation, January 16–21, 2018 (50 percent favorable, 42 percent unfavorable, 8 percent unsure).
10. To bolster this point, Republicans tend to favor President Trump's positions on both issues by a wide margin. A Quinnipiac University Poll (June 14–17, 2018) reveals that 85 percent of Republicans (as compared with 44 percent of all Americans) answered "repealed" in response to the question, "In general, would you like to see the Affordable Care Act, also known as Obamacare, remain in place, or would you like to see Obamacare repealed?" Another Quinnipiac University Poll (February 2–6, 2017) reveals that 88 percent of Republicans (as compared with 46 percent of all Americans) answered "support" in response to the question, "Now I'd like to ask you a few questions about President Trump's executive order on immigration. Do you support or oppose suspending all travel by citizens of Iraq, Syria, Iran, Libya, Somalia, Sudan, and Yemen to the US for 90 days?"
11. http://www.trumptwitterarchive.com/
12. Recall we searched the *Public Papers of the Presidents* for the term "Supreme Court." We opted to search for "court" instead given that Twitter is a forum for communication based on brevity (Perez 2018).
13. Although not all presidential comments on the Court's decisions implicate constitutional matters, the vast majority (75 percent) of cases mentioned by presidents involve constitutional interpretation, as opposed to statutory construction, administrative rule making, or federal common law (Spaeth et al. 2018).
14. Of course, we recognize that constitutional debate is not just about Supreme Court decisions (e.g., Levinson 2006; Tushnet 1999).
15. We do not, however, agree that singling out judges for characteristics such as their ethnicity, race, or gender is appropriate behavior by presidents.

References

Abraham, Henry J. 2008. *Justices, Presidents, and Senators: A History of U.S. Supreme Court Appointments from Washington to Bush II*. Lanham, MD: Rowman & Littlefield.

Adarand v. *Pena*, 515 U.S. 200 (1995).

Agence France Presse. 2012. "Did Obama Step Over Line with Supreme Court Blast?" *Agence France Presse*, April 4.

Akron v. *Akron Center for Reproductive Health*, 462 U.S. 416 (1983).

Alexander v. *Holmes County Board of Education*, 396 U.S. 19 (1969).

American Presidency Project. 2017. *Public Papers of the Presidents*. www.presidency.ucsb.edu/ (January 31, 2017).

American Presidency Project. 2018. *Public Papers of the Presidents*. www.presidency.ucsb.edu/ (January 31, 2018).

American Presidency Project. 2019. *Public Papers of the Presidents*. www.presidency.ucsb.edu/ (March 20, 2019).

Anderson, James E. 2015. *Public Policymaking*, 8th ed. Stamford, CT: Cengage.

Arizona v. *United States*, 567 U.S. 387 (2012).

Armaly, Miles T. 2018. "Extra-Judicial Actor Induced Change in Supreme Court Legitimacy." *Political Research Quarterly* 71: 600–613.

Associated Press. 2012. "McConnell Says Obama Trying to Influence Justices," *Associated Press State & Local Wire*, April 5.

Bailey, Michael A., Brian Kamoie, and Forrest Maltzman. 2005. "Signals from the Tenth Justice: The Political Role of the Solicitor General in Supreme Court Decision Making." *American Journal of Political Science* 49: 72–85.

Bailey, Michael, Lee Sigelman, and Clyde Wilcox. 2003. "Presidential Persuasion on Social Issues: A Two-Way Street?" *Political Research Quarterly* 56: 49–58.

Baird, Vanessa A. 2001. "Building Institutional Legitimacy: The Role of Procedural Justice." *Political Research Quarterly* 54: 333–354.

Baker, Peter. 2017. "Can Trump Destroy Obama's Legacy?" *The New York Times: Sunday Review*, June 23.

Baltimore Sun. 2012. "Obama and Judicial Review," *Baltimore Sun*, April 6.

Barnes, Robert. 2010. "Reactions Split on Obama's Remark, Alito's Response at State of the Union," *Washington Post*, January 29.

Barnes, Robert. 2012. "The Supreme Court, Absent from the Election Debate," *Washington Post*, September 30.

Barrett, Andrew W. 2004. "Gone Public: The Impact of Going Public on Presidential Legislative Success." *American Politics Research* 32: 338–370.

Barrett, Andrew W. 2005. "Going Public as a Legislative Weapon: Measuring Presidential Appeals Regarding Specific Legislation." *Presidential Studies Quarterly* 35: 1–10.

Barrett, Andrew. W. 2007. "Press Coverage of Legislative Appeals by the President." *Political Research Quarterly* 60: 655–668.

Barrett, Andrew W., and Jeffrey S. Peake. 2007. "When the President Comes to Town: Examining Local Newspaper Coverage of Domestic Presidential Travel." *American Politics Research* 35: 3–31.

Bartels, Brandon L., and Christopher D. Johnston. 2013. "On the Ideological Foundations of Supreme Court Legitimacy in the American Public." *American Journal of Political Science* 57: 184–199.

Baruch, Hezki. 2016. "Zionist Union: Fire Shaked for Criticizing Court," *Arutz Sheva*, March 13.

Baum, Lawrence. 2013. *The Supreme Court*, 11th ed. Thousand Oaks, CA: CQ Press.

Baum, Matthew A., and Samuel Kernell. 1999. "Has Cable Ended the Golden Age of Presidential Television?" *American Political Science Review* 93: 99–114.

Baumgartner, Frank, and Bryan D. Jones. 1993. *Agendas and Instability in American Politics*. Chicago, IL: University of Chicago Press.

Bennett, W. Lance. 2016. *News: The Politics of Illusion*, 9th ed. Chicago, IL : University of Chicago Press.

Berinsky, Adam. 2009. *In Time of War: Understanding American Public Opinion from World War II to Iraq*. Chicago, IL: University of Chicago Press.

Berinsky, Adam J., Gregory A. Huber, and Gabriel S. Lenz. 2012. "Evaluating Online Labor Markets for Experimental Research: Amazon.com's Mechanical Turk." *Political Analysis* 20: 351–368.

Bermant, Gordon, and Russell R. Wheeler. 1995. "Federal Judges and the Judicial Branch: Their Independence and Accountability." *Mercer Law Review* 46: 835–861.

Bickel, Alexander. 1962. *The Least Dangerous Branch: The Supreme Court at the Bar of Politics*. Indianapolis, IN: Bobbs-Merrill Company.

Black, Ryan C., and Ryan J. Owens. 2012. *The Solicitor General and the United States Supreme Court: Executive Influence and Judicial Decisions*. New York, NY: Cambridge University Press.

Black, Ryan C., Ryan J. Owens, and Miles T. Armaly. 2016. "A Well-Traveled Lot: A Research Note on Judicial Travel by U.S. Supreme Court Justices." *Justice System Journal* 37: 367–384.

Black, Ryan C., and James F. Spriggs, II. 2008. "An Empirical Study of the Length of U.S. Supreme Court Opinions." *Houston Law Review* 45: 621–683.

Blackman, Josh. 2016. *Unraveled: Obamacare, Religious Liberty, and Executive Power*. New York, NY: Cambridge University Press.

Blackstone, Bethany. 2013. "An Analysis of Policy–Based Congressional Responses to the U.S. Supreme Court's Constitutional Decisions." *Law & Society Review* 47: 199–228.

Blackstone, Bethany, and Greg Goelzhauser. 2014. "Presidential Rhetoric Toward the Supreme Court." *Judicature* 97: 179–187.

Boddery, Scott S., and Jeff Yates. 2014. "Do Policy Messengers Matter? Majority Opinion Writers as Policy Cues in Public Agreement with Supreme Court Decisions." *Political Research Quarterly* 67: 851–863.

Boller, Paul F., Jr., and John George. 1989. *They Never Said It: A Book of Fake Quotes, Misquotes, and Misleading Attributions*. New York, NY: Oxford University Press.

Bond, Jon R., and Richard Fleisher. 1990. *The President in the Legislative Arena*. Chicago, IL: University of Chicago Press.

Boumediene v. *Bush*, 553 U.S. 723 (2008).

Bowsher v. *Synar*, 478 U.S. 714 (1986).

Boydstun, Amber. 2013. *Making the News: Politics, the Media, and Agenda Setting*. Chicago, IL: University of Chicago Press.

Brace, Paul, and Barbara Hinckley. 1993. "Presidential Activities from Truman Through Reagan: Timing and Impact." *Journal of Politics* 55: 382–398.

Bradshaw, Seth C., Kevin Coe, and Rico Neumann. 2014. "Newspaper Attention to Major Presidential Addresses: A Reexamination of Conceptualizations, Predictors, and Effects." *Communication Reports* 27: 53–64.

Bravin, Jess. 2015. "President Obama's Supreme Court Remarks Set Him Apart," *Wall Street Journal*, June 10.

Brennan Center for Justice. 2018. "In His Own Words: The President's Attacks on the Courts." www.brennancenter.org/analysis/his-own-words-presidents-attacks-courts (March 13, 2019).

Brewer v. *Arizona Dream Act Coalition*, 138 S.Ct. 1279 (2018).

Broder, David. 2010. "Confrontation between the Branches; Justice Alito Reacts to the President, and Democrats Scurry to Disarm the Latest Supreme Court Ruling," *Newsday*, January 31.

Brown v. *Board of Education*, 347 U.S. 483 (1954).

Buckley v. *Valeo*, 424 U.S. 1 (1976).

Bullock, Charles S., III, and Charles M. Lamb, eds. 1984. *Implementation of Civil Rights Policy*. Monterey, CA: Brooks/Cole Publishing.

Bump, Philip. 2019. "Trump Is the Most Polarizing President on Record – and Almost Nobody's Opinion of Him Is Changing," *Washington Post*, January 16.

Bureau of Labor Statistics. 2017. "Databases, Tables & Calculators by Subject." www.bls.gov/data/ (July 1, 2017).

Burgess, Susan R. 1992. *Contest for Constitutional Authority: The Abortion and War Powers Debate*. Lawrence, Kansas: University Press of Kansas.

Calabresi, Steven G., and Saikrishna B. Prakash. 1994. "The President's Power to Execute the Laws." *Yale Law Journal* 104: 541–665.

Calabresi, Steven G., and Christopher S. Yoo. 2008. *The Unitary Executive: Presidential Power from Washington to Bush*. New Haven, CT: Yale University Press.

Caldeira, Gregory A. 1986. "Neither the Purse nor the Sword: Dynamics of Public Confidence in the Supreme Court." *American Political Science Review* 80: 1209–1226.

Caldeira, Gregory A. 1987. "Public Opinion and the U.S. Supreme Court: FDR's Court-Packing Plan." *American Political Science Review* 81: 1139–1153.

Caldeira, Gregory A., and James L. Gibson. 1992. "The Etiology of Public Support for the Supreme Court." *American Journal of Political Science* 36: 635–664.

Cameron, Charles, and Jee-Kwang Park. 2011. "Going Public When Opinion Is Contested: Evidence from Presidents' Campaigns for Supreme Court Nominees, 1930–2009." *Presidential Studies Quarterly* 41: 442–470.

Canes-Wrone, Brandice. 2001. "The President's Legislative Influence from Public Appeals." *American Journal of Political Science* 45: 313–329.

Canes-Wrone, Brandice. 2006. *Who Leads Whom? Presidents, Policy, and the Public.* Chicago, IL: University of Chicago Press.

Canes-Wrone, Brandice, and Kenneth W. Shotts. 2004. "The Conditional Nature of Presidential Responsiveness to Public Opinion." *American Journal of Political Science* 48: 690–706.

Canon, Bradley C., and Charles A. Johnson. 1999. *Judicial Policies: Implementation and Impact.*Washington, DC: CQ Press.

Caplan, Lincoln. 1987. *The Tenth Justice: The Solicitor General and the Rule of Law.* New York, NY: Vintage Books.

Cassens Weiss, Debra. 2018. "Kentucky Governor Criticizes 'Activist Judges' after State Supreme Court Overturns Pension Law," *ABA Journal*, December 14.

Cavari, Amnon. 2017. *The Party Politics of Presidential Rhetoric.* New York, NY: Cambridge University Press.

Chaiken, Shelly. 1980. "Heuristic Versus Systematic Information Processing and the Use of Source Versus Message Cues in Persuasion." *Journal of Personality and Social Psychology* 39: 752–766.

Chemerinsky, Erwin. 1997. *Interpreting the Constitution.* Santa Barbara, CA: Praeger.

Chemerinsky, Erwin. 2018. "Donald Trump's Threat to Judicial Independence," *Sacramento Bee*, November 28.

Chicago Daily Herald. 2012. "Let's Respect Our System of Checks and Balances," *Chicago Daily Herald*, April 8.

Chin Bak Kan v. *United States*, 186 U.S. 193 (1902).

Christenson, Dino P., and David M. Glick. 2015. "Chief Justice Roberts's Health Care Decision Disrobed: The Microfoundations of the Supreme Court's Legitimacy." *American Journal of Political Science* 59: 403–418.

Citizens United v. *Federal Election Commission*, 558 U.S. 310 (2010).

Clark, Tom. S. 2009. "The Separation of Powers, Court Curbing, and Judicial Legitimacy." *American Journal of Political Science* 53: 971–989.

Clark, Tom S. 2011. *The Limits of Judicial Independence.* New York, NY: Cambridge University Press.

Clark, Tom S., and Jonathan P. Kastellec. 2015. "Source Cues and Public Support for the Supreme Court." *American Politics Research* 43: 504–535.

Clark, Tom S., Jeffrey R. Lax, and Douglas Rice. 2015. "Measuring the Political Salience of Supreme Court Cases." *Journal of Law and Courts* 3: 37–65.

Clawson, Rosalee A., and Eric N. Waltenburg. 2003. "Support for a Supreme Court Affirmative Action Decision: A Story in Black and White." *American Politics Research* 31: 251–279.

Clifford, Scott, Ryan M. Jewell, and Philip D. Waggoner. 2015. "Are Samples Drawn from Mechanical Turk Valid for Research on Political Ideology?" *Research & Politics* 2: https://doi.org/10.1177d/2053168015622072.

Clinton v. *City of New York*, 524 U.S. 417 (1998).
Clymer, Adam. 2003. "At Rights Forum, the Target Is Bush," *New York Times*, January 18.
Cohen, Jeffrey E. 1995. "Presidential Rhetoric and the Public Agenda." *American Journal of Political Science* 39: 87–107.
Cohen, Jeffrey E. 1997. *Presidential Responsiveness and Public Policy-Making*. Ann Arbor, MI: University of Michigan Press.
Cohen, Jeffrey E. 2008. *The Presidency in an Era of 24-Hour News*. Princeton, NJ: Princeton University Press.
Cohen, Jeffrey E. 2010. *Going Local: Presidential Leadership in the Post-Broadcast Age*. New York, NY: Cambridge University Press.
Cohen, Jeffrey E., Michael A. Krassa, and John A. Hamman. 1991. "The Impact of Presidential Campaigning on Midterm US Senate Elections." *American Political Science Review* 85: 165–178.
Cohen, Jeffrey E., and Richard J. Powell. 2005. "Building Public Support from the Grassroots Up: The Impact of Presidential Travel on State-Level Approval." *Presidential Studies Quarterly* 35: 11–27.
Collins, Paul M., Jr. 2008a. *Friends of the Supreme Court: Interest Groups and Judicial Decision Making*. New York, NY: Oxford University Press.
Collins, Paul M., Jr. 2008b. "The Consistency of Judicial Choice." *Journal of Politics* 70: 861–873.
Collins, Paul M., Jr., Pamela C. Corley, and Jesse Hamner. 2015. "The Influence of Amicus Curiae Briefs on U.S. Supreme Court Opinion Content." *Law & Society Review* 49: 917–944.
Collins, Paul M., Jr., and Lori A. Ringhand. 2013. *Supreme Court Confirmation Hearings and Constitutional Change*. New York, NY: Cambridge University Press.
Collins, Todd A., and Christopher A. Cooper. 2012. "Case Salience and Media Coverage of Supreme Court Decisions: Toward a New Measure." *Political Research Quarterly* 65: 396–407.
Collins, Todd A., and Christopher A. Cooper. 2015. "Making the Cases 'Real': Newspaper Coverage of U.S. Supreme Court Cases 1953–2004." *Political Communication* 32: 23–42.
Communications Workers of America v. *Beck*, 487 U.S. 735 (1988).
Congressional Quarterly. 2018. "Supreme Court Collection." http://library.cqpress.com/scc/ (March 20, 2019).
Cooley v. *Board of Wardens*, 53 U.S. (12 How.) 299 (1852).
Cooper v. *Aaron*, 358 U.S. 1 (1958).
Corley, Pamela C., Paul M. Collins, Jr., and Bryan Calvin. 2011. "Lower Court Influence on U.S. Supreme Court Opinion Content." *Journal of Politics* 73: 31–44.
Corwin, Edward S. 1957. *The President: Office and Powers, 1787–1957*. New York, NY: New York University Press.
Dahl, Robert A. 1957. "Decision-Making in a Democracy: The Supreme Court as a National Policy-Maker." *Journal of Public Law* 6: 279–295.
Daily Mail Reporter. 2012. "Republican Senator Slams Obama as 'Stupid' over Health Care Boasts," *Daily Mail*, April 8.

Davis, Richard. 2014. "The Symbiotic Relationship Between the U.S. Supreme Court and the Press." In *Covering the United States Supreme Court in the Digital Age*, ed. Richard Davis. New York, NY: Cambridge University Press, 4–22.

Days, Drew S., III. 2001. "When the President Says 'NO': A Few Thoughts on Executive Power and the Tradition of Solicitor General Independence." *Journal of Appellate Practice and Process* 3: 509–520.

Dellinger, Walter. 1993. "Memorandum for Bernard N. Nussbaum, Counsel to the President. The Legal Significance of Presidential Signing Statements, November 3." https://scholarship.law.duke.edu/cgi/viewcontent.cgi?referer=https://www.google.com/&httpsredir=1&article=2177&context=faculty_scholarship (March 20, 2019).

Dennison, Lyle. 2018. "Chief Justice, President in a Public Feud." *Constitution Daily* https://constitutioncenter.org/blog/chief-justice-president-in-a-public-feud (March 18, 2019).

Department of the Navy v. *Egan*, 484 U.S. 518 (1988).

Devins, Neal. 2006. "Should the Supreme Court Fear Congress?" *Minnesota Law Review* 90: 1337–1362.

District of Columbia v. *Heller*, 554 U.S. 570 (2008).

Doherty, Brendan J. 2012. *The Rise of the President's Permanent Campaign*. Lawrence, KS: University Press of Kansas.

Dost, Meredith. 2015. "Dim Public Awareness of Supreme Court as Major Rulings Loom," *Pew Research Center*, May 14.

Dred Scott v. *Sandford*, 60 U.S. 393 (1857).

Druckman, James N., Donald P. Green, James H. Kuklinski, and Arthur Lupia. 2006. "The Growth and Development of Experimental Research in Political Science." *American Political Science Review* 100: 627–635.

Ducat, Craig R., and Robert L. Dudley. 1989. "Federal District Judges and Presidential Power During the Postwar Era." *Journal of Politics* 51: 98–118.

Easterbrook, Frank H. 1990. "What's so Special about Judges?" *University of Colorado Law Review* 61: 773–782.

Easton, David. 1975. "A Re-assessment of the Concept of Political Support." *British Journal of Political Science* 5: 435–457.

Editorial Board. 2012. "A More Judicious View," *The Washington Post*, April 4.

Edwards, George C., III. 2003. *On Deaf Ears: The Limits of the Bully Pulpit*. New Haven, CT: Yale University Press.

Edwards, George C., III. 2016. *Predicting the Presidency: The Path to Successful Leadership*. Princeton, NJ: Princeton University Press.

Edwards, George C., III and Andrew Barrett. 2000. "Presidential Agenda Setting in Congress." In *Polarized Politics*, eds. Jon R. Bond, and Richard Fleisher. Washington DC: CQ Press, 109–133.

Edwards, George C., III, Andrew Barrett, and Jeffrey Peake. 1997. "The Legislative Impact of Divided Government." *American Journal of Political Science* 41: 545–563.

Edwards, George C., III, and B. Dan Wood. 1999. "Who Influences Whom? The President, Congress, and the Media." *American Political Science Review* 93: 327–344.

Ellis, Richard J., and Alexis Walker. 2007. "Policy Speech in the Nineteenth Century Rhetorical Presidency: The Case of Zachary Taylor's 1849 Tour." *Presidential Studies Quarterly* 37: 248–269.

Employers' Liability Cases, 207 U.S. 463 (1908).
Engel v. *Vitale*, 370 U.S. 421 (1962).
Entman, Robert M. 2012. *Scandal and Silence: Media Responses to Presidential Misconduct*. Cambridge, MA: Polity Press.
Epstein, Lee, and Jack Knight. 1998. *The Choices Justices Make*. Washington, DC: CQ Press.
Epstein, Lee, William M. Landes, and Richard A. Posner. 2010. "Inferring the Winning Party in the Supreme Court from the Pattern of Questioning at Oral Argument." *Journal of Legal Studies* 39: 433–467.
Epstein, Lee, William M. Landes, and Richard A. Posner. 2014. "The Best for Last: The Timing of U.S. Supreme Court Decisions." *Duke Law Journal* 64: 991–1022.
Epstein, Lee, and Andrew D. Martin. 2010. "Does Public Opinion Influence the Supreme Court-Possibly Yes (But We're Not Sure Why)." *University of Pennsylvania Journal of Constitutional Law* 13: 263–281.
Epstein, Lee, and Jeffrey A. Segal. 2000. "Measuring Issue Salience." *American Journal of Political Science* 44: 66–83.
Epstein, Lee, Jeffrey A. Segal, Harold J. Spaeth, and Thomas G. Walker. 1994. *The Supreme Court Compendium: Data, Decisions & Developments*. Thousand Oaks, CA: CQ Press.
Ericson, David. 1977. "Newspaper Coverage of the Supreme Court." *Journalism Quarterly* 54: 605–607.
Erikson, Robert S., Michael B. MacKuen, James A. Stimson. 2002. *The Macro Polity*. New York, NY: Cambridge University Press.
Eshbaugh-Soha, Matthew. 2005. "The Politics of Presidential Agendas." *Political Research Quarterly* 58: 257–268.
Eshbaugh-Soha, Matthew. 2006. *The President's Speeches: Beyond "Going Public."* Boulder, CO: Lynne Reinner.
Eshbaugh-Soha, Matthew. 2010. "The Politics of Presidential Speeches." *Congress and the Presidency* 37: 1–21.
Eshbaugh-Soha, Matthew. 2011. "Presidential Public Relations." In *Political Public Relations: Principles and Applications*, eds. Jesper Stromback, and Spiro Kiousis. New York, NY: Routledge, 95–114.
Eshbaugh-Soha, Matthew. 2013. "Presidential Leadership of the News Media: The Case of the Press Conference." *Political Communication* 30: 548–564.
Eshbaugh-Soha, Matthew. 2017. "Presidential Rhetoric, Agency Turnover, and the Importance of Salience to Bureaucratic Leadership." *Social Science Journal* 54: 206–215.
Eshbaugh-Soha, Matthew. 2018. "Presidential Leadership of Partisan News." *Presidential Studies Quarterly* 48: 27–48.
Eshbaugh-Soha, Matthew, and Paul M. Collins, Jr. 2015. "Presidential Rhetoric and Supreme Court Decisions." *Presidential Studies Quarterly* 45: 633–652.
Eshbaugh-Soha, Matthew, and Ronald J. McGauvran. 2018. "Presidential Leadership, the News Media, and Income Inequality." *Political Research Quarterly* 71: 157–171
Eshbaugh-Soha, Matthew, and Tom Miles. 2008–2009. "George W. Bush's Domestic Policy Agenda." *American Review of Politics* 29: 351–369.
Eshbaugh-Soha, Matthew, and Sean Nicholson-Crotty. 2009. "Presidential Campaigning in Midterm Elections." *American Review of Politics* 30: 35–50.

Eshbaugh-Soha, Matthew, and Jeffrey S. Peake. 2005. "Presidents and the Economic Agenda." *Political Research Quarterly* 58: 127–138.

Eshbaugh-Soha, Matthew, and Jeffrey S. Peake. 2006. "The Contemporary Presidency: 'Going Local' to Reform Social Security." *Presidential Studies Quarterly* 36: 689–704.

Eshbaugh-Soha, Matthew, and Jeffrey S. Peake. 2011. *Breaking through the Noise: Presidential Leadership, Public Opinion, and the News Media*. Stanford, CA: Stanford University Press.

Eskridge, William N. 1991. "Overriding Supreme Court Statutory Interpretation Decisions." *Yale Law Journal* 101: 331–455.

Evans, Martin C. 1989. "Rights Leader Urges Protest of Supreme Court Decisions," *St. Petersburg Times*, July 14.

Fabian, Jordan. 2015. "Obama's Frustration with Courts Spills into Public Eye," *The Hill*, June 8.

Farber, Daniel A., and Suzanna Sherry. 2009. *Judgment Calls: Principle and Politics in Constitutional Law*. New York NY: Oxford University Press.

Farnsworth, Stephen J., and S. Robert Lichter. 2006. *The Mediated Presidency: Television News and Presidential Governance*. New York, NY: Rowman and Littlefield.

Ferris, Sarah. 2015. "Obama's Supreme Court Gambit," *The Hill*, June 11.

Fett, Patrick J. 1994. "Presidential Legislative Priorities and Legislators' Voting Decisions: An Exploratory Analysis." *Journal of Politics* 56: 502–512.

Fisher, Louis. 2009. *The Supreme Court and Congress: Rival Interpretations*. Washington, DC: CQ Press.

Flemming, Roy B., John Bohte, and B. Dan Wood. 1997. "One Voice Among Many: The Supreme Court's Influence on Attentiveness to Issue in the United States, 1947–1992." *American Journal of Political Science* 41: 1224–1250.

Flemming, Roy B., B. Dan Wood, and John Bohte. 1999. "Attention to Issues in a System of Separated Powers: The Macrodynamics of American Policy Agendas." *Journal of Politics* 61: 75–108.

Flood v. *Kuhn*, 407 U.S. 258 (1972).

Franklin, Charles H., and Liane C. Kosaki. 1989, "Republican Schoolmaster: The U.S. Supreme Court, Public Opinion, and Abortion." *American Political Science Review* 83: 751–771.

Friedman, Barry. 1993. "Dialogue and Judicial Review." *Michigan Law Review* 91: 577–682.

Friedman, Barry. 2009. *The Will of the People: How Public Opinion Has Influenced the Supreme Court and Shaped the Meaning of the Constitution*. New York, NY: Farrar, Straus and Giroux.

Fullilove v. *Klutznick*, 448 U.S. 448 (1980).

Furman v. *Georgia*, 408 U.S. 238 (1972).

Gailey, Phil. 1989. "Uproar over Court's Flag Ruling Threatens to Debase Old Glory," *St. Petersburg Times*, June 24.

Gallup. 2017. "Presidential Job Approval Center." www.gallup.com/poll/124922/presidential-approval-center.aspx (January 30, 2017).

Gallup. 2018a. "Supreme Court." www.gallup.com/poll/4732/supreme-court.aspx (March 22, 2019).

Gallup. 2018b. "Marriage." https://news.gallup.com/poll/117328/marriage.aspx (March 25, 2019).
Gallup. 2018c. "Americans' Views of the Affordable Care Act, November 2018 (Trends)." https://news.gallup.com/poll/245063/americans-views-affordable-care-act-november-2018-trends.aspx?g_source=link_newsv9&g_campaign=item_245057&g_medium=copy (March 13, 2019).
Gallup. 2019. "Immigration." https://news.gallup.com/poll/1660/immigration.aspx (March 13, 2019).
Gant, Scott E. 1997. "Judicial Supremacy and Nonjudicial Interpretation of the Constitution." *Hastings Constitutional Law Quarterly* 24: 359–440.
Geer, John Gray. 1996. *From Tea Leaves to Opinion Polls: A Theory of Democratic Leadership*. New York, NY: Columbia University Press.
Gerhardt, Michael J. 2000. *The Federal Appointments Process: A Constitutional & Historical Analysis*. Durham, NC: Duke University Press.
Gibson, James L., and Gregory A. Caldeira. 2009. "Knowing the Supreme Court? A Reconsideration of Public Ignorance of the High Court." *Journal of Politics* 71: 429–441.
Gibson, James L., Gregory A. Caldeira, and Lester Kenyatta Spence. 2003. "Measuring Attitudes toward the United States Supreme Court." *American Journal of Political Science* 47: 354–367.
Gibson, James L., and Michael J. Nelson. 2015. "Is the U.S. Supreme Court's Legitimacy Grounded in Performance Satisfaction and Ideology?" *American Journal of Political Science* 59: 162–174.
Gideon v. *Wainwright*, 372 U.S. 335 (1963).
Giles, Micheal W., Bethany Blackstone, and Richard L. Vining Jr. 2008. "The Supreme Court in American Democracy: Unraveling the Linkages between Public Opinion and Judicial Decision Making." *Journal of Politics* 70: 293–306.
Ginsberg v. *New York*, 390 U.S. 629 (1968).
Globe and Mail. 2010. "Yes He Can Criticize the Supreme Court," *Globe and Mail*, February 3.
Gold Clause Cases, 294 U.S. 240 (1935), 294 U.S. 317 (1935), 294 U.S. 330 (1935).
Goldman, Sheldon. 1997. *Picking Federal Judges: Lower Court Selection from Roosevelt through Reagan*. New Haven, CT. Yale University Press.
Goldstein, Amy, and Dana Milbank. 2003. "Bush Joins Admissions Case Fight," *Washington Post*, January 16.
Goodman, Ellen. 1989. "Capturing the Flag for Political Payoff," *St. Louis Post-Dispatch*, June 30.
Greeley, Horace. 1864. *American Conflict: A History of the Great Rebellion in the United States of America, 1860-'64*. Hartford, CT: O.D. Case & Company.
Graber, Doris A, and Johanna Dunaway. 2015. *Mass Media and American Politics*, 9th ed. Washington, DC: CQ Press.
Graber, Mark A. 1993. "The Nonmajoritarian Difficulty: Legislative Deference to the Judiciary." *Studies in American Political Development* 7: 35–73.
Gratz v. *Bollinger*, 539 U.S. 244 (2003).
Greenhouse, Linda. 2003. "Bush and Affirmative Action," *New York Times*, January 17.
Greenhouse Linda. 2004. "Press Room Predictions." *Perspectives on Politics* 2: 781–784.
Greenhouse, Linda. 2010. "Justice Alito's Reaction," *New York Times*, January 27.

Gregg v. *Georgia*, 428 U.S. 153 (1976).
Groeling, Tim. 2010. *When Politicians Attack: Party Cohesion in the News Media*. New York, NY: Cambridge University Press.
Groeling, Tim, and Samuel Kernell. 1998. "Is Network News Coverage of the President Biased?" *Journal of Politics* 60: 1063–1087.
Groseclose, Tim, and Jeffrey Milyo. 2005. "A Measure of Media Bias." *Quarterly Journal of Economics* 120: 1191–1237.
Gross, Justin H., and Kaylee T. Johnson. 2016. "Twitter Taunts and Tirades: Negative Campaigning in the Age of Trump." *PS: Political Science & Politics* 49: 748–754.
Grove City College v. *Bell*, 465 U.S. 555 (1984).
Grutter v. *Bollinger*, 539 U.S. 306 (2003).
Hager, Gregory L., and Terry Sullivan. 1994. "President-Centered and Presidency-Centered Explanations of Presidential Public Activity." *American Journal of Political Science* 38: 1079–103.
Haider-Markel, Donald P., Mahalley D. Allen, and Morgen Johansen. 2006. "Understanding Variations in Media Coverage of US Supreme Court Decisions: Comparing Media Outlets in Their Coverage of *Lawrence* v. *Texas*." *Harvard International Journal of Press/Politics* 11: 64–85.
Hall, Matthew E. K. 2014. "The Semiconstrained Court: Public Opinion, the Separation of Powers, and the U.S. Supreme Court's Fear of Nonimplementation." *American Journal of Political Science* 58: 352–366.
Hallin, Daniel C. 1992. "Sound Bite News: Television Coverage of Elections, 1968–1988." *Journal of Communication* 42: 5–24.
Hamdan v. *Rumsfeld*, 548 U.S. 557 (2006).
Hamilton, James T. 2004. *All the News That's Fit to Sell*. Princeton, NJ: Princeton University Press.
Hammer v. *Dagenhart*, 247 U.S. 251 (1918).
Hansford, Thomas G., and James F. Spriggs, II. 2006. *The Politics of Precedent on the U.S. Supreme Court*. Princeton, NJ: Princeton University Press.
Hart, Roderick P., Jay P. Childers, and Colene J. Lind. 2013. *Political Tone: How Leaders Talk and Why*. Chicago, IL: University of Chicago Press.
Hartman, Rachel Rose. 2012. "Jay Carney: Obama Didn't Intend to Challenge Supreme Court's Authority." *abcnews.com*, http://abcnews.go.com/Politics/OTUS/jay-carney-obama-intend-challenge-supreme-courts-authority/story?id=16074310 (September 18, 2014).
Harvey, Anna, and Barry Friedman. 2006. "Pulling Punches: Congressional Constraints on the Supreme Court's Constitutional Rulings, 1987–2000." *Legislative Studies Quarterly* 31: 533–562.
Heith, Diane J. 2013. *The Presidential Road Show: Public Leadership in an Era of Party Polarization and Media Fragmentation*. Boulder, CO: Paradigm Publishers.
Hettinger, Virginia A., and Christopher Zorn. 2005. "Explaining the Incidence and Timing of Congressional Responses to the U.S. Supreme Court." *Legislative Studies Quarterly* 30: 5–28.
Hoekstra, Valerie J. 2000. "The Supreme Court and Local Public Opinion." *American Political Science Review* 94: 89–100.
Hoekstra, Valerie J. 2003. *Public Reaction to Supreme Court Decisions*. New York, NY: Cambridge University Press.

Hoekstra, Valerie J., and Jeffrey A. Segal. 1996. "The Shepherding of Local Public Opinion: The Supreme Court and *Lamb's Chapel*." *Journal of Politics* 58: 1079–1102.

Hoffman, Karen S. 2002. "'Going Public' in the Nineteenth Century: Grove Cleveland's Repeal of the Sherman Silver Purchase Act." *Rhetoric & Public Affairs* 5: 57–77.

Holland, Kenneth M. 2004. "FDR and Charles Evans Hughes: President versus Chief Justice." *In Franklin D. Roosevelt and the Transformation of the Supreme Court*, eds. Stephen K. Shaw, William D. Pederson, Frank J. Williams, and Michael R. Williams. New York, NY: ME Sharpe, 77–112.

Hollingsworth v. *Perry*, 570 U.S. 693 (2013).

Holmes, Lisa M. 2007. "Presidential Strategy in the Judicial Appointment Process: 'Going Public' in Support of Nominees to the U.S. Courts of Appeals." *American Politics Research* 35: 567–594.

Holmes, Lisa M. 2008. "Why 'Go Public'? Presidential Use of Nominees to the U.S. Courts of Appeals." *Presidential Studies Quarterly* 38: 110–122.

Horvit, Beverly, Adam. J. Schiffer, and Mark Wright. 2008. "The Limits of Presidential Agenda Setting: Predicting Newspaper Coverage of the Weekly Radio Address." *International Journal of Press/Politics* 13: 8–28.

Hunter, Robert. 1975. "Franklin's Tower." *Blues for Allah* (Grateful Dead Records).

Ignagni, Joseph, and James Meernik. 1994. "Explaining Congressional Attempts to Reverse Supreme Court Decisions." *Political Research Quarterly* 47: 353–371.

INS v. *Chadha*, 462 U.S. 919 (1983).

Iyengar, Shanto, and Donald R. Kinder. 1987. *News That Matters: Television and American Opinion*. Chicago, IL: University of Chicago Press.

Jacobs, Lawrence R., and Robert Y. Shapiro. 2000. *Politicians Don't Pander: Political Manipulation and the Loss of Democratic Responsiveness*. Chicago, IL: University of Chicago Press.

Jacoby, Tamar, Ann McDaniel, and Peter McKillop. 1989. "A Fight for Old Glory," *Newsweek*, July 3.

Janus v. *AFSCME*, 16–1466 (2018).

Jennings v. *Rodriguez*, 15–1204 (2018).

Johnsen, Dawn E. 2004. "Functional Departmentalism and Nonjudicial Interpretation: Who Determines Constitutional Meaning? *Law & Contemporary Problems* 67: 105–147.

Johnson, Timothy R. 2003. "The Supreme Court, the Solicitor General, and the Separation of Powers." *American Politics Research* 31: 426–451.

Johnson, Timothy R., Ryan C. Black, Jerry Goldman, and Sarah A. Treul. 2009. "Inquiring Minds Want to Know: Do Justices Tip Their Hands with Questions at Oral Argument in the U.S. Supreme Court." *Washington University Journal of Law & Policy* 29: 241–261.

Johnson, Timothy R., and Andrew D. Martin. 1998. "The Public's Conditional Response to Supreme Court Decisions." *American Political Science Review* 92: 299–309.

Johnson, Timothy R., and Jason M. Roberts. 2004. "Presidential Capital and the Supreme Court Confirmation Process." *Journal of Politics* 66: 663–83.

Johnson, Tyler, and Erica Socker. 2012. "Actions, Factions, and Interactions: Newsworthy Influences on Supreme Court Coverage." *Social Science Quarterly* 93: 434–463.

Kahneman, Daniel, Jack L. Knetsch, and Richard H. Thaler. 1991. "Anomalies: The Endowment Effect, Loss Aversion, and Status Quo Bias." *Journal of Economic Perspectives* 5: 193–206.

Kaiser Family Foundation. 2018. http://www.pollingreport.com/health.htm. (March 22, 2019).

Kastellec, Jonathan P., and Eduardo L. Leoni. 2007. "Using Graphs Instead of Tables in Political Science." *Perspectives on Politics* 5: 755–771.

Kent v. *Dulles*, 357 U.S. 116 (1958).

Keele, Luke J., Brian J. Fogarty, and James A. Stimson. 2004. "Presidential Campaigning in the 2002 Congressional Elections." *PS: Political Science and Politics* 37: 827–832.

Kelleher, Christine A., and Jennifer Wolak. 2007. "Explaining Public Confidence in the Branches of State Government." *Political Research Quarterly* 60: 707–721.

Kelley, Christopher S., and Bryan W. Marshall. 2010. "Going it Alone: The Politics of Presidential Signing Statements from Reagan to Bush II." *Social Science Quarterly* 91: 168–187.

Kernell, Samuel. 1997. *Going Public: New Strategies of Presidential Leadership*, 3rd ed. Washington, DC: CQ Press.

Kernell, Samuel, and Laurie L. Rice. 2011. "Cable and the Partisan Polarization of the President's Audience." *Presidential Studies Quarterly* 41: 693–711.

Kiefer, Heather Mason. 2005. "Support Cooling for Flag-Burning Amendment." https://news.gallup.com/poll/17491/support-cooling-flagburning-amendment.aspx (March 20, 2019).

King v. *Burwell*, 135 S.Ct. 475 (2014).

King, Kimi Lynn, and James Meernik. 1999. "The Supreme Court and the Powers of the Executive: The Adjudication of Foreign Policy" *Political Research Quarterly* 52: 801–824.

Kingdon, John W. 1995. *Agendas, Alternatives, and Public Policies*, 2nd ed. New York, NY: Longman.

Kramer, Larry D. 2004. *The People Themselves: Popular Constitutionalism and Judicial Review*. New York, NY: Oxford University Press.

Kreis, Ramona. 2017 "The 'Tweet Politics' of President Trump." *Journal of Language and Politics* 16: 607–618.

Krosnick, Jon A. 1988. "The Role of Attitude Importance in Social Evaluation: A Study of Policy Preferences, Presidential Candidate Evaluations, and Voting Behavior." *Journal of Personality and Social Psychology* 55: 196–210.

Krutz, Glen S., Richard Fleisher, and Jon R. Bond. 1998. "From Abe Fortas to Zöe Baird: Why Some Presidential Nominations Fail in the Senate." *American Political Science Review* 92: 871–881.

Kumar, Martha Joynt. 2007. *Managing the President's Message: The White House Communications Operation*. Baltimore, MD: Johns Hopkins University Press.

Landis, Richard J., and Gary G. Koch. 1977. "The Measurement of Observer Agreement for Categorical Data." *Biometrics* 33: 159–174.

Lane, Charles. 2018. "What We Should Take Away from the Trump Roberts Kerfuffle," *Washington Post*, November 26.

Laracey, Mel. 2002. *Presidents and the People: The Partisan Story of Going Public*. College Station, TX: Texas A&M University Press.

Laracey, Mel. 2009. "*The Rhetorical Presidency* Today: How Does It Stand Up?" *Presidential Studies Quarterly* 39: 908–931.

Laurence, Charles. 2003. "I Opened that Letter and Said: 'Can We Sue Them?,'" *Sunday Telegraph*, January 19.

Leighley, Jan E. 2003. *Mass Media and Politics: A Social Science Perspective*. Boston, MA: Houghton Mifflin.

Leuchtenburg, William E. 1966. "The Origins of Franklin D. Roosevelt's 'Court-Packing' Plan." *Supreme Court Review* 1966: 347–400.

Levinson, Sanford. 2006. *Our Undemocratic Constitution: Where the Constitution Goes Wrong (And How We the People Can Correct It)*. New York, NY: Oxford University Press.

Lewis, Anthony. 1989. "Abroad at Home: What Is America?," *New York Times*, June 29.

Lewis, John. 2003. "Bush's Strategy of Racial Innuendo a Telling and Troubling Sign," *Atlanta Journal-Constitution*, January 20.

Lewis, Neil A. 2003. "Bush and Affirmative Action: Constitutional Questions," *New York Times*, January 16.

Light, Paul. 1999. *The President's Agenda*, 3rd ed. Baltimore, MD: Johns Hopkins University Press.

Lim, Elvin T. 2008. *The Anti-Intellectual Presidency: The Decline of Presidential Rhetoric from George Washington to George W. Bush*. New York, NY: Oxford University Press.

Linos, Katerina, and Kimberly Twist. 2016. "The Supreme Court, the Media, and Public Opinion: Comparing Experimental and Observational Methods." *Journal of Legal Studies* 45: 223–254.

Liptak, Adam. 2010. "Supreme Court Gets a Rare Rebuke, in Front of a Nation," *New York Times*, January 28.

Liptak, Adam. 2018. "Chief Justice Defends Judicial Independence After Trump Attacks 'Obama Judge,'" *New York Times*, November 21.

Lithwick, Dahlia. 2017. "Why Trump Has Declared War on the Judiciary," *Slate*, February 10.

Long, Scott. 1997. *Regression Models for Categorical and Limited Dependent Variables*. Thousand Oaks, CA: Sage Publications.

Loughlin, Sean. 2003. "Bush: Court Should Decide Role of Race in Admissions," *CNN*, January 21.

Lowi, Theodore J. 1985. *The Personal President: Power Invested, Promise Unfulfilled*. Ithaca, NY: Cornell University Press.

Luckey, John R. 2009. "Flag Protection: A Brief History and Summary of Recent Supreme Court Decisions and Proposed Constitutional Amendments." CRS Report for Congress https://fas.org/sgp/crs/misc/95-709.pdf (March 12, 2019).

Magnuson, Eric J., and Chelsea A. Walcker. 2017. "The Decline in News Coverage of Appellate Court Decisions." www.robinskaplan.com/resources/articles/the-decline-in-news-coverage-of-appellate-court-decisions (March 12, 2019).

Maltese, John Anthony. 1995a. *The Selling of Supreme Court Nominees*. Baltimore, MD: Johns Hopkins University Press.

Maltese, John Anthony. 1995b. "Speaking Out: The Role of Presidential Rhetoric in the Modern Supreme Court Confirmation Process." *Presidential Studies Quarterly* 25: 447–455.

Maltzman, Forrest, and Paul J. Wahlbeck. 2003. "Salience or Politics: New York Times Coverage of the Supreme Court." Presented at the Annual Meeting of the Midwest Political Science Association, Chicago, IL.

Marbury v. *Madison*, 5 U.S. 137 (1803).

March, James G., and Johan P. Olsen. 2004. *The Logic of Appropriateness*. Oslo: University of Oslo Centre for European Studies.

Mark, Alyx, and Michael A. Zilis. 2018. "Restraining the Court: Assessing Accounts of Congressional Attempts to Limit Supreme Court Authority." *Legislative Studies Quarterly* 43: 141–169.

al-Marri v. *Spagone*, 555 U.S. 1220 (2009).

Marshall, Thomas R. 1989. *Public Opinion and the Supreme Court*. Boston, MA: Unwin Hyman.

Marshall, Thomas R. 2008. *Public Opinion and the Rehnquist Court*. Albany, NY: SUNY Press.

Marshall, Thomas R. 2018. "Justice Anthony Kennedy in the Court of Public Opinion." Presented at the Annual Meeting of the American Political Science Association, Boston, MA.

Massachusetts v. *Environmental Protection Agency*, 549 U.S. 497 (2007).

Mauro, Tony. 1989. "Presidential Peril Seen in Leading Fight for Flag," *USA Today*, June 28.

Mauro, Tony. 2018. "Judges Push Back at Trump's Anti-Judiciary Tweets," *National Law Journal*, December 13.

Mayer, Kenneth R. 2001. *With the Stroke of a Pen: Executive Orders and Presidential Power*. Princeton, NJ: Princeton University Press.

Mayhew, David R. 1974. *Congress: The Electoral Connection*. New Haven, CT: Yale University Press.

Mayhew, David. 1991. *Divided We Govern*. New Haven, CT: Yale University Press.

McCarthy, Justin. 2015. "U.S. Support for Gay Marriage Stable After High Court Ruling," *Gallup*, July 17.

McCutcheon v. *FEC*, 572 U.S. 185 (2014).

McGauvran, Ronald J., and Matthew Eshbaugh-Soha. 2017. "Presidential Speeches amid a More Centralized and Unified Congress." *Congress and the Presidency* 44: 55–76.

McGuire, Kevin T., and James A. Stimson. 2004. "The Least Dangerous Branch Revisited: New Evidence on Supreme Court Responsiveness to Public Preferences." *Journal of Politics* 66: 1018–1035.

McKenna, Marian C. 2002. *Franklin Roosevelt and the Great Constitutional War: The Court-Packing Crisis of 1937*. New York, NY: Fordham University Press.

McMahon, Kevin J. 2004. *Reconsidering Roosevelt on Race: How the Presidency Paved the Road to Brown*. Chicago, IL: University of Chicago Press.

Mears, Bill. 2012. "Holder: Obama Recognizes Supreme Court's Authority," *CNN*, April 5.

Medhurst, Martin J., ed. 2008. *Before the Rhetorical Presidency*. College Station, TX: Texas A&M University Press.
Mercer, Ilana. 2003. "Bush's Affirmative Action Ambush," *The Globe and Mail*, January 21.
Meese III, Edwin. 1987. "Law of the Constitution." *Tulane Law Review* 61: 979–990.
Mitchell, Amy. 2018. "Americans Still Prefer Watching to Reading the News – and Mostly Still Through Television," *Pew Research Center*, December 3.
Moe, Terry. 1985. "The Politicized Presidency." In *The New Direction in American Politics, eds*. John E. Chubb and Paul E. Peterson. Washington, DC: Brookings Institution, 235–271.
Mondak, Jeffery J. 1994. "Policy Legitimacy and the Supreme Court: The Sources and Contexts of Legitimation." *Political Research Quarterly* 47: 675–692.
Mondak, Jeffery J., and Shannon Ishiyama Smithey. 1997. "The Dynamics of Public Support for the Supreme Court." *Journal of Politics* 59: 1114–1142.
Monroe, Alan D. 1998. "Public Opinion and Public Policy, 1980–1993." *Public Opinion Quarterly* 62: 6–28.
Moore, Acel. 2003. "Bush's King Day Strategy," *Philadelphia Inquirer*, January 20.
Morehead v. *New York ex rel. Tipaldo*, 298 US 587 (1936).
Morin, Richard. 1989. "*Wapner* v. *Rehnquist*: No Contest: TV Judge Vastly Outpolls Justices in Test of Public Recognition," *Washington Post*, June 23.
Mullinix, Kevin J., Thomas J. Leeper, James N. Druckman, and Jeremy Freese. 2015."The Generalizability of Survey Experiments." *Journal of Experimental Political Science* 2: 109–138.
Murphy, Walter F. 1986. "Who Shall Interpret? The Quest for the Ultimate Constitutional Interpreter." *Review of Politics* 48: 401–442.
Nagel, Stuart S. 1964. "Court-Curbing Periods in American History." *Vanderbilt Law Review* 18: 925–944.
Nagourney, Adam. 2003. "Bush and Affirmative Action: The Context," *New York Times*, January 16.
Nathan, Richard P. 1983 *The Administrative Presidency*, 2nd ed. New York, NY: Wiley.
National Federation of Independent Business v. *Sebelius*, 132 S.Ct. 2566 (2012).
Nelson, Michael. 1988. "The President and the Court: Reinterpreting the Court-Packing Episode of 1937." *Political Science Quarterly* 103: 267–293.
Nelson, Michael J., and Alicia Uribe-McGuire. 2017. "Opportunity and Overrides: The Effect of Institutional Public Support on Congressional Overrides of Supreme Court Decisions." *Political Research Quarterly* 70: 632–643.
Nemacheck, Christine L. 2007. *Strategic Selection: Presidential Nomination of Supreme Court Justices from Herbert Hoover through George W. Bush*. Charlottesville, VA: University of Virginia Press.
Neustadt, Richard E. 1990. *Presidential Power and the Modern Presidents: The Politics of Leadership from Roosevelt to Reagan*. New York, NY: The Free Press.
New York Daily News. 2003. "Affirmative Action is Needed – For Now Bush Talks the Talk of Equality, but Doesn't Walk the Walk," *New York Daily News*, January 19.
New York Times. 1988. "Thousand March Against Abortion," *New York Times*, January 23.
New York Times. 2003. "A Crucial Decision on Race," *New York Times*, January 15.

Nicholson, Chris, and Paul M. Collins, Jr. 2008. "The Solicitor General's Amicus Curiae Strategies in the Supreme Court." *American Politics Research* 36: 382–415.

Nicholson, Stephen P., and Thomas G. Hansford. 2014. "Partisans in Robes: Party Cues and Public Acceptance of Supreme Court Decisions." *American Journal of Political Science* 58: 620–636.

Nixon v. *Shrink Missouri Government PAC*, 528 U.S. 377 (2000).

NLRB v. *Jones & Laughlin Steel Corporation*, 301 U.S. 1 (1937).

Obergefell v. *Hodges*, 135 S.Ct. 2584 (2015).

Olmstead v. *L.C.*, 527 U.S. 521 (1999).

Oyez. 2018. https://www.oyez.org/ (March 20, 2019).

Pacelle, Richard L., Jr. 1991. *The Transformation of the Supreme Court's Agenda: From the New Deal to the Reagan Administration*. Boulder, CO: Westview.

Pacelle, Richard L., Jr. 2003. *Between Law and Politics: The Solicitor General and the Structuring of Race, Gender, and Reproductive Rights Litigation*. College Station, TX: Texas A&M University Press.

Pacelle, Richard L., Jr., Brett W. Curry, and Bryan W. Marshall. 2011. *Decision Making by the Modern Supreme Court*. New York, NY: Cambridge University Press.

Packham, Ben. 2011. "Julia Gillard Attacks High Court's Asylum Ruling," *The Australian*, September 1.

Paulsen, Michael Stokes. 1994. "The Most Dangerous Branch: Executive Power to Say What the Law Is." *Georgetown Law Journal* 83: 217–345.

Paulsen, Michael Stokes. 2008. "Lincoln and Judicial Authority." *Notre Dame Law Review* 83: 1227–1301.

Peake, Jeffrey S. 2001. "Presidential Agenda Setting in Foreign Policy." *Political Research Quarterly* 54: 69–86.

Peake, Jeffrey S., and Matthew Eshbaugh-Soha. 2008. "The Agenda-Setting Impact of Major Presidential TV Addresses." *Political Communication* 25: 113–137.

Pegram v. *Herdrich*, 530 U.S. 211 (2000).

Perez, Sarah. 2018. "Twitter's Doubling of Character Count from 140 to 280 Had Little Impact on Length of Tweets." *Techcrunch* https://techcrunch.com/2018/10/30/twitters-doubling-of-character-count-from-140-to-280-had-little-impact-on-length-of-tweets/ (March 12, 2019).

Peters, B. Guy. 2012. *Institutional Theory in Political Science: The "New Institutionalism."* New York, NY: Continuum International Publishing.

Peterson, Mark A. 1990. *Legislating Together: The White House and Capitol Hill from Eisenhower to Reagan*. Cambridge, MA: Harvard University Press.

Petty, Richard E., and John T. Cacioppo. 1986. *Communication and Persuasion: Central and Peripheral Routes to Attitude Change*. New York: Springer-Verlag.

Pickerill, J. Mitchell. 2004. *Constitutional Deliberation in Congress: The Impact of Judicial Review in a Separated System*. Durham, NC: Duke University Press.

Pollitt, Daniel H. 1992. "Reflection on the Bicentennial of the Bill of Rights – The Flag Burning Controversy: A Chronology." *North Carolina Law Review* 70: 553–614.

Poole, Keith. 2015. "Common Space Scores Congresses 75–113" http://voteview.com/readmeb.htm (March 12, 2019).

Post, Robert, and Reva Siegel 2004. "Popular Constitutionalism, Departmentalism, and Judicial Supremacy." *California Law Review* 92: 1027–1043.

Powell, Richard J. 1999. "'Going Public' Revisited: Presidential Speechmaking and the Bargaining Setting in Congress." *Congress and the Presidency* 26: 153–170.

Presser, Stephen B. 2012. "Obama Should Know Better on Supreme Court's Role," *CNN*, April 3.

Printz v. *United States*, 521 U.S. 898 (1997).

Provalis. 2017. "Sentiment Dictionaries." https://provalisresearch.com/products/content-analysis-software/wordstat-dictionary/sentiment-dictionaries/ (April 24, 2017).

Quinnipiac University Poll. 2017. www.pollingreport.com/immigration.htm (March 22, 2019).

Quinnipiac University Poll. 2018a. www.pollingreport.com/immigration.htm. (March 22, 2019).

Quinnipiac University Poll. 2018b. www.pollingreport.com/health.htm. (March 22, 2019).

Ragsdale, Lyn. 1984. "The Politics of Presidential Speechmaking, 1949–1980." *American Political Science Review* 78: 971–984.

Ragsdale, Lyn. 2014. *Vital Statistics on the Presidency*, 4th ed. Washington, DC: CQ Press.

Rapanos v. *United States*, 547 U.S. 715 (2006).

Reddish, Martin H. 1995. "Federal Judicial Independence: Constitutional and Political Perspectives." *Mercer Law Review* 46: 697–731.

Regents of the University of California v. *Bakke*, 438 U.S. 265 (1978).

Reynolds v. *Sims*, 377 U.S. 533 (1964).

Rice, Douglas. n.d. "Placing the Ball in Congress' Court: Supreme Court Requests for Congressional Action." *American Politics Research* forthcoming.

Ringquist, Evan J., Jeff Worsham, and Marc Allen Eisner. 2003. "Salience, Complexity, and the Legislative Direction of Regulatory Bureaucracies." *Journal of Public Administration Research and Theory* 13: 141–164.

Rhode Island v. *Massachusetts*, 37 U.S. 657 (1838).

Roberts John G., Jr. 2005. "Oral Advocacy and the Re-emergence of a Supreme Court Bar. *Journal of Supreme Court History* 30: 68–81.

Roe v. *Wade*, 410 U.S. 113 (1973).

Rogol, Natalie C., Matthew D. Montgomery, and Justin T. Kingsland. 2018. "Going Public: Presidential Impact on Supreme Court Decision-Making." *Justice System Journal* 39: 210–227.

Rosen, Jeffrey. 2017. "Not Even Andrew Jackson Went as Far as Trump in Attacking the Courts." *The Atlantic*, February 9.

Rosenberg, Gerald N. 1991. *The Hollow Hope: Can Courts Bring About Social Change?* Chicago, IL: University of Chicago Press.

Rottinghaus, Brandon. 2006. "Rethinking Presidential Responsiveness: The Public Presidency and Rhetorical Congruency, 1953–2001." *Journal of Politics* 68: 720–732.

Rottinghaus, Brandon. 2010. *The Provisional Pulpit: Modern Presidential Leadership of Public Opinion*. College Station, TX: Texas A&M University Press.

Rush, Mark. 2018. "The Law: Presidential Signing Statements and Coordinate Constitutional Interpretation." *Presidential Studies Quarterly* 48: 168–182.

Sager, Lawrence G. 2004. *Justice in Plainclothes: A Theory of American Constitutional Practice*. New Haven, CT: Yale University Press.

Salamone, Michael F. 2014. "Judicial Consensus and Public Opinion: Conditional Response to Supreme Court Majority Size." *Political Research Quarterly* 67: 320–334.

Salokar, Rebecca Mae. 1992. *The Solicitor General: The Politics of Law*. Philadelphia, PA: Temple University Press.

Schattschneider, E .E. 1960. *The Semisovereign People: A Realist's View of Democracy in America*. New York, NY: Holt, Rinehart, and Winston.

Schechter Poultry Corp. v. *United States*, 295 U.S. 495 (1935).

Schwarz, Hunter. 2015. "Obama and Clinton Love to Celebrate Gay Marriage Now. Here's How Late They Were to the Party," *Washington Post*, June 26.

Scigliano, Robert. 1971. *The Supreme Court and the Presidency*. New York, NY: The Free Press.

Segal, Jeffrey A., and Harold J. Spaeth. 2002. *The Supreme Court and the Attitudinal Model Revisited*. New York, NY: Cambridge University Press.

Sessions v. *Dimaya*, 138 S. Ct. 1204 (2018).

Sherman, Mark. 2018. "Roberts, Trump Spar in Extraordinary Scrap over Judges," *AP News*, November 21.

Shogan, Colleen J. 2006. *The Moral Rhetoric of American Presidents*. College Station, TX: Texas A&M University Press.

Sill, Kaitlyn L., Emily T. Metzgar, and Stella M. Rouse. 2013. "Media Coverage of the Supreme Court: How Do Journalists Assess the Importance of Court Decisions?" *Political Communication* 30: 58–80.

Slotnick, Eliot E., and Jennifer A. Segal. 1998. *Television News and the Supreme Court: All the News That's Fit to Air?* New York, NY: Cambridge University Press.

Smith, Lamar. 2012. "President Obama Wrong to Bully the Supreme Court," *Politico*, April 10.

Soroka, Stuart N. 2012. "The Gatekeeping Function: Distributions of Information in Media and the Real World." *Journal of Politics* 74: 514–528.

Soroka, Stuart N., Dominik A. Stecula, and Christopher Wlezien. 2015 "It's (Change in) the (Future) Economy, Stupid: Economic Indicators, the Media, and Public Opinion." *American Journal of Political Science* 59: 457–474.

Soroka, Stuart, and Christopher Wlezien. 2015. "On the Sources of Public Responsiveness to Policy." Presented at the Annual Meeting of the American Political Science Association, San Francisco, CA.

South Dakota v. *Wayfair Inc.*, 17–494 (2018).

Spaeth, Harold, Lee Epstein, Ted Ruger, Keith Whittington, Jeffrey Segal, and Andrew D. Martin. 2017. *The Supreme Court Database: LEGACY Database*. http://scdb.wustl.edu/index.php (March 20, 2019).

Spaeth, Harold, Lee Epstein, Ted Ruger, Keith Whittington, Jeffrey Segal, and Andrew D. Martin. 2018. *The Supreme Court Database*. http://scdb.wustl.edu/index.php (March 20, 2019).

Spriggs, James F. 1996. "The Supreme Court and Federal Administrative Agencies: A Resource-Based Theory and Analysis of Judicial Impact." *American Journal of Political Science* 40: 1122–1151.

St. Louis Post-Dispatch. 1989. "America's Flag: Our Obsession," *St. Louis Post-Dispatch*, July 11.

St. Louis Post-Dispatch. 2003. "A Missed Opportunity," *St. Louis Post-Dispatch*, January 16.
Stampp, Kenneth M. 1990. *America in 1857: A Nation on the Brink*. New York, NY: Oxford University Press.
Steilen, Matthew. 2013. "Collaborative Departmentalism." *Buffalo Law Review* 61: 345–411.
Steilen, Matthew J. 2014. "Judicial Review and Non-Enforcement at the Founding." *University of Pennsylvania Journal of Constitutional Law* 17: 479–568.
Stevenson, Richard W. 2003. "Conservative Positions by Bush Could Cost Votes from Center, Moderates Warn," *New York Times*, January 21.
Sullivan, John L., Amy Fried, and Mary G. Dietz. 1992. "Patriotism, Politics, and the Presidential Election of 1988." *American Journal of Political Science* 36: 200–234.
Swaine, Jon. 2012. "Barack Obama Accused of Bullying' US Supreme Court Over Controversial Healthcare Reforms," *The Telegraph*, April 5.
Swann v. *Charlotte-Mecklenburg Board of Education*, 402 U.S. 1 (1971).
Swanson, Rick A. 2007. "The Dynamics of Specific and Diffuse Support for the U.S. Supreme Court: A Panel Study." *Social Science Journal* 44: 645–663.
Tanenhaus, Joseph, and Walter F. Murphy. 1981. "Patterns of Public Support for the Supreme Court: A Panel Study." *Journal of Politics* 43: 24–39.
Targeted News Service. 2010. "PFAW Applauds Obama for Criticizing Citizens United Decision," *Targeted News Service*, January 27.
Teten, Ryan Lee. 2008. "The Evolution of the Rhetorical Presidency and Getting Past the Traditional/Modern Divide." *Presidential Studies Quarterly* 38: 308–314.
Texas v. *Johnson*, 491 U.S. 397 (1989).
Tiefer, Charles. 1992. "The Flag-Burning Controversy of 1989–1990: Congress' Valid Role in Constitutional Dialogue." *Harvard Journal on Legislation* 29: 357–398.
Toma, Eugenia Froedge. 1991. "Congressional Influence and the Supreme Court: The Budget as a Signaling Device." *Journal of Legal Studies* 20: 131–146.
Trump v. *Hawaii*, 138 S. Ct. 2392 (2018).
Trump v. *International Refugee Assistance Project*, 138 S.Ct. 353 (2017).
Tulis, Jeffrey K. 1987. *The Rhetorical Presidency*. Princeton, NJ: Princeton University Press.
Tulis, Jeffrey K. 2000. "The Two Constitutional Presidencies." In *The Presidency and the Political System*, ed. Michael Nelson. Washington, DC: CQ Press, 57–87.
Turzai v. *League of Women Voters of Pennsylvania*, 17A909 (2018).
Tushnet, Mark. 1999. *Taking the Constitution Away from the Courts*. Princeton, NJ: Princeton University Press.
Tushnet, Mark, and Katya Lezin. 1991. "What Really Happened in *Brown* v. *Board of Education*." *Columbia Law Review* 91: 1867–1930.
Tyler, Tom R. 2006. *Why People Obey the Law*. Princeton, NJ: Princeton University Press.
United States v. *Butler*, 297 U.S. 1 (1936).
United States v. *Cannelton Sewer Pipe*, 364 U.S. 76 (1960).
United States v. *Darby Lumber Co.*, 312 U.S. 100 (1941).
United States v. *Eichman*, 496 U.S. 310 (1990).
United States v. *Nixon*, 418 U.S. 683 (1974).
United States v. *Texas*, 136 S. Ct. 2271 (2016).

United States v. *The Amistad*, 40 U.S. 518 (1841).

United States v. *Trans-Missouri Freight Association*, 166 U.S. 290 (1897).

United States v. *Windsor*, 186 L.Ed.2d 808 (2013).

Uribe, Alicia, James F. Spriggs, and Thomas G. Hansford. 2014. "The Influence of Congressional Preferences on Legislative Overrides of Supreme Court Decisions." *Law & Society Review* 48: 921–945.

U.S. Newswire. 2003. "Black Conservatives Support Bush Stand on Affirmative Action Challenge," *U.S. Newswire*, January 16, 2003.

Villalobos, José D., and Cigdem V. Sirin. 2012. "Agenda Setting from the Oval Office: An Experimental Examination of Presidential Influence over the Public Agenda." *International Journal of Public Opinion Research* 24: 21–41.

Wahlbeck, Paul J. 1997. "The Life of the Law: Judicial Politics and Legal Change." *Journal of Politics* 59: 778–802.

Wallsten, Peter, and Robert Barnes. 2012. "Obama's Supreme Court Comments Lead Some to Question His Strategy," *The Washington Post*, April 4.

Wanta, Wayne, Mary Ann Stephenson, Judy Van Slyke Turk, and Maxwell E. McCombs. 1989. "How Presidents State of Union Talk Influenced News Media Agendas." *Journalism Quarterly* 66: 537–541.

Ward, Artemus, and David L. Weiden. 2006. *Sorcerers' Apprentices: 100 Years of Law Clerks at the United States Supreme Court*. New York, NY: New York University Press.

Washington v. *Glucksberg*, 521 U.S. 702 (1997).

Waterman, Richard, Carol L. Silva, and Hank Jenkins-Smith. 2014. *The Presidential Expectations Gap: Public Attitudes Concerning the Presidency*. Ann Arbor, MI: University of Michigan Press.

Weaver, Warren, Jr. 1973. "Nixon Asks New Sentencing System for Capital Crimes," *New York Times*, March 15.

Webster v. *Reproductive Health Services*, 492 U.S. 490 (1989).

Weiss, Brennan. 2018. "RANKED: The 15 Most Polarizing US Presidents, According to Political Scientists," *Business Insider*, March 6.

Welch, Reed L. 2003. "Presidential Success in Communicating with the Public through Televised Addresses." *Presidential Studies Quarterly* 33: 347–356.

West, Darrell M. 1988. "Activists and Economic Policymaking in Congress." *American Journal of Political Science* 32: 662–680.

Whitford, Andrew B., and Jeff Yates. 2009. *Presidential Rhetoric and the Public Agenda: Constructing the War on Drugs*. Baltimore, MD: Johns Hopkins University Press.

Whittington, Keith E. 1999. *Constitutional Construction: Divided Powers and Constitutional Meaning*. Cambridge, MA: Harvard University Press.

Whittington, Keith E. 2001. "Presidential Challenges to Judicial Supremacy and the Politics of Constitutional Meaning." *Polity* 33: 365–395.

Whittington, Keith E. 2003. "Legislative Sanction and the Strategic Environment of Judicial Review." *International Journal of Constitutional Law* 1: 446–474.

Whittington, Keith E. 2005. "'Interpose Your Friendly Hand': Political Supports for the Exercise of Judicial Review by the United States Supreme Court." *American Political Science Review* 99: 583–596.

Whittington, Keith E. 2007. *Political Foundations of Judicial Supremacy: The Presidency, the Supreme Court, and Constitutional Leadership in U.S. History*. Princeton, NJ: Princeton University Press.

Whittington, Keith E. 2009. *Constitutional Construction: Divided Powers and Constitutional Meaning*. Cambridge, MA: Harvard University Press.

Wilson, Patricia. 2003. "Bush Opposes Race-based Admissions," *Globe and Mail*, January 16.

Wohlfarth, Patrick C. 2009. "The Tenth Justice? Consequences of Politicization in the Solicitor General's Office." *Journal of Politics* 71: 224–237.

Wolf, Richard. 2012. "Other Presidents Took on High Court Before Obama," *USA Today*, April 6.

Wolf, Z. Byron. 2018. "Trump's Attacks on Judge Curiel Are Still Jarring to Read," *CNN*, February 27.

Wood, B. Dan. 2007. *The Politics of Economic Leadership*. Princeton, NJ: Princeton University Press.

Wood, B. Dan. 2009. *The Myth of Presidential Representation*. Cambridge, MA: Cambridge University Press.

Wood, B. Dan, and Jeffrey S. Peake. 1998. "The Dynamics of Foreign Policy Agenda Setting." *American Political Science Review* 92: 173–184.

Wood, B. Dan, and Richard W. Waterman. 1994. *Bureaucratic Dynamics: The Role of Bureaucracy in a Democracy*. Boulder, CO: Westview Press.

Worcester v. *Georgia*, 31 U.S. (6 Pet.) 515 (1832).

Yalof, David Alistair. 1999. *Pursuit of Justices: Presidential Politics and the Selection of Supreme Court Nominees*. Chicago, IL: University of Chicago Press.

Yates, Jeff. 2002. *Popular Justice: Presidential Prestige and Executive Success in the Supreme Court*. Albany, NY: SUNY Press.

Yates, Jeff, and Andrew B. Whitford. 1998. "Presidential Power and the US Supreme Court." *Political Research Quarterly* 51: 539–550.

Young, Lori, and Stuart Soroka. 2012. "Affective News: The Automated Coding of Sentiment in Political Texts." *Political Communication* 29: 205–231.

Youngstown Sheet & Tube Company v. *Sawyer*, 343 U.S. 579 (1952).

Zaller, John R. 1992. *The Nature and Origins of Mass Opinion*. New York, NY: Cambridge University Press.

Zarefsky, David. 1986. *President Johnson's War on Poverty: Rhetoric and History*. Tuscaloosa, AL: University of Alabama Press.

Zelman v. *Simmons-Harris*, 536 U.S. 639 (2002).

Zink, James R., James F. Spriggs, and John T. Scott. 2009. "Courting the Public: The Influence of Decision Attributes on Individuals Views of Court Opinions." *Journal of Politics* 71: 909–925.

Index

www.ingramcontent.com/pod-product-compliance
Lightning Source LLC
LaVergne TN
LVHW011810200926
848484LV00005B/1134
* 9 7 8 1 1 0 8 4 9 8 4 8 7 *